#1 INTERNATIONAL BESTSELLER

PODCAST SECRETS

FOR ENTREPRENEURS

Second Editon

https://podcastsecrets.biz/s/kit

PODCAST SECRETS

FOR ENTREPRENEURS

Second Editon

JOHN NORTH | JAMES NORTH

Podcast Secrets for Entrepreneurs
1st Edition. 2023
2nd Edition. 2024
Version 7.5

ASIN: B0BQVBG948 (Amazon Kindle)
ISBN: 978-0-6454380-7-9 (Amazon Paperback)
ISBN: 978-0-6454380-8-6 (Amazon Hardcover)
ISBN: 978-1-923223-41-7 (Ingram Spark) PAPERBACK
ISBN: 978-1-923223-42-4 (Ingram Spark) HARDCOVER
ISBN: 978-1-923223-43-1 (e-Book)
ISBN: 978-1-923223-53-0 (Lulu)

CONTACT THE AUTHOR:
Business Name: EVOLVE SYSTEMS GROUP PTY LTD
Author Website: www.johnnorth.com.au
Main Website: www.podcastsecrets.app
All In One Platform: www.evolvepreneur.app
LinkedIn: https://au.linkedin.com/in/johnnorth1085
X: @johnnorth7 and @evolvepreneur
Email: john@evolvesys.com.au
Phone: 1300 889 383
Fonts/size: Headings - Montserrat 19pt / Paragraphs - Myriad Pro 9.5pt

TRADEMARKS

TABLE OF CONTENTS

ABOUT THE AUTHOR - JOHN NORTH

Transforming Entrepreneurs through Cutting-Edge Publishing and Software Solutions...

John North is the Swiss Army knife of entrepreneurship—versatile, sharp, and ready to tackle just about anything.

A 9-time #1 best-selling author (Amazon, USA Today, and Wall Street Journal approved), he's not just a leader; he's a pioneer in publishing, marketing, and business innovation.

As the CEO of Evolve Systems Group, John doesn't just run businesses; he creates tools that revolutionize them.

Platforms like **Evolvepreneur.app**, an all-in-one solution that helps entrepreneurs take control of their future without relying on social media, or **Evolve Global Publishing**, where authors can launch their books in as little as 90 days—without even lifting a pen.

His mission is clear: empower entrepreneurs with smarter, faster ways to succeed.

Some highlights that define John's career:

Over **30 years** leading in business and marketing, with hands-on expertise in fields ranging from IT to personal development $25M+ in sales for his clients and himselfCreator, publisher, or contributor to **3,500+ books** (8 of his own hit #1)Mastermind behind industry-shaking tools like **PodcastSecrets.app** and beyond

And then there's the rest of the story:

John once turned a struggling software distribution company into the #2 global distributor in under three years. He's helped countless entrepreneurs boost their marketing intelligence, reimagine their strategies, and create lasting impact.

When he's not innovating in the business world, John is on the squash court in Sydney, Australia, where he plays competitively five days a week. His drive to win extends to every facet of life, making him a powerhouse for anyone ready to scale smarter, faster, and better.

John's style is about simplicity, impact, and results—and his tools, from publishing to podcasting, are designed with that same ethos.

He's the rare combination of visionary and hands-on creator, building systems that change the game for entrepreneurs everywhere.

ABOUT THE AUTHOR - JAMES NORTH

Meet **James North**: the co-author of Podcast Secrets for Entrepreneurs and the go-to expert for taking creative projects from concept to polished perfection.

As the son of renowned CEO John North—who co-wrote the book with him—James was raised in a world where ideas, innovation, and execution were part of daily life.

Over the past seven years at Evolve, he's honed his craft, mastering the art of editing, publishing, and digital design.

For Podcast Secrets for Entrepreneurs, James didn't just contribute; he ensured every idea, tip, and insight was expertly refined. His precision as an editor and deep understanding of the podcasting space bring clarity to the book's roadmap for aspiring podcasters.

Whether shaping a compelling chapter or untangling technical jargon, James is all about making big ideas accessible and actionable for readers.

This isn't James' first publishing venture. He also played a key role in editing *Book Publishing Secrets for Entrepreneurs*, helping authors turn their visions into reality. His attention to detail and ability to weave structure into creativity have made him a trusted force behind countless successful projects.

But James' talents go beyond words on a page. As the lead UI designer for Evolvepreneur. app, he's brought his design expertise to life, helping to create an intuitive platform that entrepreneurs rely on to manage their businesses seamlessly.

Though he thrives behind the scenes, James is an entrepreneur at heart, constantly learning and innovating. His ability to juggle editing, publishing, design, and strategy makes him an invaluable asset to every project he touches.

With *Podcast Secrets for Entrepreneurs*, he has opened the door for creators to step into the spotlight—just as he's quietly mastered the art of shining behind it.

FREE PODCAST SECRETS RESOURCE KIT

To help you implement the strategies outlined in Podcasting Secrets for Entrepreneurs, we've put together a comprehensive Podcast Secrets Resource Kit, which is available for free.

This kit contains tools, templates, and guides to streamline your podcasting process, from the initial planning stages to audience growth and monetization.

What's Included in the Podcast Secrets Resource Kit?

1. Podcast Episode Planning Template

What it is: A downloadable template to help you plan each episode from start to finish, including key talking points, guest details, and post-production notes.

Why you need it: Streamline your episode creation process and ensure every episode is well-structured and aligned with your podcast's vision.

How to use it: Fill out the template before each recording session to keep your podcast organized and focused.

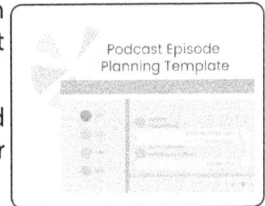

2. Content Calendar Template

What it is: A pre-built content calendar template in Excel or Google Sheets to help you map out your podcast episodes for weeks or months in advance.

Why you need it: Consistency is critical to podcast success. This calendar will keep your publishing schedule on track and ensure a steady flow of content.

How to use it: Plan your episodes, schedule guest interviews, and align your content with major events or industry trends.

3. Podcast Launch Checklist

What it is: A detailed checklist that walks you through every step of the podcast launch process, from choosing the right equipment to submitting your podcast to platforms like Apple Podcasts, Spotify, and Google Podcasts.

Why you need it: To ensure you don't miss any crucial steps when preparing to launch your podcast.

How to use it: Follow the checklist to ensure your podcast is ready for a successful launch.

4. Podcast Hosting Selection Guide

What it is: A guide to help you choose the right podcast hosting platform based on your specific needs and budget.

Why you need it: Choosing the right hosting platform is critical for long-term success. This guide breaks down the key features you should look for, from storage limits and analytics to monetization options and ease of use.

How to use it: Review the guide to select the best podcast hosting platform that aligns with your goals and technical requirements.

5. Podcast Monetization Blueprint

What it is: A step-by-step guide on monetising your podcast, including sponsorship outreach templates, membership ideas, and premium content strategies.

Why you need it: Monetization is a key goal for many podcasters, and this blueprint provides proven methods to turn your podcast into a profitable venture.

How to use it: Implement this guide's strategies to generate revenue through ads, sponsorships, or premium content offerings.

6. Podcast Growth Strategy Roadmap

What it is: A roadmap that outlines essential steps to grow your podcast audience through organic marketing, social media promotion, and guest collaborations.

Why you need it: Audience growth is critical to long-term success, and this roadmap will give you actionable tactics to increase your listener base.

How to use it: Follow the roadmap as a guide to scale your podcast using proven growth techniques.

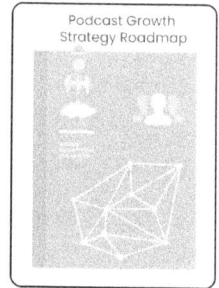

7. Guest Outreach Email Templates

What it is: Pre-written email templates for inviting guests to your podcast, following up, and promoting episodes once they're live.

Why you need it: Effective communication with guests is key to building relationships and securing great interviews.

How to use it: Customize these templates for your show and use them to streamline your guest outreach process.

8. Listener Engagement Toolkit

What it is: A toolkit with strategies to engage your audience, including sample social media posts, listener Q&A ideas, and engagement metrics to track.

Why you need it: Building a community around your podcast requires active listener engagement, and this toolkit helps you foster deeper relationships with your audience.

How to use it: Use these resources to encourage more interaction with listeners on social media and during your episodes.

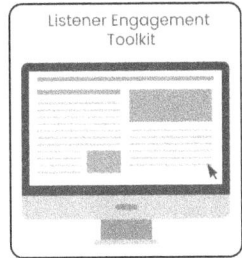

Listener Engagement Toolkit

9. Analytics Tracking Spreadsheet

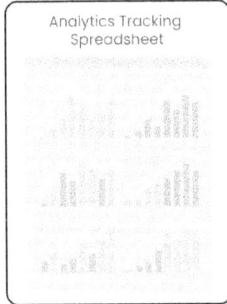

Analytics Tracking Spreadsheet

What it is: A customizable spreadsheet to help you track key podcast metrics like downloads, listener retention, and episode performance.

Why you need it: Monitoring analytics is essential for optimizing your content and growing your audience. This spreadsheet makes it easy to track progress and identify areas for improvement.

How to use it: Input your data regularly to track your podcast's performance and adjust your strategy based on the insights you gather.

PODCAST RESOURCES KIT
Grab it here:

https://podcastsecrets.biz/s/kit

To help you implement the strategies outlined in Podcasting Secrets for Entrepreneurs, we've put together a comprehensive Podcast Secrets Resource Kit, which is available for free.

This kit contains tools, templates, and guides to streamline your podcasting process, from the initial planning stages to audience growth and monetization.

https://podcastsecrets.biz/s/kit

Introduction

CHAPTER 1

PODCASTING - MY JOURNEY

"The journey of a thousand miles begins with one step." – **Lao Tzu**

Ever wondered what it really takes to start a podcast? Here's a behind-the-scenes look at our journey—the ups, the downs, and all the messy middle.

We'll take you through the moments that inspired us to hit "record" for the first time, the hurdles we didn't see coming, and the moments that reminded us why we started.

Consider this your backstage pass to podcasting, where we share our story so you can feel prepared and fired up to begin your own.

We launched the "Evolvepreneur (After Hours) Show" as a way of creating a multiple host and guest process and system.

Our goal with Evolvepreneur (After Hours) was to create a profitable podcast by interviewing our ideal customers—entrepreneurs interested in podcasting and publishing. Each episode was more than just a conversation; it was a chance to build a real relationship.

By providing value and showcasing our expertise, we aimed to earn their trust. If they resonated with our approach, we'd introduce them to our sales team to explore how we could support them further with their own podcasting or book publishing goals. This strategy allowed us to connect meaningfully with potential clients while keeping the podcast engaging and relevant.

Over a period of 12 months we hired and trained 7 hosts and created over 1,200 episodes. Along the way we invested over $50,000 in building systems from hiring and training the hosts to marketing to get guests to the entire workflow from interview to publishing and promotion. It was a wild ride but in the end we had built an entirely integrated and robust podcast platform.

To make Evolvepreneur (After Hours) run smoothly and professionally, we developed a full host application and interview system through our Evolvepreneur.app platform. Hosts went through a structured training course, complete with survey forms, assessments, and a final quiz they had to pass before starting interviews.

We set up contracts and a commission-based system so hosts earned a percentage whenever they successfully handed off a guest to sales. Additionally, we used an episode outcome form that automated production tasks and followed up with listeners interested in our products. This setup allowed us to streamline the entire process, ensuring quality control and maximizing engagement with each episode.

We built a smooth, automated guest journey to keep our production efficient and professional. It started with a guest application page and survey, where potential guests shared their information and interest. If approved, our system auto-generated an episode from a template, which made it easy to move forward. The guest was then sent to a group calendar to book their interview time, where a relevant host could claim the episode.

For the hosts, we created a one-screen "Host Hub"—a simple dashboard with all the interview details, questions, and even a recording option. After the interview, the host filled out an Outcome Form, which triggered automated follow-ups, emails, and notified production to edit and schedule the episode.

Guests had access to their own "Guest Hub," containing everything they needed, from interview prep to resources, plus a status update for their episode. Once the episode was scheduled, guests received an email notification, and another when it went live. The episode was then posted automatically to social media via our RSS feed and sent to our subscriber email list.

With such a streamlined system, we produced so many episodes that we had to release one every day for almost six months. Thanks to automation, our virtual assistant spent just 5-10 minutes per episode on production and scheduling.

In the end, we created a truly turnkey system that handled everything from guest onboarding to episode promotion with minimal manual effort.

The Genesis of a Vision

Starting the "Evolvepreneur (After Hours) Show" wasn't an overnight decision—it was the result of a lot of thought and a real passion for creating something meaningful for entrepreneurs.

Early on, I spent hours figuring out what I wanted Evolvepreneur (After Hours) to be: more than just business talk, but a place to share real stories, challenges, and wins.

My goal was simple—to build a show that inspires, educates, and connects entrepreneurs who are all on their own journeys.

I finally came up with this as a statement of who the show was for:

"As a time-poor, typically underfunded online entrepreneur who receives so much conflicting advice about the best ways to grow your business, how can you compete with the big end of town without any of the resources they have at their disposal?"

The process involved some planning and strategizing. I reflected on these questions:

- 🎙 What unique angle could my podcast offer?
- 🎙 How could it add value to the entrepreneurial community?
- 🎙 What were the stories and insights that needed to be shared?

The answers to these questions formed the foundation of the podcast, guiding its direction and purpose.

We crafted a clear mission statement for the podcast. This mission statement was more than a few words; it was a guiding principle for every decision, every episode, and every interview. It encapsulated what we wanted to achieve: to empower, educate, and connect entrepreneurs from all walks of life.

"Are you a startup entrepreneur or looking to pivot and re-invent your business and struggling with the complexity?

The question in my mind is...

How do you create or re-launch a highly profitable and successful 6 to 7 figure business?

With so much conflicting advice about the best ways to start and grow your business, how do you get it right the first time!"

Building the Foundation

With over a decade of podcasting and several shows already under my belt, I knew what it took to make a show work.

But with Evolvepreneur (After Hours), I wanted to go further—creating something truly impactful for entrepreneurs. I focused on refining the format, dialing in on audience engagement strategies, and making sure the content would hit home.

Even with my experience, launching this show came with its own set of challenges, but my team and I was ready to put in the work to make it resonate.

Crafting a Unique Podcast Identity

We knew that for Evolvepreneur (After Hours) to stand out, it needed a clear, unique identity—not just a series of interviews, but a voice and style that listeners would recognize instantly. I thought hard about what I wanted the show to represent and how it could genuinely reflect the goals and values of the entrepreneurial community. The goal was to create something memorable, something that would resonate with listeners and keep them coming back for more.

For Evolvepreneur (After Hours), we wanted a unique, recognizable style—something that felt real and engaging. So, we recorded each episode more like a live radio show, keeping edits to a minimum to capture authentic conversations. We experimented with different episode lengths too, trying out shorter 10-minute episodes alongside longer ones up to 30 minutes. This variety helped us find what resonated most with our audience while keeping the format fresh and flexible.

Visual and Audio Branding

A significant part of creating this identity was visual and audio branding. The logo, color scheme, and overall design aesthetic were carefully chosen to represent the podcast's branding. These elements were visual cues that communicated the essence of the Evolvepreneur (After Hours) Show to its audience.

Consistency Across Episodes

Consistency was key. Each episode, regardless of the topic or guest, needed to align with the overall identity of the podcast. This tone, style, and content consistency helped build a brand that listeners could trust and relate to. Consistency in podcasting is not just about regular episode releases; it's also about maintaining a consistent quality and style that becomes your trademark. We spent some time training our hosts to pay attention to this when interviewing guests.

A Unique Blend of Content

The content of the Evolvepreneur (After Hours) Show was designed to reflect its unique identity. We didn't just focus on success stories; we also delved into entrepreneurs' challenges, failures, and real-life experiences. This approach set our podcast apart, making it a source of genuine insight and inspiration for our listeners.

Diverse Perspectives and Topics

To ensure diversity and richness in our content, we invited guests from various sectors within the entrepreneurial world. This diversity brought different perspectives and experiences to the show, making each episode a unique learning opportunity. We discussed the latest trends in entrepreneurship, shared success stories, and, importantly, talked about failures and the lessons learned from them.

Creating Engaging and Actionable Content

Each episode was crafted to be engaging and actionable. I wanted listeners to come away with insights, practical tips and strategies they could apply in their own entrepreneurial journeys. This focus on actionable content sets the Evolvepreneur (After Hours) Show apart, making it a valuable resource for our audience.

Continuous Learning and Adaptation

We continuously sought feedback from our guests to adapt and evolve our content. This feedback loop was instrumental in keeping our content relevant and engaging and helped build a stronger connection with our audience.

Developing content that resonated with our audience was a dynamic and ongoing process. It required understanding the audience, strategic planning, and a commitment to delivering valuable and engaging content. These principles were the cornerstone of our content development strategy and played a significant role in the success of the Evolvepreneur (After Hours) Show.

Fostering Meaningful Connections with Guests

The Art of Selecting and Engaging Guests

Selecting the right guests has been essential to the success of Evolvepreneur (After Hours). Our goal was to feature guests who could offer real value to our audience—those with unique insights, relevant experience, and stories that would resonate. Using the Evolvepreneur.app platform, we developed a structured approach for finding and engaging with ideal guests.

We evaluated each potential guest through a series of targeted questions, covering everything from their business background and turnover to their future goals. This approach didn't just help us select the best guests; it also gave us a rich set of data and insights, adding layers of depth and variety to our episodes. Each guest brought something unique to the table, helping us keep the content fresh, relevant, and engaging for our listeners.

Preparation and Research

Preparation and research were key components in making the most of each guest's appearance. Before each interview, We invested time in understanding the guest's background, achievements, and areas of expertise. This preparation allowed for deeper and more meaningful conversations. It also showed respect for our guests' time and contributions, fostering appreciation and mutual respect.

We built an entire "Host Hub" as part of our platform's podcast module to make this process seamless for our hosts.

Creating a Comfortable and Open Environment

Creating a comfortable and open environment for our guests was paramount. The Evolvepreneur.app platform facilitated this by streamlining the communication process, making it easy for guests to understand the show's format and expectations. As much of the process as possible happened inside this one platform, making the experience convenient for guests. This clarity and ease of interaction set the stage for open, honest, and engaging conversations.

Guests had their own "Guest Hub," which was designed to give them a central place to track their episode from start to finish and provide access to promotional links and resources.

Leveraging Guest Networks

In addition to the value each guest brought to the podcast regarding content, their networks also significantly expanded our reach. Guests often shared their episodes within their networks, introducing new audiences to the Evolvepreneur (After Hours) Show. This cross-promotion benefited both the podcast and the guests, creating a symbiotic relationship.

We developed an automated email system to let the guest know when their episode was scheduled and when it was released.

These efforts enhanced the quality of our episodes and played a significant role in the growth and popularity of the Evolvepreneur (After Hours) Show.

Technical Mastery for Quality Production

Prioritizing Sound Quality and Production

The technical quality of a podcast can significantly influence its success. The top priority for the Evolvepreneur (After Hours) Show was to prioritise sound quality and overall production value. Investing in high-quality recording equipment, microphones, and editing software was the first step in this process.

Monetizing the Podcast Effectively

Exploring Diverse Revenue Streams

It's important to monetize a podcast effectively to ensure its sustainability and growth. Exploring diverse revenue streams for the Evolvepreneur (After Hours) Show was a strategic decision. This included affiliate marketing, and leveraging the podcast's content for other products, such as books or online courses.

We created the "Evolvepreneur (After Hours) Show Volume 1" Book which featured Hosts and Guests and a full directory of episodes. Grab a copy here: *https://getmybook.club/show-book/B0CQL1KSYV*

We have also added shorts of each episode to our YouTube channel to promote the guests.

Affiliate Marketing

Affiliate marketing was also integrated into our strategy. By recommending products or services that were relevant and beneficial to our audience, we were able to generate revenue through affiliate commissions. This approach required careful selection to ensure the products and services promoted aligned with our audience's interests and needs.

Building and Nurturing a Loyal Community

Introducing the VIP Boost Offer

As I've detailed in "Podcasting Secrets for Entrepreneurs," building and nurturing a community is as crucial as producing content in the podcasting journey. The Evolvepreneur (After Hours) Show aimed to attract listeners and create an engaged community.

To enhance this community-building effort and cover operational costs, we introduced the VIP Boost Package.

The VIP Boost Concept

The VIP Boost Package was designed to give our guests an extraordinary experience and additional exposure. Recognizing that every interview is unique, we wanted to offer something extra to make each episode stand out. The package included a series of exclusive benefits:

Facebook Ads Push: We allocated a budget of $100 for Facebook Ads for each VIP episode, ensuring that these episodes received heightened exposure and reached a broader audience. This not only benefited the guests but also brought more listeners to our show.

Original Content Files: VIP guests received the original video and audio interview files. This allowed them to share and repurpose their content, extending the life and reach of their episode.

Custom Promo Video and Images: We provided professionally edited promo videos and images with the guest's headshot. These were tailored to promote the show and the guest, enhancing their personal brand.

Bite-sized Social Media Content: Understanding the power of social media, we created up to three 'reels' from each VIP episode. These short, engaging clips captured attention and drew new listeners to the full episode.

Why VIP Boost?

The VIP Boost was more than just a monetization strategy; it was a way to add value and elevate the experience for our guests. It distinguished our podcast in a market saturated with content, offering our guests a platform not just to share their story but to truly shine.

This approach was aligned with the principles in "Podcasting Secrets for Entrepreneurs," where I emphasize the importance of creating unique value propositions in your podcasting venture.

Limited and Exclusive Offering

The VIP Boost was a limited offer exclusive to those who were eager to amplify their impact and stand out in the crowd. It was a testament to our commitment to producing quality content and supporting our guests in maximizing their reach and influence.

The VIP Boost Package was a strategic initiative that helped build and nurture our podcast community. It provided additional value to our guests, covered operational costs, and enhanced the overall quality and reach of the Evolvepreneur (After Hours) Show. This innovative approach, inspired by the strategies in "Podcasting Secrets for Entrepreneurs," played a significant role in the growth and success of our podcast.

Evolvepreneur (After Hours) was built on the idea that a podcast can do more than just share information—it can drive real relationships and profitable results. By investing in a streamlined, automated system, we were able to connect with our ideal clients while producing high-quality episodes at scale.

If you're looking to build your own successful podcast, focus on creating a strong guest journey, automating where you can, and finding ways to add real value for your audience and guests. Remember, it's not just about recording episodes; it's about crafting a platform that serves your goals and resonates with listeners.

In the chapters ahead, we'll guide you through each step to create your own podcasting success—from developing a clear vision and setting up workflows, to mastering audience engagement and monetization strategies. Let's get started on building a podcast that stands out.

To help you implement the strategies outlined in Podcasting Secrets for Entrepreneurs, we've put together a comprehensive Podcast Secrets Resource Kit, which is available for free.

This kit contains tools, templates, and guides to streamline your podcasting process, from the initial planning stages to audience growth and monetization.

https://podcastsecrets.biz/s/kit

CHAPTER 2

THE POWER OF PODCASTING FOR ENTREPRENEURS

"Success usually comes to those who are too busy to be looking for it."
– Henry David Thoreau

Podcasting is more than just a platform—it's a tool for growth, connection, and influence.

As an entrepreneur, a podcast gives you a unique voice in your industry, allowing you to reach your audience directly and share insights they won't find anywhere else.

In this chapter, we'll explore how podcasting can supercharge your brand, attract new clients, and open doors you never thought possible.

Ready to see why podcasts are an entrepreneur's secret weapon?

Let's dive in!

Over the last twenty years, podcasting has established itself as a prominent form of media, but it has truly taken off and captured the attention of a wide audience only in the last six years. Several factors contribute to this surge in popularity.

It's estimated that over 2 million podcast shows are growing daily, with over 420 million listeners.[*1]

2006 only 22% of the adult population was aware of podcasting.

That number is now 79% in 2022, and they estimate there will be over 100 million listeners (in the USA alone) in 2024, growing to 144 million in 2025.

Analysts project that podcast advertising spending in 2023 will surpass the 2 billion mark.

Experts predict the podcast industry will generate 4 billion in revenues by 2024.

If you are an entrepreneur, one effective strategy you can employ is leveraging the power of podcasting. By doing so, you can reach a wide and highly engaged audience and establish and enhance your brand and reputation.

Podcasting presents an opportunity to monetize your content and generate revenue.

In the upcoming chapter, we will examine in depth the wide array of benefits that podcasting brings to entrepreneurs and the compelling reasons it deserves serious consideration as an impactful marketing and content strategy.

One of the biggest advantages of podcasting is its ability to reach a highly targeted and engaged audience. According to recent statistics, over 79% of all Americans and 90% of Australians are aware of podcasting.

This means there is a vast and growing audience for podcast content, and as an entrepreneur, you can tap into this audience and get your message out there.

Another key benefit of podcasting is its ability to build trust and credibility with your audience. By sharing your expertise and insights through a podcast, you can establish yourself as an expert in your industry and build trust with your audience. This is especially important for entrepreneurs, as building trust is key to attracting customers and building a successful business.

Podcasting can also be a powerful marketing tool. By creating a podcast, you can drive traffic to your website, build your email list, and monetize your content through advertising and sponsorships.

Podcasting can be a great way to have fun and connect with your audience on a deeper level. By sharing your story and insights through a podcast, you can build a loyal community of listeners engaged with your content and brand. This can be a rewarding and fulfilling experience for entrepreneurs, and can help you build a successful and sustainable business.

Podcasting can be a powerful tool for entrepreneurs looking to reach a targeted and engaged audience, build trust and credibility, and grow their businesses. Whether you are just starting out or have been in business for years, podcasting is worth considering as a marketing and content strategy.

We also introduce you to a concept we call "Profitable Podcasting", which is a unique way to launch a podcast. It requires a change in mindset and might even sound counter-intuitive compared to the traditional way podcasting is done.

This book is a comprehensive guide to podcasting for your business, from the concept and strategy to implementation and, finally, marketing.

Sources:
https://www.statista.com/topics/3170/podcasting/
https://influencermarketinghub.com/podcast-statistics

CHAPTER 3

WHY PODCASTING

"The secret of getting ahead is getting started." – **Mark Twain**

For many entrepreneurs, starting a podcast sits high on their bucket list, but it often feels like a daunting project, with worries about time, complexity, and tech setup.

The reality?

Creating a podcast can be one of the simplest and most effective marketing tools in your arsenal. With the right approach, you can launch an audio-only podcast in just a few hours, giving your brand a powerful voice and a unique way to connect with your audience.

In this chapter, we'll walk you through the key reasons to consider podcasting, essential setup tips, and the basics to get started—no stress, no endless hours, just practical steps to make it happen.

Despite their interest in doing it, they perceive it as a task that demands a substantial amount of time and complexity in terms of setup and maintenance.

Surprisingly, creating a podcast is not as daunting as one might think.

To create a podcast show is, in reality, one of our top suggestions for effortless marketing strategies.

If you're curious, it is possible to create and deploy an audio-only podcast in just a few hours.

If you are considering podcasting, there are some key demographics and facts that you should consider:

- Out of the 60% of respondents aged 35+ years, 22% of those aged 50 or above in the US listened to a podcast within the preceding month in 2022. Respondents aged 35-54 years make up 38%[1].

- All generations except Gen X preferred podcasts with video. With 31% stating their preference for podcasts without video, Gen X leaned more towards no video.

- Slightly outweighing female listeners, male listeners (mostly white) hold a share of 53%, but in recent years, podcasts have gained popularity among Hispanic and African-American listeners.

- Surprisingly, Amazon has entered the podcasting realm by acquiring Wondery, the leading independent podcast network, and Art19, a prominent ad marketplace dedicated to podcasts.

- Even Amazon acknowledges the potential of podcasting and shows the growing significance of the industry by joining through its platform Amazon Music. It is quite easy to observe the seamless integration of the two components.

- With Spotify (25%) being considered the most popular app for listening to podcasts in the US, the tables turned on Apple (20%) in 2020.

- The most popular genre is comedy, with education and news following closely behind.

- 49% of listeners choose to engage in podcast listening from the comfort of their own homes. Following closely behind, 22% of listeners choose to indulge in podcasts while commuting in their cars. It is interesting to note that a significant portion of listeners, about 93%, enjoy this activity in solitude.

- While engaging in work or study-related activities, a substantial number of listeners, approximately 33%, find themselves engrossed in podcasts.

Completely free to decide, you have the option of choosing the frequency of your show, whether it be on a daily or weekly basis, with no pressure. It would be beneficial to prioritize the swift completion of 3-5 episodes and subsequently plan their release in a synchronized manner, with each episode being unveiled weekly.

By having a lead time of 3-5 weeks ahead of the latest episode, you can record multiple episodes at once, allowing you to stick to the planned schedule.

To ensure that your podcast is up and running, the following components are necessary:

- The strategy takes into consideration the show's title and its subject.

- Take some time to develop a comprehensive content plan for the show and also explore the possibility of inviting some guests to join us.

- To create a show vision, consult the "Vision" section in this book.

- Hosting Platform for your show's metadata (such as title, description, author name, etc.) and audio files for episodes.

- Show art to use as a cover for your podcast.

- Because of its ease of setup and use, as well as its reasonable quality, the Blue Yeti is a popular beginner choice for a decent microphone.

- Learn to use audio editing tools or hire someone to assist.

- A strategy to get subscribers listening to your show on your mailing list.

This is how the process operates:

- To have a complete podcast platform setup, include all the relevant details, such as the show title, categories, and description.

- In addition, it is important to recognize the importance of generating your RSS feed URL, which functions as a news feed providing platforms with the required information to host and stream your episodes, as previously mentioned.

- You can improve your episodes by recording and editing them.

- Upload and schedule your completed episodes.

- Once you have signed up for Apple Podcasts, the largest podcasting platform, you can list your show on other platforms.

🎤 To build up subscribers, it is important to officially launch your show and regularly post your episodes on social media and in your mailing list as you release them.

With over a decade of podcasting experience, we have discovered crucial elements for a show.

This includes:

🎤 Detailed Podcast Show Page

🎤 Awesome Show Art with strong branding

It is essential that you strongly value the freedom of owning your RSS Feed, as it is something you should never be willing to surrender. Having your own RSS Feed, specifically using your own domain, is something that you should seriously consider.

Many of the popular platforms enforce the use of their domain name for your RSS feed, which can cause a loss of flexibility. By renting the feed that is used to send the episodes to platform distribution sites, such as Apple Podcasts, you ensure that your content reaches a wider audience.

It's not something that crosses your mind until you decide to switch your hosting platform. With our platform, you are the sole owner of your RSS Feed, giving you autonomy and control.

Most Podcasters make this crucial mistake, and rectifying it can become an absolute nightmare later on.

Here are some game-changers:

🎤 Upsell products straight off your Show and Episode Page

🎤 You can have a video on the podcast page as well, providing extra value

🎤 Ability to have email subscribers and alert them automatically when a new episode comes out. Almost no one does this; if they do, they never give you the email addresses.

🎤 Using those email addresses, it is possible to create a show community. They can access the website's backend to see what you offer.

🎤 Create a course and membership (free or paid) to grow your revenue

🎤 Track your statistics to help grow your show

By implementing a Guest Host System makes efficiently managing guests for your show simple, thanks to its seamless application and pre-interview process. Guest hosts receive their own profile page for added visibility.

If you're not using PodcastSecrets.app for your podcast, you most likely have to set up a similar system through another platform like WordPress.

If you are new to podcasting and what to fast-track your setup and launch consider one of our **Evolvepreneur Podcast Packages.**

Our Podcast Show packages are designed to help you from start to finish and remain available for you after the setup.

You can find out more about podcastsecrets.biz

There are several phases:

- 🎤 **Your Success Manager in Phase 1** will dedicate 60 minutes to ensure strategic alignment of your ideas and concepts. It's great to have an expert sounding board before you dive in.

- 🎤 **Phase 2 - Setup & Design**—The setup phase is where we will design your show page and artwork and create your show pages. Your Success Manager will spend 60 minutes with you to create the best designs for your podcast.

- 🎤 **Phase 3 - Create Your Episodes**—Now it's your turn! We have a Podcast Host Course to guide you through all the technical and art of the podcast. You can also ask our Expert Support Team questions along the way. If you need your episodes edited, we can arrange this as an additional service.

- 🎤 **Phase 4 - Launch and Grow**—By now, you have created your initial episodes and are ready to launch. Our expert team will help get you ready to launch the show.

- 🎤 **Phase 5 - Revenue!**

If you take the "Done For You Package", Your Success Manager will spend 60 minutes discussing the best ways to leverage the platform to earn revenues. Using your show as the conversation starter, we aim to go from $0 to $5,000 a month in recurring revenue.

Podcasting might seem like a big leap, but with the right guidance, it can be a straightforward and rewarding venture. You have the flexibility to craft a show that suits your schedule, brand, and goals, all while building a lasting connection with your listeners.

By taking charge of your content and distribution, you're creating a platform that grows with you—an extension of your brand that's always working to expand your reach.

So go ahead, take that first step, and turn podcasting from a "someday" goal into an active part of your entrepreneurial journey.

Your audience is ready to tune in!

Sources:

https://www.statista.com/topics/3170/podcasting/

https://influencermarketinghub.com/podcast-statistics

CHAPTER 4

WHY CREATE YOUR OWN SHOW?

"Do not wait to strike till the iron is hot; but make it hot by striking." – **William Butler Yeats**

With so many podcasts out there, why start your own?

This chapter is all about discovering the unique value your voice and perspective bring to the table. We'll explore what makes your podcast stand out, how it can serve as a powerful business tool, and why the world needs your ideas.

Whether you want to inspire, educate, or entertain, we'll help you uncover the reasons why creating your own show might be the best business decision you make.

When entrepreneurs promote their businesses, they typically run ads or social media posts that are random and inconsistent. There's no overall strategy involved.

Successful individuals often host TV or Radio Shows.

What if we backward-engineered this concept?

If you created your own "show", it would not only allow you to formalize your content logically and sequentially; but it would also give your future customers a closer connection with you.

In the world of marketing, there are 2 very different key marketing strategies.

- 🎤 **Spray and Pray** involves creating and publishing enormous volumes of posts, videos, blogs, and other content.
- 🎤 **Narrow and Deep**—create less content but narrowly focused and comprehensive.

Let's explore the depths of the Narrow and Deep. If you did your initial research well enough, you will have a good idea of your ideal prospect and buyer.

By going deep into your topic, your content will stand out.

At this stage, you don't want to overthink the concept of a show. If you are not confident on video, start with audio.

If you have guests, try to capture both video and audio. If the video doesn't work out, it's fine since you only planned for audio.

But sometimes, you can re-purpose portions of your video for promotional purposes.

Many entrepreneurs at this stage mistakenly attempt to create, produce, and promote simultaneously.

This quickly becomes confusing and often results in some steps not getting the attention they need.

So, we suggest this plan:

Podcast Production and Promotion Plan

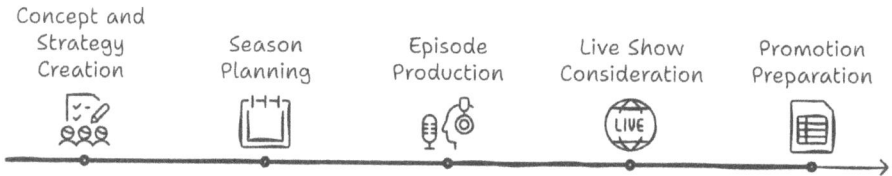

| Concept and Strategy Creation | Season Planning | Episode Production | Live Show Consideration | Promotion Preparation |

- Spend a few days creating the concept and strategies for your show.
- Plan on a "season" of 12-13 episodes at a rate of 1 per week.
- That means you could, in theory, have 3-4 seasons a year.
- Produce your episodes. If you are pre-recording, it will be a lot easier than going live on Facebook.
- You may do a live show, but remember both platforms can premiere or essentially fake a live show. This takes the pressure off, especially in the early days when you aren't yet a confident veteran podcaster.
- At the promotion stage, you should have scheduled your content and can prepare your marketing materials. For example, creating short outtakes of 1-2 minutes.

You need to consider where your primary show platform is. For most podcasts, that's Apple Podcasts. There are plenty of other platforms, like Google Podcasts and Spotify, but Apple Podcasts remain one of the most popular today.

So, be clear on your goals. Each platform has its own approach. It's a bit like choosing a TV channel and sticking to it.

Repurpose your content. For example, transcribe your episode and make it a blog post, or create a LinkedIn Article—however you reach people. Include the text on the actual episode itself, too. Your goal here should be to build email subscribers, offering bonus materials for them to sign up.

Level Up Ideas

One of the best ways to promote engagement is to hold a Q&A mini-show every so often, covering feedback and questions the main show content has highlighted. This is on-the-fly content creation during your promotion stage that encourages some live interaction with your viewers.

- Create a free membership club where listeners can subscribe to get extra bonuses and content from you.
- Get guest appearances on other podcast shows so you can cross-promote yourself.
- Create some front-end surveys to gain insight into your subscribers.

CHAPTER 5

OUR PODCAST BLUEPRINT

"A goal without a plan is just a wish." – **Antoine de Saint-Exupéry**

After many years of launching and growing podcasts, we've developed our own "Podcast Secrets Blueprint", which covers the five key phases of creating a successful podcast and reaping its benefits.

Podcast Creation Process

Vision   Create   Publish   Cultivate   Amplify

1. Vision

Developing a clear vision is the first step towards building a podcast that achieves success. The first step in creating a successful show is to identify your target audience.

Next, focus on determining the theme that will resonate with them. Last, it is crucial to define your unique value proposition to attract and engage your audience.

Take some time to consider the subjects that ignite your passion and the specific message you want to convey to your audience when reflecting on it.

It is important to emphasize that this phase is crucial for the success of your podcast.

It plays a pivotal role in not only shaping the overall direction of your podcast but also in ensuring that it aligns with your goals and resonates with your intended audience.

2. Create

The creation phase of the process involves the design of episodes that are both engaging and informative, intending to reflect your individual personality and style. To ensure that your podcast is both relevant and entertaining, it may be necessary to invest time in researching and planning each episode, depending on its nature.

If your goal is to produce compelling interviews, it may be worthwhile to prioritize the search for fascinating and entertaining individuals to interview. Regardless of any challenges you may face, it is crucial that you dedicate your efforts to establishing a cohesive format and tone for your podcast.

Consider incorporating distinctive elements that will distinguish your podcast from others within your niche.

By incorporating high-quality audio production techniques and implementing a crafted script, we can ensure that the final product exudes professionalism and polish.

3. Publish

The essential step of streamlining the publication process is crucial in order to maximize the reach of your podcast to your desired audience.

When selecting a hosting platform, it is important to consider various factors.

These factors include pricing, features offered by the platform, storage capabilities, the platform's ability to host the feed on your own domain, and obtaining analytics tools.

Take some time to think about the various ways you could present your completed episode.

If you focus on creating appealing cover art and writing compelling show notes, you will establish a stronger connection with a wider range of listeners.

4. Cultivate

Adopting a strategic approach to cultivating meaningful connections with your ideal prospects can have a dual benefit of enriching your podcast content and driving sales for your products or services.

If interviews are a major part of your podcast, select guests who align with your show's theme and resonate with your target audience.

When engaging in conversation, strive to cultivate a nurturing atmosphere that fosters open dialogue.

Encourage your guests to express their expertise and share their unique experiences, while subtly highlighting the advantages and pertinence of what you offer.

By building rapport and establishing trust with these guests, you create an organic pathway for potential business opportunities, transforming your podcast into a powerful marketing tool.

5. Amplify

To maximize the chances of your podcast being successful, it is crucial that you make efforts to amplify your brand.

Enhance the visibility of your show by implementing a comprehensive promotion strategy that encompasses various channels, such as social media, email marketing, and collaborating with other podcasters.

One way to engage with your audience is to encourage them to write reviews, which can spark discussions within your community.

Collaborate with influential individuals in your field and engage in podcasting communities to expand your audience and establish a firm presence in the growing podcast industry.

The focus of this book is to delve deeper into the 5 phases of podcasting and provide detailed guidance on how to establish a profitable and sustainable podcasting business.

Short Implementation Plan:

Timeline Overview

- Weeks 1-2: Focus on the Vision stage. Finalize your podcast concept, niche, and audience.
- Weeks 3-4: Move into Creation by planning episodes, recording, and editing. Complete a content calendar.
- Week 5: Publish your podcast. Set up hosting, distribute to platforms, and promote your launch.
- Weeks 6-8: Begin Cultivating your audience through engagement tactics, guest appearances, and cross-promotion.Ongoing: Amplify your reach. Use analytics, optimize marketing strategies, and explore monetization.

To help you implement the strategies outlined in Podcasting Secrets for Entrepreneurs, we've put together a comprehensive Podcast Secrets Resource Kit, which is available for free.

This kit contains tools, templates, and guides to streamline your podcasting process, from the initial planning stages to audience growth and monetization.

https://podcastsecrets.biz/s/kit

CHAPTER 6

BUILDING A PERSONAL BRAND THROUGH PODCASTING

"Be yourself; everyone else is already taken." – **Oscar Wilde**

Your brand is your business card—and podcasting is one of the most powerful ways to build that brand authentically.

In this chapter, we'll cover how to use your podcast to craft a personal brand that resonates with listeners, builds trust, and showcases your expertise.

We'll dive into strategies for showing up consistently, sharing your story, and creating a podcast that feels like a true reflection of who you are and what you offer.

Let's turn your voice into your brand's most valuable asset!

Podcasting offers a unique opportunity to craft and communicate your personal brand in an authentic and engaging way. Whether you're looking to establish yourself as an expert in your industry, promote your business, or share your ideas with a broader audience, podcasting can be the cornerstone of your personal branding strategy.

Through consistent episodes, thoughtful content, and genuine interaction, your podcast can help position you as a thought leader and influencer in your field.

Defining Your Personal Brand

Before you start building your personal brand through your podcast, you must define what your brand stands for. Your brand is a reflection of who you are, what you believe in, and the unique value you bring to your listeners.

Identify Your Core Message

Your core message is the foundation of your personal brand—it's the central idea you want to communicate to your audience. This message should align with your values, expertise, and the needs of your target listeners.

Ask yourself:

- What am I passionate about?
- What unique knowledge or experience do I bring to the table?
- How do I want to help my audience, and what problems can I solve for them?

Your podcast episodes should consistently reflect this core message. Whether you're offering advice, sharing personal experiences, or interviewing guests, everything should tie back to the central theme that defines your brand.

Building a Personal Brand Through Podcasting

Brand Growth

Audience Engagement

Content Consistency

Brand Personality

Niche Clarification

Core Message

Clarify Your Niche

To stand out in the crowded podcasting space, it's important to clearly define your niche. Instead of trying to appeal to everyone, focus on a specific audience segment that aligns with your expertise. This allows you to position yourself as an authority in that niche, making it easier to grow a loyal listener base. The more specific and focused your niche, the stronger your brand will be.

For example, if you're a marketing consultant, you might focus your podcast on digital marketing for small businesses or social media strategies for solopreneurs. By honing in on a particular niche, you differentiate yourself from broader marketing podcasts and become the go-to expert for that audience.

Develop Your Brand Personality

Your personal brand is also about how you present yourself. Your tone, style, and personality all contribute to how your audience perceives you. Are you approachable and conversational? Authoritative and data-driven? Inspirational and motivational?

Choose a brand personality that reflects your authentic self and resonates with your audience. Consistency is key here. Your listeners should feel like they know you, and that familiarity helps build trust and loyalty.

Crafting Valuable and Consistent Content

Once you've defined your personal brand, the next step is to craft valuable and consistent content that reinforces your brand's message and engages your audience.

Align Your Content with Your Brand

Every podcast episode should serve a purpose and reinforce your personal brand's core message. Whether you're educating, entertaining, or inspiring, your content should align with your brand's values and your audience's interests. Over time, your listeners will come to associate your podcast with the specific value you deliver.

For example, if your brand is centered around personal development, your episodes could include practical advice for self-improvement, interviews with successful entrepreneurs, or stories of overcoming challenges. The key is to create content that consistently delivers on your brand promise.

Be Consistent in Frequency and Format

Consistency is one of the most important elements of building a strong personal brand. This means delivering episodes on a regular schedule, maintaining a consistent format, and ensuring that your tone and messaging remain cohesive across episodes.

When listeners know what to expect from your podcast, they're more likely to become regular subscribers and engage with your content over the long term. Whether you publish weekly, bi-weekly, or monthly, stick to a schedule that works for you and ensures you can maintain quality and consistency.

Leverage Guest Interviews to Expand Your Reach

Featuring guest interviews on your podcast is an excellent way to add value to your content and grow your audience. By inviting thought leaders, industry experts, or influencers in your niche, you not only provide your listeners with diverse perspectives, but you also expose your podcast to your guest's audience.

However, be selective about your guests—each interview should align with your brand and add value to your core message. Your guests should complement your expertise, not overshadow it, and help reinforce your position as an authority in your niche.

Engaging with Your Audience

A strong personal brand isn't built in isolation—it's built through genuine interaction and engagement with your audience. Podcasting allows you to create a two-way relationship with your listeners, which is crucial for building long-term trust and loyalty.

Create Opportunities for Listener Interaction

One of the best ways to engage your audience is by encouraging interaction. You can do this by inviting listener questions, feedback, or topic suggestions. Use social media, email, or your podcast's website to facilitate this interaction, and feature listener questions or comments in your episodes.

For example, you might say, "Have a question you'd like answered on the show? Send it to [email] or leave us a voice message on our website, and we'll feature it in an upcoming episode!" This involvement engages your audience and gives you valuable insight into what your listeners care about most.

Share Personal Stories

Personal stories are one of the most effective ways to connect with your audience and build a strong personal brand. When you share your own experiences—whether they're successes, failures, or lessons learned—you create a sense of authenticity and relatability. Your listeners will feel like they know you on a personal level, which strengthens their trust in your brand.

Don't be afraid to be vulnerable or transparent about your journey. Authenticity is key to building a lasting personal brand, and sharing your real experiences can inspire and motivate your listeners.

Build a Community Around Your Brand

Fostering a community around your podcast is a powerful way to strengthen your personal brand. Consider creating private groups, forums, or social media communities where your listeners can interact with each other and with you. This deepens engagement and gives your audience a space to connect beyond just listening to your episodes.

A community platform can provide a sense of exclusivity and belonging, where members can discuss episodes, share their thoughts, and engage with your brand on a more personal level. You can also host live Q&A sessions, webinars, or virtual events to further enhance your community engagement.

Leveraging Podcasting for Brand Growth

Podcasting offers many opportunities to grow your personal brand beyond the podcast itself. By repurposing content, cross-promoting your podcast, and strategically aligning your podcast with other platforms, you can expand your reach and amplify your brand.

- **Repurpose Podcast Content for Multiple Platforms.** Don't limit your content to the podcast alone—repurpose it across other platforms to reach a wider audience. Transcribe episodes into blog posts, create social media snippets, or turn your podcast into video content for YouTube. This not only increases your visibility but also helps reinforce your personal brand across different channels.

  ▷ For example, a particularly insightful episode could be repurposed as an article on LinkedIn, while key quotes or sound bites can be shared on Instagram or Twitter. The more platforms you use, the more touchpoints you create for potential audience members to discover your brand.

- **Collaborate with Other Creators.** Collaboration is a great way to grow your personal brand by tapping into new audiences. Consider partnering with other podcasters, guesting on other shows, or co-creating content with industry experts. These collaborations can introduce your brand to new listeners who are already interested in your niche.

- **Monetize Strategically.** As your personal brand grows, podcast monetization becomes an opportunity to further solidify your brand's authority. Whether through sponsorships, affiliate marketing, or premium content, your monetization strategies should align with your brand values and provide value to your audience.

Be selective about the partnerships or sponsors you work with, ensuring they complement your personal brand and resonate with your audience. Authenticity is crucial in maintaining the trust you've built with your listeners, so only endorse products or services you genuinely believe in.

Building a personal brand through podcasting is a powerful strategy for establishing yourself as an authority in your niche, growing a loyal audience, and creating long-term success.

By defining your brand message, delivering consistent and valuable content, and engaging with your listeners in a meaningful way, your podcast can become the foundation of a thriving personal brand.

Podcasting is a platform for building a legacy.

To help you implement the strategies outlined in Podcasting Secrets for Entrepreneurs, we've put together a comprehensive Podcast Secrets Resource Kit, which is available for free.

This kit contains tools, templates, and guides to streamline your podcasting process, from the initial planning stages to audience growth and monetization.

https://podcastsecrets.biz/s/kit

CHAPTER 7

SETTING YOUR GOALS AND OBJECTIVES

"You miss 100% of the shots you don't take." – **Wayne Gretzky**

Before you hit record, it's important to know where you're headed. This chapter is all about setting clear, achievable goals for your podcast.

Are you looking to build a loyal audience?

Generate leads?

Position yourself as a thought leader?

Whatever your vision, we'll guide you through setting objectives that keep you focused, motivated, and on track.

Let's make sure every episode you produce brings you closer to your podcasting goals.

This will help you focus your efforts and ensure your podcast aligns with your overall business goals.

Consider what you hope to achieve through your podcast to set your goals and objectives.

Are you looking to build your brand and reputation, drive traffic to your website, generate leads, or monetize your content?

By clearly defining your goals, you can ensure your podcast aligns with your overall business objectives.

Besides setting overall goals, it can also be helpful to set specific, measurable, achievable, relevant, and time-bound (SMART) objectives.

For example, you might set a goal to increase your podcast's subscriber base by 20% in the next six months or generate a certain amount of revenue through advertising and sponsorships. By setting SMART objectives, you can track your progress and measure the success of your podcast.

You must also consider your target audience when setting your goals and objectives.

Who are you trying to reach through your podcast, and what are their interests and needs?

By understanding your target audience, you can tailor your content and marketing efforts to meet their needs better and engage them with your podcast.

Finally, it is important to be realistic when setting your goals and objectives.

While you should aim high and strive for success, you must be realistic about what you can achieve. Setting realistic goals and objectives allows you to avoid disappointment and stay motivated to continue growing and improving your podcast.

Achieving targets and goals is a major challenge in every entrepreneur's life. Despite your success, the longing for more persists.

Setting goals is not only a way to accomplish your entrepreneurial success, but also an essential human need.

If you want to fill your life with purpose and accomplishment, you must start with worthwhile goals that are most important to you.

Just getting through the day is not enough. The skill of setting goals can be learned and practiced.

Goal-setting works because your brain is a mechanical goal-seeking device.

Our unique ability to possess and achieve goals sets us apart from other forms of life.

After you have defined your objective and begun taking steps to accomplish it, it is important to guarantee that you stay aligned with your target.

Develop the habit of assessing your progress regularly and making any necessary changes or corrections to effectively stay on target.

You build your life and success through your thoughts; a winning self-concept is the first step to building yourself. Who you believe you are and who you are is your potential.

What you believe will become reality (if you have faith in your mind's goal-seeking mechanism).

What you believe grows from an idea, vision, or dream into your life's reality. If you dwell on your eventual success, you will achieve it. Focus on problems negatively, and they will grow and overwhelm you.

The images you see will become real. The more often you concentrate on them, the sooner you will attain them.

When setting your goals, focus on the result or outcome rather than the actual process.

Focusing on outcomes is a critical element if you want to succeed. Try to avoid making your goal smaller.

You may have to compromise, which is a fact of life.

The trick is to pay the right price for the right thing.

You also need to write your goals down—otherwise, you can easily change them in your mind!

Some ideas:

- 🎤 How many listeners do I want?
- 🎤 How many podcast episodes in three years?
- 🎤 How many new monthly subscribers to my email list do I want to receive from my podcast?
- 🎤 What are my lifetime goals?

- 🎤 What is my desired situation in 5 years?
- 🎤 What is my ideal situation in 3 years?
- 🎤 What is the most important current ambition?

You should write goals in result terms rather than activity terms.

For example:

Activity Terms

I want to improve as a podcaster.

Result Terms

I want to get the top 100-ranked podcast in the XX Category

The message here is clear. You may learn and know more about Product Y than anyone else.

The entire purpose of writing goals in result terms is to achieve a positive result. Test the validity of a goal. Try to write in result terms, focused on achieving a specific, positive, and worthwhile result. Output forces you to focus and act.

Here are a few ideas to help achieve your goals...

Balance your picture – ask yourself whether your goals fit your total lifestyle picture.

Align your goals – this means working in an orderly and consistent way. Smaller goals should work towards achieving bigger long-term goals.

Co-operate with others – if others are involved, and you need cooperation, ask for it. Most people are glad to help. Be prepared to return the favor for their goals in the future.

Imagine your desires, not your fears. This principle is crucial for success. Always focus on what you want until it becomes the dominant thought.

If you visualize what you don't want, it becomes the dominant thought you will surely get!

It is interesting to observe that a significant number of negative individuals in life often end up receiving the things they least desire. Instead of focusing on their desires, they choose to focus on their fears.

Visualize your desired outcome. – traditional methods of achieving your goals don't consider the power of your mind and the role visualization plays.

Success requires mastering visualization and believing in its crucial role. If you can't see it, you can't do it.

Accept Responsibility – It's up to you. If you don't do it, it won't get done. It's your goal; it's your responsibility. You will look at life differently once you accept absolute responsibility for your actions and goals.

Actions gain new meaning.

It's your choice to determine your desires. Prioritize self-control before exercising this right or power.

"By [date], it'll be done."

Measure your achievement – It's important to define clearly how you will know when you have accomplished your goal. Measure the progress made.

It is vital to record it so others can also understand, as you often need others to help you achieve your goals.

Check your progress–Set dates of review. Constantly check your progress, destination, and punctuality. If not, why not?

How do you plan to get back on target again?

Taking things as they come will almost guarantee that you achieve less than you could.

Write the "how-to" of your plan–put your goals in writing. That's the vital key. Then prepare a detailed activity plan to achieve your goals. You need a separate activity plan for each goal you set.

The real issue lies in the means to achieve your desires. Without a list of activities, you're just stuck in the "want to" phase.

Strong desire is necessary to achieve something.

Many people believe they can keep their goals in their head. Let's say you have 6 goals, which have 10-20 activities for each goal to achieve them.

- 🎙 Each goal requires an average of 15 sequential activities.
- 🎙 This means a total of 90 activities; some may even be mini-goals in themselves!
- 🎙 Do you believe you can handle 90 activities in your head?

If you don't write your goals and activities, you must do them as they occur to you. Taking a chance, you will get it right.

Write them in the future tense.

Now that we have spoken about setting personal goals, we can move on to setting goals for your business.

One of the biggest problems in any business is the owner!

Yes, you… Why?

Because you don't have anyone keeping you honest with your business goals, you can always make a trade-off in your mind and make excuses. Would you accept some of these excuses from a staff member?

Probably not. In fact, you might even consider firing them!

If you want your business to grow, you must decide how it will look when it's finished. Envision your destination for the next 3, 5, and 10 years.

Remember, if you are not following your plan, you are probably following someone else's. What plans do they have for you? Usually, not much!

What and When!

Set some time frames for your podcast's growth regarding turnover, guests, sponsorship, clients, billing time, etc. Once you reach these targets, consider putting someone into your business who can take over some of your daily functions.

A brilliant book to read BEFORE employing anyone is The E-Myth by Gerber. Don't wait for the perfect candidate, but rather, get your business ready for new employees.

Start by filling out an organizational chart, noting key job positions. Next, complete job descriptions for each position. Sign it. Once you know each position, document it to facilitate hiring in the future. Never hire someone based on their skills and then create a position for them. It's a recipe for disaster. You will end up doing whatever they don't want to do.

After all, who is the boss?

The side benefit of documentation is your business becomes much more saleable. In fact, clients feel more comfortable when they know how you run your business.

You can use it as a selling tool. We have often shown a prospect, our client training system checklist and manual or even our job descriptions.

Sometimes, they don't even have it in their business, which instantly gives them confidence that you know what you are doing.

Goal-Writing Workshop

Choose a goal that you wish to achieve in the next 12 months:

Outline the specific actions needed to reach the bigger goal.

1._____WHEN:

2._____WHEN:

3._____WHEN:

4._____WHEN:

To help you implement the strategies outlined in Podcasting Secrets for Entrepreneurs, we've put together a comprehensive Podcast Secrets Resource Kit, which is available for free.

This kit contains tools, templates, and guides to streamline your podcasting process, from the initial planning stages to audience growth and monetization.

https://podcastsecrets.biz/s/kit

CHAPTER 8

WHAT IS AN RSS FEED AND WHY DO I CARE? 🔊

"Don't limit your challenges. Challenge your limits." – **Anonymous**

RSS feeds may sound technical, but they're actually the magic behind how your podcast reaches listeners worldwide.

This chapter breaks down what an RSS feed is, how it works, and why it's essential for getting your podcast out there.

We'll cover everything you need to know to set up your feed without the headache, so you can focus on what you do best—creating amazing content.

Most podcasts are distributed through something called an RSS feed, which is a page written in XML that holds information necessary to distribute your podcast.

RSS feeds are over 20 years old at the time of writing, and they have found other applications over time. They were originally designed for users to keep up with frequently-updated information such as blogs or news sites, and they are still used in those areas today.

Even YouTube publishes RSS feeds for channels!

This often stops the new podcaster in their tracks and is the main reason they put off starting a podcast for so long.

We think this is a little ironic, as RSS stands for Really Simple Syndication—it's meant to make your life easier, not harder! There isn't much to them, really.

This feed will be created by your hosting platform, although we believe you should "own" your feed.

More on that later.

You can see an example of an RSS feed here:

https://evolvepreneursecrets.show/feed/podcast

If you look closely, it will quickly start to make some sense. You can see the show details, followed by links to and details about the episodes.

The truth is, podcast platforms like Apple Podcasts (the biggest platform on the market currently) don't actually host anything; descriptions, episode files, and show artwork are taken from RSS feeds like this. They simply hook into this feed, which is updated every time you make changes on your hosting platform—which, in our case, is Evolvepreneur, a fully-featured podcasting solution.

Once they acquire the information they need, they stream it on-demand via their website, or in the case of Apple Podcasts, their app. It's stupidly simple to distribute your podcast on several platforms, because all you need is the link to your RSS feed. You don't need to upload audio files, show artwork, fill in the show description, or any of those details on the distribution platform—they get it from the feed.

And if you need to make a change, you don't need to make the same change on dozens of different platforms; you just need to change it on the RSS feed, and every platform will pick up on the change. If you decide you don't like an episode you've already produced, simply delete it from your feed and it's gone forever.

All these distribution platforms come to you to get your podcast.

The best part is you don't need to know much create and manage an RSS feed; all podcast hosting platforms worth their salt will automatically generate an RSS feed and update it whenever you make changes. You simply take the link to your RSS feed and plug it into a podcasting distribution platform like Apple Podcasts.

How an RSS Feed Looks

The RSS feed is essentially an XML file with a series of tags that contain the data for your podcast.

Key Fields Explained

Channel Information (Podcast Level)

This section gives directories the main details about your entire podcast:

- 🎙 **<title>:** Your podcast's title.**<link>:** A link to your podcast's main webpage.
- 🎙 **<description>:** A brief summary of what your podcast is about.
- 🎙 **<language>:** Language code, like "en-us" for American English.
- 🎙 **<itunes:author>:** Your name or brand.
- 🎙 **<itunes:category>:** Primary category to help users find your show.
- 🎙 **<itunes:image>:** Link to the podcast cover art, typically 1400x1400 to 3000x3000 pixels.
- 🎙 **<itunes:explicit>:** Whether your content is explicit ("yes" or "no").

Item Information (Episode Level)

Each <item> tag represents a single podcast episode:

- 🎙 **<title>:** The episode's title.
- 🎙 **<description>:** A brief description or summary of the episode.
- 🎙 **<enclosure>:** The audio file URL. Includes attributes for the file type (usually "audio/mpeg") and file size.
- 🎙 **<guid>:** A unique identifier for the episode, usually the audio file's URL.
- 🎙 **<pubDate>:** The date and time the episode was published.
- 🎙 **<itunes:duration>:** Episode length in HH:MMformat.

How the RSS Feed Works

Once your RSS feed is set up and linked to your podcast hosting platform, it updates automatically each time you publish a new episode. Podcast directories regularly check your RSS feed for updates, so any new episodes or changes to existing ones are picked up and updated for subscribers.

In short, an RSS feed is the backbone of your podcast's distribution. It ensures that your show reaches listeners across all platforms and keeps everything up-to-date.

That's it! You're done! This is the hardest aspect of podcasting to get your head around. It only gets easier from here!

To help you implement the strategies outlined in Podcasting Secrets for Entrepreneurs, we've put together a comprehensive Podcast Secrets Resource Kit, which is available for free.

This kit contains tools, templates, and guides to streamline your podcasting process, from the initial planning stages to audience growth and monetization.

https://podcastsecrets.biz/s/kit

Vision

Conceptualizing your vision is the foundation for creating a successful podcast. Start by identifying your target audience, determining your show's theme, and defining your unique value proposition.

Consider the topics you are passionate about and the message you want to convey to your listeners.

This phase is crucial, as it shapes the direction of your podcast, ensuring it aligns with your goals and resonates with your intended audience.

CHAPTER 9

DEVELOPING YOUR PODCAST IDEA

"Creativity is intelligence having fun." – **Albert Einstein**

Every great podcast starts with a spark—an idea that's unique, intriguing, and just won't let go.

But how do you take that spark and turn it into a full-fledged show that people actually want to listen to?

In this chapter, we'll explore the art of developing a podcast idea that stands out in a sea of shows. From finding your niche to defining the voice and personality of your show, we'll help you shape an idea that's bursting with potential.

So grab a notebook (or a napkin—no judgment!) and get ready to bring that podcast vision to life!

One of the first steps in creating a successful podcast is developing a clear and compelling idea. This will be the foundation of your podcast, and will help you attract and engage listeners.

Start by considering your strengths and expertise.

What are you passionate about and knowledgeable in? This could be a particular industry, hobby, or topic you are well-versed in. By focusing on your strengths and expertise, you can create an authentic, engaging, and informative podcast for your audience.

Next, consider your target audience.

Who are you trying to reach through your podcast, and what are their interests and needs? By understanding your target audience, you can tailor your podcast idea to meet their needs better and engage them with your content. More on this in the Defining Your Target Audience chapter.

It can also be helpful to conduct market research to see what types of podcasts are currently popular in your industry or niche. This can give you ideas for your podcast and help you stand out in a crowded marketplace.

Once you have a clear idea for your podcast, testing it out and getting feedback from potential listeners is important. Produce a pilot episode, direct your list to it, and examine the response. This can help you refine your concept and ensure it is compelling and resonates with your target audience. Negative feedback is valuable, too, because you can use it to change the parts listeners weren't a fan of.

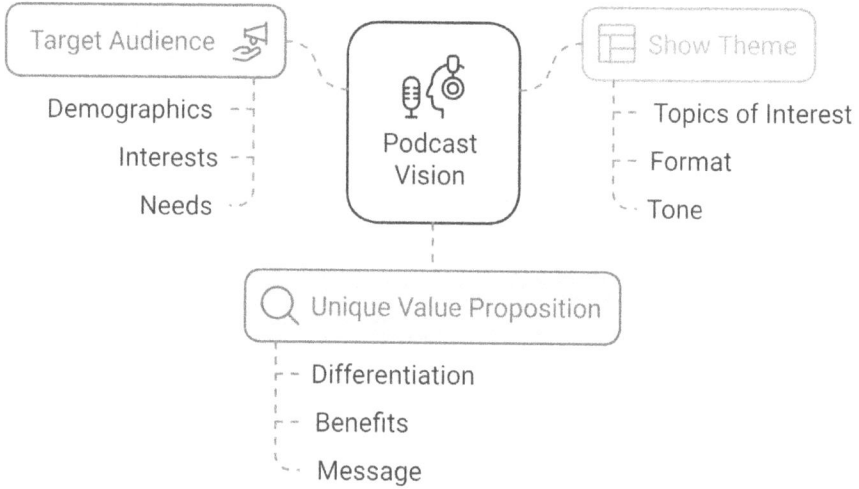

By focusing on your strengths and expertise and understanding your target audience, you can create an authentic podcast, engaging, and resonates with your listeners. That's the content part—but there's more to it than that. You have to consider how the podcast is presented.

Here are a few ideas for branding a podcast:

- Choose a catchy and memorable name that reflects the theme or focus of the podcast.
- Develop a unique and consistent visual identity, including a logo and cover art that represents the podcast and distinguishes it from other shows.
- Create consistent art for each episode that matches your overall show art.
- Create a tagline or motto that sums up the essence of the podcast memorably and concisely.
- Use social media and other online platforms to promote the podcast and engage with listeners.
- Consider creating merchandise such as t-shirts, stickers, or other items that feature the podcast's branding.
- Utilize a consistent and professional-sounding intro and outro that helps establish the podcast's identity and tone.
- Consider working with a professional designer or branding expert to help develop a cohesive and effective branding strategy.

Remember, the key to successful branding is consistency. By consistently using the same name, visual identity, and messaging across all platforms and materials, you can help establish a strong and recognizable brand for your podcast.

CHAPTER 10

CHOOSING YOUR FORMAT AND STRUCTURE

"Simplicity is the ultimate sophistication." – **Leonardo da Vinci**

S hould your podcast be interview-based, solo, narrative-driven, or a mix of everything? Choosing the right format and structure is essential to making your podcast engaging and sustainable.

In this chapter, we'll explore different formats, help you figure out what suits your strengths, and guide you in crafting a structure that flows.

Let's make sure your podcast has a format that keeps listeners hooked and feels easy to produce.

There are many different formats and structures to choose from, and the right one for you will depend on your goals, content, and target audience.

One common format for podcasts is the interview or conversation style.

This involves having one or more hosts interview a guest or guests on a particular topic or theme. This format is great for building relationships, sharing expertise, and engaging with your audience.

We also call this "Guest Hosting", and it's a fast and potentially very profitable way to launch a podcast. We cover this idea later in the book, so read this important chapter!

Another popular format is the solo or monologue style, where hosts share their insights and experiences on a particular topic. This format is great for sharing personal stories, sharing expertise, and offering a unique perspective.

Other formats to consider include roundtable discussions, panel discussions, and group conversations. These formats are great for bringing together multiple experts or perspectives on a particular topic and fostering a sense of community and collaboration.

In terms of structure, breaking your podcast into distinct segments or episodes can be helpful. This can make your content more digestible and help to keep your listeners engaged.

Each episode should have a consistent structure or format, starting with an introduction, then an interview or discussion, and ending with a conclusion or call to action.

This is an important step in refining your podcast concept, so it's important to get it right.

Refining Your Podcast Concept

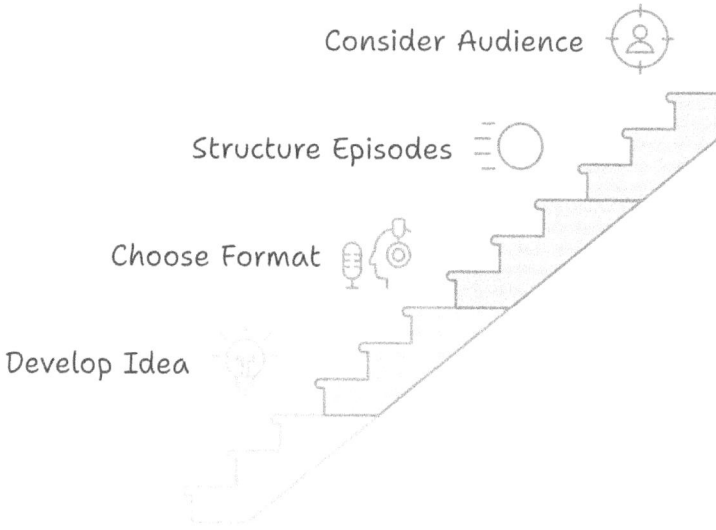

Consider Audience

Structure Episodes

Choose Format

Develop Idea

Consider your goals and content when deciding on a format and structure.

Your target audience will also influence this decision, so you may want to read the next chapter on Defining Your Target Audience before you finalize your format.

CHAPTER 11

DEFINING YOUR TARGET AUDIENCE

"To be yourself in a world that is constantly trying to make you something else is the greatest accomplishment." – **Ralph Waldo Emerson**

Who is your podcast really for?

Defining your target audience isn't just about demographics; it's about understanding who will benefit most from your content and how to speak directly to them.

In this chapter, we'll help you identify and connect with your ideal listeners, making sure every episode you create is tuned to their needs, interests, and desires.

The clearer your audience, the more powerful your impact.

Key Factors for a Successful Podcast

Monetization Opportunities

Defining Target Audience

Connecting with Listeners

·LIVE·

Tailoring Content

Marketing Strategies

Messaging Strategies

One of the most crucial steps in launching a successful podcast is identifying and understanding your target audience. Your target audience is the group of people most likely to be interested in your podcast's content and theme. By defining your target audience, you can tailor your content, messaging, and marketing strategies to attract and engage the right listeners.

It enables you to connect more deeply with your listeners by creating relevant content that provides value to them and allows you to develop effective promotional strategies that speak to their interests and challenges. It also helps you identify suitable monetization opportunities, such as sponsorships or premium content that are relevant to your listeners, which gives you one way to make your podcast sustainable.

This chapter will guide you through the process of defining your target audience and using that information to create a podcast that resonates with them.

Identifying Your Target Audience And Creating Listener Personas

To define your target audience, start by considering the general demographics of your potential listeners, such as their age, gender, location, income, and occupation. This can give you a better understanding of who your podcast is most likely to appeal to.

Next, consider the interests and needs of your potential listeners. What are they interested in, and what do they hope to get from your podcast? By understanding the interests and needs of your target audience, you can tailor your content and marketing efforts to meet their needs better and engage them with your podcast.

It can also be helpful to conduct market research to understand your target audience better. This can include things like surveying your email list, conducting focus groups, or analyzing data from social media or other online platforms.

There are a few other ways to pin down your target audience:

- **Psychographics:** Analyze your potential listeners' interests, hobbies, values, attitudes, and lifestyle preferences. This will help you better understand their needs and create content that resonates with them.

- **Listening Habits:** Examine the listening habits of your potential audience, such as when and where they typically listen to podcasts, their preferred podcast platforms, and their favorite podcast genres. This information can guide your content format, episode length, and distribution strategy.

- **Pain Points & Desires:** Dig deeper into who your listeners are and what they want. Understanding what your audience wants and needs from a podcast will help you create content addressing those concerns. Everyone has something that makes them hurt—sometimes physically! Medical podcasts are a great example of hitting both pain points and desires. They help you understand what ails you while satisfying your desire to learn new things.

Tailoring Your Podcast to Your Target Audience

By understanding who your ideal listeners are and what they value, you can create a podcast that resonates with them and meets their needs. This, in turn, will increase your chances of attracting loyal subscribers, growing your podcast, and creating a sustainable and profitable podcasting venture.

Here's how you can tailor your podcast to your target audience:

- 🎙 **Content and Format:** Use your understanding of your target audience to develop content and a format that speaks to their interests and preferences. Consider episode length, frequency, and structure, as well as the tone and style of your podcast.

- 🎙 **Branding and Messaging:** Develop a brand and messaging strategy that appeals to your target audience. This includes elements such as your podcast's name, logo, tagline, overall visual identity, and the language and tone used in your marketing materials.

- 🎙 **Promotion and Distribution:** Align your promotional and distribution strategies with your target audience's preferences and habits. Choose popular podcast platforms and marketing channels among your target listeners and create promotional materials that resonate with their interests and needs.

The mistake many new entrepreneurs and podcasters alike make is trying to sell something no one wants to buy.

Many of these entrepreneurs target a broad audience based on their industry or vague demographics, such as age or sex. This strategy is doomed to fail.

The broader you go, the worse it gets. Go too far, and you'll end up as nothing to no one. For your podcast to attract listeners, you must be something to someone.

But first, you need to find out who that someone is.

What we discuss next can easily be done in less than a day, saving you a lot of time and money.

The first rule of marketing is that you should be able to describe your target audience so well that they think you must have been stalking them!

The first step is to discover what keywords your market uses. This can be accomplished in a few ways:

- 🎙 Google "Google Keyword Planner"
- 🎙 Use Google Insights
- 🎙 Google alerts; signup for keywords
- 🎙 Search Amazon
- 🎙 Insert quotes on either side of a phrase and paste it into search.twitter.com. Look for tweets for those that are frustrated, would directly benefit, or are suggestive of a wish—ignore advertisers
- 🎙 Search "YoutubeSetup"
- 🎙 Do a Facebook search

Dedicate some time to researching your market by pasting your chosen subject into the search box to see what pops up on these platforms.

Create a spreadsheet of all posts and comments with the longest, most engaged or most passionate text.

Look for patterns—does your research suggest a contrarian position?

At this stage, you are looking for the top 5-10% of relevant results to refine your spreadsheet to focus on what angles you might take in your marketing.

You are looking for one critical need you could use to differentiate yourself from your competitors in the market.

In your research, look for "hyper-responsive text".

Even in your surveys, people who respond in detail are more likely to buy a product or service, because they are passionate about the problem or solution.

There are three questions you want to ask your ideal prospect or customer.

- 🎙 The WHAT question—e.g. "what is your single biggest question about...
- 🎙 "The WHY question—e.g. "Why would that make a difference in your life?"
- 🎙 The HOW HARD question—e.g. How hard has it been for you to find a good answer about....?"

And just like that, you've filled out a fairly detailed profile of your target audience, and you can now work on being a better something for that someone.

CHAPTER 12

CREATING A CONTENT CALENDAR

"By failing to prepare, you are preparing to fail." – **Benjamin Franklin**

I f you've ever sat down to record an episode and thought, "Wait... what am I even talking about today?" you're not alone. Welcome to the magic of the podcast content calendar—a tool that keeps you from scrambling for ideas and ensures your episodes flow seamlessly week after week.

Think of it as your roadmap for content greatness, helping you plan topics, schedule guest interviews, and align with key dates or trends. In this chapter, we'll walk through creating a calendar that'll make your podcast look organized and intentional, even if you're still recording in your pajamas. Ready to bring some structure to the chaos? Let's map it out!

Once you have developed a clear and compelling podcast idea, chosen your format and structure, and defined your target audience, the next step is to create a content calendar. A content calendar is a schedule that outlines the topics and themes for each episode of your podcast, as well as any deadlines or milestones.

How to plan a podcast?

Frequency
Decide how often to release new episodes (weekly, biweekly, monthly).

Length
Determine the ideal length of each episode (specific length or variable).

Topics
Choose the topics and themes to cover (niche-specific or wide range).

Guests
Decide whether to have guests and how to find them.

There are a few key things to consider when creating a content calendar:

🎙 **Frequency:**

▷ How often do you want to release new podcast episodes?

▷ Will you release new episodes weekly, biweekly, monthly, or on another schedule?

▷ More frequent episodes are not necessarily a good thing; listeners can find that overwhelming.

▷ You need to give listeners just the right amount of you. On the other hand, listeners are more accepting of monthly episodes if a lot of work has gone into production.

▷ Consistency is important, regardless of how often you release new episodes.

🎙 **Length:**

▷ How long will each episode of your podcast be?

▷ Will you aim for a specific length, or will it vary depending on the topic and format?

▷ Do you need to trim parts of your recorded content to match that length?

▷ These are things to keep in mind during the recording stage.

🎙 **Topics:**

▷ What topics and themes will you cover in each podcast episode?

▷ Will you focus on a specific niche or industry or cover a wider range of topics?

🎙 **Guests:**

▷ Will you have guests on your podcast, and if so, who will they be?

▷ How will you find and schedule guests for your podcast?

🎙 **Promotion:**

▷ How will you promote each episode of your podcast?

▷ Will you use social media, email marketing, or other tactics to get the word out?

By creating a content calendar, you can stay organized and on track with your podcasting efforts and consistently release new and interesting content for your audience.

If you choose "Guest Hosting", building an exact content calendar becomes harder. You might want to break your show into seasons that handle key concepts or ideas and attract potential guests who can compliment this strategy.

Consistency is important whether you choose to release a new episode weekly, fortnightly, or monthly. Insofar as it relates to the release schedule, listeners find predictability to be reassuring. This doesn't mean you can't take breaks when needed, but you should always stick to a schedule.

If you can, you should record episodes weeks ahead of time to give yourself leeway.

CHAPTER 13

YOUR PODCAST SCRIPTS

"The best preparation for tomorrow is doing your best today." – **H. Jackson Brown, Jr.**

Every episode of your podcast will have clips that always appear:

- 🎤 Intro
- 🎤 Outro
- 🎤 Mid-roll Advertisements

Getting the scripts for these clips right at the outset is important. Spend time reviewing these, because they will stick with you throughout all your podcast episodes.

Podcast Intro Writing Guide

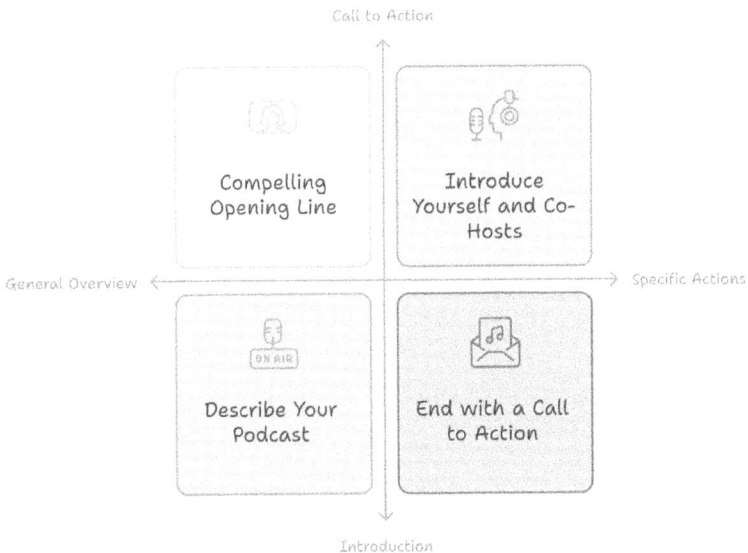

Call to Action

Compelling Opening Line	Introduce Yourself and Co-Hosts
Describe Your Podcast	End with a Call to Action

General Overview ← → Specific Actions

Introduction

Here are some steps for writing a podcast intro:

- 🎙️ **Craft a compelling opening line:** Your intro should start with a compelling opening that grabs the listener's attention and sets the tone for your podcast. This can be a question, a statement, or a compelling anecdote.

- 🎙️ **Introduce yourself and your co-hosts:** Next, introduce yourself and any co-hosts, and provide a brief overview of your backgrounds and qualifications.

- 🎙️ **Describe your podcast:** After introducing yourself and your co-hosts, describe your podcast in more detail. This should include an overview of the topic, format, and any unique features or perspectives.

- 🎙️ **End with a call to action:** You may choose to end your intro with a call to action that encourages listeners to subscribe, leave a review, or engage with your podcast in some other way, or you may choose to only mention in your outro.

Following these steps, you can write a compelling and effective podcast intro that engages and informs your listeners.

Working Example:

We wrote this outline document for creating the scripts for Evolvepreneur Secrets For Entrepreneurs Show. We recommend answering all these questions for your podcast to create powerful scripts.

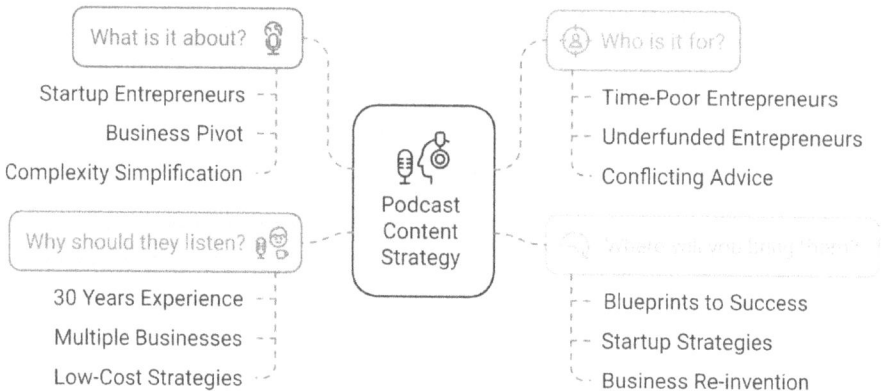

What is it about?

Are you a startup entrepreneur or looking to pivot and re-invent your business and struggling with the complexity?

Who is it for?

As a time-poor, typically underfunded online entrepreneur who receives so much conflicting advice about the best ways to grow your business, how can you compete with the big end of town without any of the resources they have at their disposal?

Where will you bring them (result)?

Help create the blueprints to success for any startup or pivot

Why should they listen (why you)?

In the past 30 years I've started many new businesses (from IT to software, marketing and back to software) and created the blueprints to starting quickly and at low cost to lower the risk and increase the chance of success.

Desire

How can you create a profitable and successful 6 to 7-figure business?

As a time-poor, typically underfunded entrepreneur with so much conflicting advice about the best ways to start and grow your business, how do you get it right, the first time?

Backstory

In the past 30 years, I've started and grown many new businesses from Accounting, and IT to software, coaching, consulting, marketing and back to software. I took a failing distribution company and turned it into the 2nd largest on the planet for a major accounting software brand in less than 3 years, I thought I knew it all, but boy was I wrong!

Wall

This company came under attack from my own supplier which lead to a brutal 7 years of war for survival.

At one point, I was diagnosed with deadly cancer, which I truly believe was caused by the extreme stress of trying to save this business. This leads me to quit and start all over again for the 3rd time. This failure cost me millions of dollars and easily set me back 15 years, and I had to start again with virtually no money and no time to waste.

Journey/Epiphany

Failure is a great teacher, but it doesn't have to be this way!

I had to admit defeat, so the next day I started a new marketing company to help entrepreneurs avoid the pitfalls.

Along the way, I finally learnt not only how to start a new business or product fast but also how to avoid the pitfalls that cost me a lot of money and focus in the past.

But soon faced a major challenge on how to help them create a world-class website experience for their customers. It often meant cobbling up to 10 solutions together using plugins and third-party tools to get a functioning website capable of engaging and convincing visitors to buy from them.

Plan

In frustration, I set out to create the "ultimate all-in-one business system" which is a unique combination of software, coaching and implementation services to help implement the secret blueprints to success for any startup or pivot. These blueprints need to help you can start quickly, at a low cost, risk and have a high chance of success.

Conflict

The real question is, How do I do it?

How do I grow this system to deliver the results that entrepreneurs really need?

Join me on my personal journey to find out as we build these blueprints together and share ideas from real entrepreneurs who are fighting every day to build and grow their own businesses.

Achievement

My mission is to start a revolution that will help entrepreneurs easily establish their own complete business system that can compete with the big end of town and mainstream social media platforms.

I want to help entrepreneurs make a real difference and navigate the messy world of startup or re-launch.

My name is John North and this is the Evolvepreneur Secrets for Entrepreneurs Show.

Join me today where we dig deep with our guests and get you the best blueprints so you can fast track your business.

Bringing it all together

Using all of that, we were able to create a powerful, succinct intro for our podcast. We also used it to create our first episode, which introduces the podcast. You may or may not want to create a similar introductory episode for your podcast. You may wish to jump right in with a guest interview.

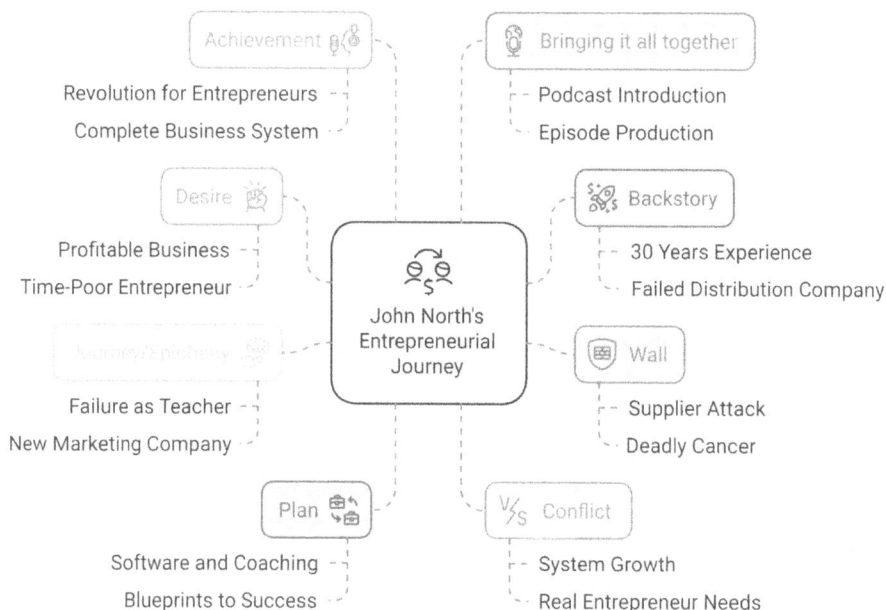

We also used this outline document for producing our mid-roll advertisements and creating our outro. You can see the scripts for each below.

Entrepreneurial Journey and Lessons

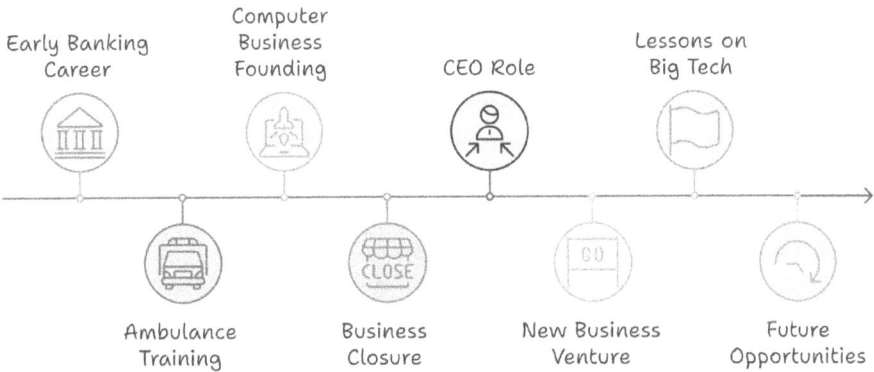

Early Banking Career | Computer Business Founding | CEO Role | Lessons on Big Tech

Ambulance Training | Business Closure | New Business Venture | Future Opportunities

EPISODE INTRO:

The question in my mind is...

How do you create or re-launch a highly profitable and successful 6 to 7-figure business?

With so much conflicting advice about the best ways to start and grow your business, how do you get it right, the first time?

I want to help entrepreneurs make a real difference and navigate the messy world of startup or re-launch

My name is John North and this is the Evolvepreneur Secrets for Entrepreneurs Show

Join me today, where we dig deep with our guests and get you the best blueprints so you can fast-track your business.

This episode is sponsored by Evolvepreneur.app your "all-in one" online business system.

Make sure you subscribe for future episodes at evolvepreneursecrets.show right now.

So let's get into today's episode...

EPISODE ONE:

The question in my mind is...

How do you create or re-launch a highly profitable and successful 6 to 7-figure business?

With so much conflicting advice about the best ways to start and grow your business, how do you get it right, the first time?

In the past 30 years, I've started and grown many new businesses, including my first business which was an IT and Accounting software business that got wiped out almost overnight when a new sales tax was introduced in Australia.

So I took over the failing accounting software distribution company that was my supplier and relocated my family to Sydney.

Time to put my experience to work!

This started a journey to re-launch this company, and I turned it into the 2nd largest distributor on the planet in less than 3 years.

At that point... I was thought I was bulletproof after creating millions of dollars of recurring income plus 23 staff

Our revenue was growing rapidly every day with new opportunities from all directions.

Life was looking pretty good. I had made it. I could only go up from here!

I thought I knew it all, boy was I so wrong!

Bizarrely my success caused my company to come under direct attack from my own supplier.

What I didn't factor in was that I had no control over the brand or the supply chain, and through a twist of fate we became a target. I basically owned nothing and essentially could be terminated anytime.

This led to brutal 7 year war for our survival, fighting on all fronts with rapidly decreasing revenues. We tried everything, including starting new sub-businesses, pricing strategies, launches, and even an alternative supplier.

Finally, I had to admit defeat, it simply wasn't worth fighting any longer, and things were getting pretty desperate.

I had failed... again!

So I after a year, I finally managed to sell the distribution business that had cost me millions of dollars.

So determined to get it right next time I decided to start a new business branded "Evolve"

(seemed a good name given the circumstances!)

I was a new online marketing company designed to help entrepreneurs grow their businesses using books, social media and websites.

This time was 100% owned and controlled.

But things took an even worse turn ...

The king-hit.... that i wasn't expecting...

I was diagnosed with deadly cancer which I truly believe was caused by the extreme stress of trying to save my accounting business

At the same time, because of an early diagnosis I was able to get surgery and was cancer free in less than a week.

Scary times and make you really appreciate what is important.

Failure can be a great teacher but it doesn't have to be this way!

My new marketing company quickly hit the wall because we struggled to help them create a world-class website experience for their customers that could generate sales and leads. It often meant cobbling up to 10 solutions together using plugins and third-party tools.

There must be a better way! Less complex and faster!

In frustration, I set out to create the "ultimate all-in-one business platform" to help implement our secret blueprints.

I called it evolvepreneur.app

The real question for me now is,

How do I get the right features to the best customer for us and grow a community around our idea?

Join me on my personal journey to find out as we improve and implement these blueprints together and share ideas from real entrepreneurs who are fighting every day to build and grow their own businesses.

I want to help entrepreneurs make a real difference and navigate the messy world of startup or re-launch

My name is John North, and this is the Evolvepreneur Secrets for Entrepreneurs Show

Join me today, where we dig deep with our guests and get you the best blueprints so you can fast-track your business.

How many times have you bought a membership product to see you move from the initial web landing page to a separate e-commerce platform to a back-end checkout system, and finally to another platform's login area? And in the end, you are taken off to join their Facebook Group.

Take a leaf from these big online corporations: your business needs to be its own "platform" where you control your own community and customers. Don't become a cog in the machine; create your own machine.

Take control of your own destiny and sleep better a night!

MID ROLL AD:

Do you want to Control Your Destiny and Create a Complete Business System for your online business?

Evolvepreneur.app offers an easy and cost-effective way to build your online business by helping you avoid the pain and stress of implementing multiple systems, giving you the freedom to automate and scale.

Support our sponsor by grabbing a free copy of the "Evolvepreneur Secrets for Entrepreneurs" book at evolvepreneur.app

MID ROLL AD:

Do you want simple and effective ways to get started that don't cost a fortune in time or money?

Discover the best steps for each strategy we teach and the most important areas to focus on, and even connect with your best customers and grow an online community.

Grab your free copy of "Evolvepreneur Secrets for Entrepreneurs" at. www.evolvepreneur secrets.show

END ROLL OUTRO:

Well, That's a wrap on another awesome guest episode for the Evolvepreneur Secrets for Entrepreneurs Show

Just Before you go...

If you liked this episode, we would be very grateful for a 5-star review!

Please also consider recommending the show to a friend or two!

Make sure you subscribe for future episodes at www.evolvepreneursecrets.show right now.

Until next time and if you an entrepreneur make a start on your next great idea today!

CHAPTER 14

DEVELOPING A STRATEGIC OBJECTIVE

"Setting goals is the first step in turning the invisible into the visible." – **Tony Robbins**

A podcast without a strategy is like a boat without a rudder—it may float, but it won't get far.

This chapter will help you develop a strategic objective for your podcast, aligning your content with your long-term goals.

We'll dive into how to build each episode around this objective, ensuring that your podcast doesn't just attract listeners but drives meaningful results for your business or brand.

Creating a strategic objective for your podcast is a crucial step in ensuring the success and sustainability of your podcasting endeavor. A well-defined strategic objective serves as your podcast's foundation and guiding principle, influencing every aspect of its creation, promotion, and growth. Here are some key reasons why you should establish a strategic objective for your podcast:

Strategic Podcasting Framework

Monetization and Sustainability

Purpose and Direction

Marketing and Promotion

Consistency and Focus

Differentiation

Prioritization and Decision-Making

Measurable Goals

- 🎙 **Purpose and direction:** A strategic objective provides your podcast's clear purpose and direction. It helps you define your podcast's overarching goal and vision, which can guide you in making informed decisions about content creation, format, target audience, and branding.

- 🎙 **Consistency and focus:** With a strategic objective in place, you can maintain consistency and focus in your podcast content. This helps you stay on track with your podcast's main theme and message, ensuring that your episodes are coherent and engaging for your listeners.

- 🎙 **Prioritization and decision-making:** A strategic objective enables you to prioritize your resources and efforts effectively. By understanding the core purpose of your podcast, you can allocate your time, energy, and budget more efficiently, making it easier to navigate challenges and make crucial decisions.

- 🎙 **Measurable goals:** Establishing a strategic objective allows you to set measurable goals and key performance indicators (KPIs) for your podcast. This helps you track your progress, evaluate your podcast's performance, and make necessary adjustments to improve its growth and impact.

- 🎙 **Differentiation:** A well-defined strategic objective can help you differentiate your podcast from others in the same niche. By clearly outlining what sets your podcast apart and its unique value, you can position your podcast as a valuable resource for your target audience, increasing your chances of gaining loyal listeners.

- 🎙 **Marketing and promotion:** A strategic objective is a foundation for your podcast's marketing and promotional efforts. By understanding your podcast's purpose and target audience, you can develop more effective marketing strategies and create promotional materials that resonate with potential listeners.

- 🎙 **Monetization and sustainability:** A strategic objective can guide you in creating a sustainable and potentially profitable podcast. You can build a business model that supports your podcast's growth and longevity by aligning your podcast's goal with potential revenue streams (such as advertising, sponsorships, or premium content).

But what is a strategic objective, exactly?

Your strategic objective is a precise written statement of what your podcast will look like when it's complete. It's a detailed picture of the future—your vision of how your podcast will be seen, what themes it will cover, and what listeners it will attract. It's the culmination of all the planning we've been doing throughout the past few chapters.

Strategic objectives are regularly written for businesses, but not so often for podcasts. In this book, we're teaching you how to make your podcast profitable, so it makes a lot of sense to get your strategic objective right.

This subject is too big for one chapter. Instead, we will go over the concepts and leave it up to you to create this statement after this module.

Below is an example of a Strategic Objective:

"XYZ Computer Services is a service-oriented company providing high-quality business software and computer hardware solutions to Australia's small business owners on-time and within budget, every time. Our clients see us a problem solvers and the key to their business success through access to critical business information and savings in efficiency.

Our clients have a strong connection with us as they appreciate our attention to detail and personalized service. They feel we are more than a software or computer supplier, they treat us like a business partner and often cite our company as fundamental in the success of their business. We will inspire our clients to dramatically increase their efficiency and profitability for their business.

XYZ Computer Services' target market is represented by small to medium sized businesses with 2 to 50 employees. Typically, our clients are the owners who are also responsible for the day-to-day running of the business. Many industries are serviced, including commerce, service, retail, and manufacturing, and often our clients are at the start of their growth stage. The majority of system sales are financed through the company's Technology Rental Plan which provides for regular two-yearly rollovers which allow our clients to keep up with technology without the high cost of replacement.

XYZ Computer Services will be a premier provider of business systems and software Australia-Wide within the next five years.

By June XXXX, with annual sales in excess of $5M and a net profit rate of 20%, the company will be floated on the Australian Stock Exchange to fund further expansion into global markets and establishment of in-house Rental Finance facility. XYZ Computer Services will have a full-time staff (in Sydney) of 25 with a network of 50 commission-based consultants in key geographical areas Australia-wide.

For our company to achieve success, our primary influencers' needs must be satisfied. The four primary influencers are our customers, our employees, our suppliers and our lenders. Each of these groups will prefer to choose us over all other companies. Our company's systems will be far superior to our competition. Because of our company's ability to control our systems, we will be able to encourage customers to choose us over other competitors, generate the highest profit margins in the computer industry, pay the highest salaries in the industry, pay all of our suppliers on time, every time, and pay all of our lenders on time and within credit terms.

XYZ Computer Services will have a reputation for employing quality staff and creating a work environment envied by its competitors. Staff incentive and recreation policies will be well above industry standards and the subject of favourable comparison against our competitors.

Goods and services are delivered to our clients using an innovative and comprehensive module-based training system. Our training system is delivered through a series of workbooks, audios, telephone conference calls, and on-site visits from our consultants.

Every client will receive professional service from every department within the company. The company will be known for its neat and highly-organized staff. Every aspect of the company's operation is standardized and tightly controlled.

Our centralized HelpDesk Centre provides high-quality telephone and remote support. Each support call is tracked and monitored, and problems are resolved within 2 hours.

All of our people wear distinctive corporate wardrobes. XYZ Computer Services is known in the marketplace for its innovative use of technology to assist small businesses in achieving success in areas of computerization and profitability.

XYZ Computer Services continually seeks the input of staff and customers to improve its efficiency and creates an atmosphere of a success-driven company."

Your Strategic Objective should have the following elements:

- Basic Characteristics
- Line of business and products offered
- Company Size and Growth Objectives
- Geographic Scope (markets, where are your listeners?)
- Target Markets and Market Positioning
- Timing (years to completion)
- The Basis of Competition (what will be your competitive advantage?)
- Distinguishing/Unique Characteristics
- Distinctive elements of your product or service
- Distinctive Marketing Methods
- Distinctive Behaviour/Dress/Qualifications of Hosts
- Distinctive Operations
- Other Unique or Distinctive Characteristics

Your Strategic Objective is like a mini-business plan. Something that will stand the test of time and is easy to read by all interested parties. The old rule is that if it isn't written down it's meaningless and easy to change!

Who is your target market?

One of the single biggest mistakes most entrepreneurs make, you'll remember, is trying to sell something to everyone. To be successful, you need to narrow your focus.

It is vital to work out who your ideal listener is and actively look for them. This is represented in your advertising and marketing efforts. A poorly defined target market is the single biggest reason why your marketing will not work.

You need to know how your prospective listener thinks and feels, what their problems are, how they feel about you and your competitors.

These are known as psychographic characteristics. Additionally, you need to know their demographic characteristics, such as age, sex, occupation, habits, and lifestyle.

Some questions to ask about your ideal listener:

- What are their concerns and problems?
- What do they want from life?
- What makes them feel good?
- What's their biggest problem that you can solve?
- What are their priorities for their money?
- What do they want for themselves?
- About your products/service:
- Do they really want or do they really need it?

- What are their concerns about it?
- What problems does it answer?
- Where does it rate in their thinking?
- What will it really do for them?
- Answer this for both you and your competition:
- What do they like?
- What do they dislike about?
- Why would they choose?
- How do they perceive?
- Why would they buy?
- What is unique and special about them?
- Demographic – "How they measure up":
- Age Range?
- Owners/manages/works in the business?
- Sex?
- Marital?
- Education level?
- Job/Title?
- Industry?
- Income?
- Reads what newspapers?
- Reads what magazines?
- Belongs to Clubs/Associations/Communities?

To help you implement the strategies outlined in Podcasting Secrets for Entrepreneurs, we've put together a comprehensive Podcast Secrets Resource Kit, which is available for free.

This kit contains tools, templates, and guides to streamline your podcasting process, from the initial planning stages to audience growth and monetization.

https://podcastsecrets.biz/s/kit

CHAPTER 15

MEASURING SUCCESS AND GROWTH

"What gets measured gets managed." – **Peter Drucker**

Y ou've put in the work, released episodes, and maybe even scored a few loyal listeners—but how do you know if your podcast is actually growing?

And what does "success" look like, anyway?

In this chapter, we'll dive into the metrics that matter and show you how to track progress without getting buried in numbers. From listener growth to engagement rates, we'll help you define what success means for your show and how to measure it in a way that keeps you motivated.

Let's turn those downloads into data you can use to level up!

Without KPIs, (Key Performance Indicators) running your podcast is a bit like driving with a blindfold on—you'll have no clue how it's going, what's working, or which parts need a tune-up!

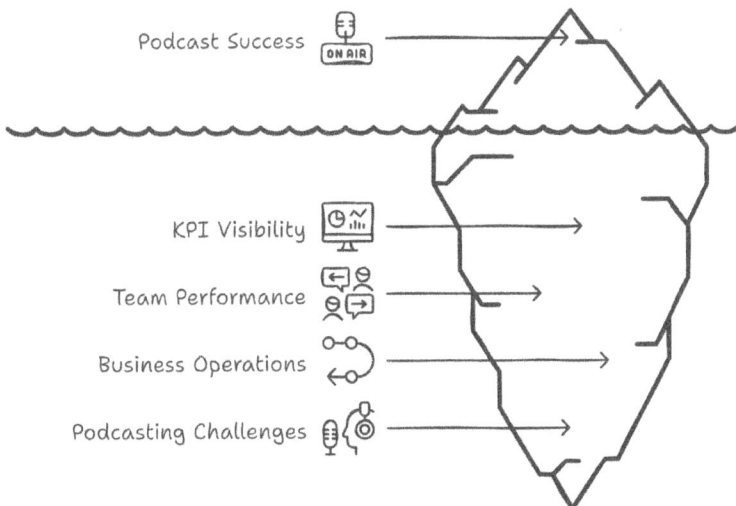

Podcast Success

KPI Visibility

Team Performance

Business Operations

Podcasting Challenges

One popular example of transparent KPI tracking in podcasting is Entrepreneurs on Fire, hosted by John Lee Dumas. Dumas not only built a highly successful podcast, but he also sets himself apart by publicly sharing his monthly income reports, complete with key performance metrics and revenue breakdowns. Each month, he posts detailed reports on his website that show stats like downloads per episode, sponsorship revenue, affiliate income, and total expenses.

By sharing these metrics, Entrepreneurs on Fire gives its audience a rare behind-the-scenes look at what it takes to run a profitable podcasting business. Dumas uses these reports to show exactly how much revenue the podcast generates, breaking down sources like sponsorships, affiliate deals, and his own product sales. This level of transparency not only builds trust with his listeners but also provides valuable insights for aspiring podcasters looking to monetize their shows.

For podcasters and entrepreneurs, following Entrepreneurs on Fire's example can be an effective way to keep themselves accountable, motivate their teams, and inspire their listeners who are looking to follow a similar path.

The practice of tracking and sharing KPIs like downloads, ad revenue, and listener engagement can turn vague goals into clear, measurable targets that show how each area of the podcast impacts growth and revenue over time.

Here's how it works:

Imagine you're on a tropical island with only your phone. Once a week, you can make a single, 60-minute call to check in with a few people on your team about your podcast. At the end of each day, what numbers (typically 5-10) would you want to see on your phone screen to get a clear picture of how the podcast is performing, how the team is executing, and where the show is headed?

What metrics would give you the insights to guide your team effectively while you're "away"?

Here's a sample list of common KPIs that successful podcasters track:

- Downloads per Episode
- Listener Retention Rate
- New Subscribers per Week
- Episode Completion Rate
- Average Listener Duration per Episode
- Website Clicks from Podcast Links
- Email Signups from Podcast
- Social Media Engagement per Episode
- Sponsorship Revenue per Episode
- Conversion Rate from Episode CTA
- Total Monthly Revenue
- New Sponsorship Deals Closed
- Cost per Acquisition (New Listener)
- Listener Feedback and Ratings

🎙 Podcast Review Volume and Rating Score

Key Questions as You Craft Your Podcast KPI System:

🎙 How often do you want to review your KPIs? (Daily, weekly, after each episode)

🎙 Which roles or team members are critical to measure? (Editors, social media managers, content planners)

🎙 Which KPIs are most important to gauge growth and engagement? (Downloads, average listener duration, CTA conversions)

🎙 How should the information be delivered? (Email summary, spreadsheet, podcast management dashboard)

🎙 How will you communicate these KPIs with your team? (Weekly check-ins, dashboard access)

🎙 What indicates strong performance for each position?

🎙 What are the big-picture goals for your podcast?

🎙 How do you define and measure success over time?

Tracking these KPIs will give you a clear and actionable view of your podcast's growth, audience engagement, and revenue potential—all while you're sipping piña coladas.

To help you implement the strategies outlined in Podcasting Secrets for Entrepreneurs, we've put together a comprehensive Podcast Secrets Resource Kit, which is available for free.

This kit contains tools, templates, and guides to streamline your podcasting process, from the initial planning stages to audience growth and monetization.

https://podcastsecrets.biz/s/kit

Create

The creation phase involves designing engaging and informative episodes that reflect your unique personality and style. Depending on the nature of your podcast, this might involve researching and planning each episode meticulously to ensure that the content is relevant and entertaining.

If you want to create interviews, you might focus on finding interesting and entertaining people to sit down with. Regardless, you should focus on developing a consistent format and tone, while also incorporating elements that differentiate your podcast from others in the same niche. High-quality audio production and careful scripting will contribute to a professional and polished final product.

CHAPTER 16

MANAGING PODCAST WORKFLOWS

"Efficiency is doing things right; effectiveness is doing the right things." – **Peter Drucker**

Podcasting has a lot of moving parts—recording, editing, publishing, promoting, and more.

In this chapter, we'll guide you through creating a streamlined workflow that keeps you on track and reduces stress. From planning your content calendar to organizing your files, you'll learn how to set up a process that lets you focus more on creating and less on managing the details.

While a content calendar helps you plan your episodes, managing the production workflow is just as crucial for the success of your podcast.

Producing a podcast involves multiple stages—from research and recording to editing and promotion—and having a streamlined workflow ensures nothing falls through the cracks.

Key Factors for a Successful Podcast

Monetization Opportunities

Defining Target Audience

Connecting with Listeners

· LIVE

Tailoring Content

Marketing Strategies

Messaging Strategies

Why You Need a Well-Defined Workflow

Podcasting can be time-consuming, especially as your show grows. A structured workflow helps you:

- 🎤 Stay Efficient: Breaking each episode into manageable steps allows you to work systematically and avoid last-minute stress.

- 🎤 Ensure Consistency: A repeatable workflow means that each episode is produced with the same level of quality, ensuring a professional result every time.

- 🎤 Collaborate Effectively: If you have a team helping with production, a defined workflow ensures everyone knows their responsibilities and timelines.

- 🎤 Planning and Research: This is the first stage of your workflow, where you plan the episode topic, research your content, and gather any needed materials. If you're interviewing guests, this stage also involves booking the interview, preparing questions, and coordinating schedules.

Tools: Obsidian, Trello, Asana, or Google Docs for organizing research and planning.

Recording

Once your topic and research are prepared, it's time to record. Whether you're doing a solo episode or an interview, ensure your recording setup is professional and has clear audio quality. Record multiple takes if necessary and ensure that guests are prepared.

Tools: Audacity, Adobe Audition, or GarageBand for recording.

Editing

After recording, you move into the editing phase. This is where you'll clean up audio, remove any background noise, and add music or sound effects. This stage also involves trimming unnecessary content for interview episodes to keep the episode concise.

Tools: Audacity, Adobe Audition, or Descript for editing.

Review and Quality Check

Once your episode is edited, listen through it again to ensure everything sounds polished and professional. This is also a good time to check for factual errors, missing segments, or areas needing more clarification.

Publishing and Distribution:

When your episode is ready, upload it to your podcast hosting platform. Ensure that show notes, a compelling episode title, and any relevant links or resources mentioned in the episode are included.

Tools: Libsyn, Anchor, Buzzsprout, or Evolvepreneur.app for publishing.

Promotion

Promotion is a critical part of your workflow. Once your episode is live, share it across social media channels, embed it on your website, and send it to your email list. Consider creating audiograms or short video snippets to promote the episode on platforms like Instagram or Twitter.

Tools: Buffer, Hootsuite, or Canva for social media scheduling and graphics.

Analyze Performance

After the episode has been live for a while, analyze its performance using analytics tools. How many downloads did it get? What is the listener retention rate? Use this data to optimize future episodes and refine your workflow.

Tools: Apple Podcasts Connect, Spotify for Podcasters, or OP3 for performance tracking.

Tips for Streamlining Your Workflow

- 🎤 **Batch Your Tasks:** If possible, batch similar tasks together. For instance, record multiple episodes in one sitting or edit several episodes simultaneously. This helps you stay focused and avoid switching between tasks.

- 🎤 **Automate Where Possible:** Use automation tools to handle repetitive tasks like social media promotion or episode scheduling. This frees up more time to focus on content creation.

- 🎤 **Use Checklists:** A simple checklist can ensure that every step of the production process is completed without oversight. You can create a checklist for each episode, covering everything from research to publishing.

By managing your podcast workflow efficiently, you'll be able to produce high-quality episodes consistently, reduce stress, and maintain a smooth production process.

To help you implement the strategies outlined in Podcasting Secrets for Entrepreneurs, we've put together a comprehensive Podcast Secrets Resource Kit, which is available for free.

This kit contains tools, templates, and guides to streamline your podcasting process, from the initial planning stages to audience growth and monetization.

https://podcastsecrets.biz/s/kit

CHAPTER 17

ESSENTIAL PODCASTING EQUIPMENT

"The best tools are the ones we already know how to use." – **Anonymous**

Think you need a studio full of high-end gear to start podcasting? Think again.

This chapter breaks down the essential equipment needed to create a professional-sounding podcast without emptying your wallet.

We'll cover must-haves, nice-to-haves, and a few pro tips on setup, so you're ready to record episodes that sound great, even if you're on a budget.

You must invest in some essential podcasting equipment to create a professional-quality podcast. While there are many options to choose from, a few key pieces of equipment are essential for most podcasts.

Choosing The Right Microphone

The one thing you can't do without: a microphone. A good microphone is essential for capturing high-quality audio. There are many options to choose from, ranging from budget-friendly USB microphones to more expensive condenser microphones. What you choose will depend on your situation. Each type is designed for a different environment.

Microphone connections will generally come in two forms—XLR and USB. USB microphones connect directly to your computer, while XLR microphones connect through audio.

For a beginner, the easiest microphones to get started with are USB microphones. The Blue Yeti remains an ever-popular recommendation for beginners due to its low cost, ease of setup, and wide applicability in various situations. It's a **condenser-type** microphone, which is the more sensitive types. It will pick up a wider range of sound from further away.

If you don't want to think too hard, you can't go wrong with the Blue Yeti. All you need to do is plug the USB-A cable into your computer.

If, however, you want to know your options, read on.

As previously mentioned, the first type of microphone is the **Condenser** type. It stands in contrast to the second type, the **Dynamic** type. While condenser microphones allow you to change the polar patterns on the microphone so it detects sound more clearly from different angles (omnidirectional detects a sound from all directions, cardioid detects sound more clearly from the front than the back, etc.), dynamic microphones detect sound only from in front of the microphone and block sound from everywhere else.

Dynamic microphones, as a consequence of being far less sensitive than condenser microphones, are harder to damage and, thus easier to care for. Dynamic microphones are also an ideal choice for interviews; it won't pick up the other speaker's voice on that microphone. They also tend to be cheaper to produce and purchase.

Both types of microphones make sense for a podcast host with no physical guests—if you're meeting with your guests online, you can route the meeting audio from your guest to your headphones instead of speakers, preventing your microphone from picking up your guest's voice.

The last type of microphone we'll mention is the **Lavalier** microphone, which is a great option for travelling podcasters. It's a small microphone you can clip to your shirt, which has many of the same properties as a dynamic microphone, such as blocking background noise.

The primary difference is that you no longer have to consider the microphone's location and speak directly into it. Even if you move, the microphone will follow you. They allow you to concentrate completely on the conversation. For this reason, some podcasters might use a Lavalier microphone for podcasting at a static studio location.

Of these types, condenser microphones are the most expensive. They capture the crispest sound because of their high sensitivity, but this makes them harder to care for and means you need to setup a quiet studio environment for recording. Dynamic microphones handle noisier situations, are more durable, and tend to be cheaper. The lavalier microphone is suitable for a narrower range of situations, but are the only logical choice for podcasters on the go.

Consider the type of your podcast you are recording, and purchase a microphone based on your criteria.

USB versus XLR and Audio Interfaces

As mentioned, microphones come with two main connections: USB or XLR. The difference between them is that an audio interface is built-in to USB microphones. This makes them easier to set up, as every computer has a USB port, but the audio interface is lower quality than a standalone one.

If you are unfamiliar, the audio interface is the component responsible for controlling the volume, or gain of your audio, as well as converting your analog audio to digital audio your computer can understand. More advanced audio interfaces allow you to apply effects prior to digital conversion. A common effect is noise gating, which drops all noise quieter than a certain level.

Audio interfaces don't have a USB input for a microphone; you need an XLR microphone to plug into the interface. The interface is what plugs into your computer via a USB connection.

Condenser, dynamic, and lavalier microphones can be found with both USB and XLR connections.

Microphone Accessories

These aren't *essential*, but they can be handy to have:

- 🎤 A pop filter can help to reduce plosives (hard "p" and "b" sounds) and improve the overall sound quality of your podcast.
- 🎤 A shock mount are useful in minimizing handling noise and vibrations from the surrounding environment, ensuring cleaner and clearer audio recordings for a more professional and enjoyable listening experience.

Recording Software

You will need recording software to capture and edit your podcast. There are many options to choose from, which we will cover in greater detail in What Software Do You Need?

Audacity is a great, free, cross-platform option for beginners for recording and editing your podcast. If you plan to interview guests, Zoom is a popular meeting service that allows you to record your meetings.

Headphones

Investing in a good pair of headphones can help you monitor your audio and ensure you capture high-quality sound. You can plug these into your audio interface if you're using an XLR-based setup. USB microphones like the Blue Yeti have an audio interface built-in to the microphone. In this case, you can plug your headphones into your computer, instead.

Investing in essential podcasting equipment is an important step in creating a professional-quality podcast. By choosing the right microphone, recording software, headphones, and other equipment, you can ensure that you capture high-quality audio and create an engaging and professional podcast.

To help you implement the strategies outlined in Podcasting Secrets for Entrepreneurs, we've put together a comprehensive Podcast Secrets Resource Kit, which is available for free.

This kit contains tools, templates, and guides to streamline your podcasting process, from the initial planning stages to audience growth and monetization.

https://podcastsecrets.biz/s/kit

CHAPTER 18

SETTING UP A RECORDING SPACE

"Success is where preparation and opportunity meet." – **Bobby Unser**

S o, you're ready to record—fantastic!
But before you dive in, let's talk about the space where the magic happens. Whether you're working with a closet full of pillows or a full-on soundproof studio, setting up your recording space can make or break your audio quality (and your sanity).

This chapter is all about creating a setup that sounds professional without breaking the bank—or driving your roommates crazy. From DIY hacks to pro tips, we'll make sure your sound is as sharp as your content. Get ready to transform that corner of your home into a podcasting powerhouse!

Your recording space needs to have these characteristics:

1. It needs to be *quiet.*

No screaming children were in the background, no emergency services blaring their sirens every half-hour, and no other sudden loud noises. You need to be uninterrupted for at least the duration of the episode. This is an ideal scenario, of course; most of us live in areas that are noisy in some way or another. If you can't eliminate the noise, do what you can to block it out. A dynamic microphone is best suited to this sort of podcaster-hostile situation.

2. It needs to sound right.

Two of the most annoying sounds a listener can detect are echo and background noise. Echo is caused by the sound bouncing off the walls in the room. Sticking sound-absorbing foam on the walls is an easy way to reduce echo. It will absorb some of the sounds before it has a chance to bounce, reducing echo. Background noise can come from many sources, not just sudden loud sounds.

The most common type is the microphone picking up sounds like your computer's fan, or the air conditioning unit. It may sound quiet to you, but when you listen to the audio later, that background noise might be overwhelming. Rather than eliminating it in post, it's better to do what you can to curtail it before recording. Turn down your microphone's gain, for example, or turn on noise gating below a certain level.

3. If you're recording a video, it needs to look nice.

While most podcasts are audio-only, you can provide video to add value for your listeners or to make conversation with your guest easier. If you are going to do this, you need to make sure your recording space looks nice. One of the easiest ways to do this is to plaster sound-absorbing foam to the wall. It reduces echo, but it also looks professional. You could also put a green screen in the background so you can transform your background into anything you like.

Once you've set up a recording space that meets these standards, don't forget to test your audio! Ensure the sound is coming through correctly and there is no overwhelming background noise. Deal with as many audio problems as possible before recording your episodes—this will make your life much easier.

CHAPTER 19

CHOOSING YOUR HOSTING PLATFORM

"Choices are the hinges of destiny." – **Edwin Markham**

Your hosting platform is the home base of your podcast, so choosing the right one is key.

In this chapter, we'll walk you through the different hosting options, what to look for, and how to find the platform that suits your needs.

With the right host, you'll be ready to publish, distribute, and manage your podcast with ease.

If you haven't already, read *What Is an RSS Feed and Why Do I Care?*

It explains one of the key considerations in choosing the right platform - whether it allows you to host your RSS feed on your domain.

Choosing a podcast platform is a crucial step in your podcasting journey.

Here are some key features to consider when making your choice:

Distribution Reach

- **Platforms Supported:** Look for a podcast host that distributes your content to multiple platforms like Apple Podcasts, Spotify, Google Podcasts, etc.-
- **Global Reach:** Consider whether the platform supports distribution to listeners in multiple countries.

Ease of Use

- **User Interface:** The dashboard and upload process should be intuitive.
- **Technical Support:** Check if they offer good customer service and technical support.

Analytics

- **Listener Insights:** Platforms that offer detailed analytics on listener demographics, listening platforms, and episode performance can be invaluable
- **Download Stats:** Comprehensive download statistics can help you understand your audience better.

Monetisation Options

- 🎙 **Ads and Sponsorships:** Some platforms offer built-in ad networks or sponsorship opportunities.
- 🎙 **Subscription Models:** Check if the platform allows you to offer premium or subscriber-only content.

Storage and Bandwidth

- 🎙 **Unlimited Hosting:** Some platforms offer unlimited hosting but may have restrictions on individual file sizes or bandwidth.
- 🎙 **Quality:** Make sure the platform doesn't compromise the audio quality during the upload process.

Cost

- 🎙 **Free Plans:** Some platforms offer free plans but with storage, analytics, or monetisation limitations.-
- 🎙 **Paid Plans:** Compare the features offered in the paid plans to see if they meet your needs.

Social Media Integration

- 🎙 **Sharing Options:** Look for platforms that make it easy to share your episodes on social media.-
- 🎙 **Embedding:** A good platform will offer a range of embedding options for your website or blog.

SEO and Discoverability

- 🎙 **Metadata:** The ability to add detailed metadata can help improve the discoverability of your podcast.-
- 🎙 **Search Features:** Some platforms offer in-audio search features that make your episodes more discoverable.

Reliability and Uptime

- 🎙 **Server Uptime:** Choose a platform known for good server uptime to ensure your podcast is always available.-
- 🎙 **Backup:** Check if the platform offers automated backup features.

Community and Networking

- 🎙 **Collaboration:** Some platforms offer features that make it easy to collaborate with other podcasters.-
- 🎙 **Community Support:** Platforms with active community forums can provide extra support and networking opportunities.

Each of these factors can vary in importance depending on your specific needs, so weigh them when deciding.

There are many podcast hosting platforms out there—we'll cover some of them.

- 🎙 **Buzzsprout**—this platform offers free hosting for 90 days, but after that period of time, you need to pay between $12-24 a month, which allows you to upload 3-12 hours of audio every month.

- 🎙 **Captivate**—they offer unlimited storage for all their plans, starting at $17 a month, for as much as $90 a month. The pricing is determined by how many downloads your podcast gets monthly. As your podcast grows more successful, Captivate will charge you more to host your podcast.

- 🎙 **Blubrry**—they will offer you a free WordPress site to host your podcast on for $10 a month, with 125MB of monthly storage, or an advanced plan for $17 a month with 400MB of monthly storage. Blubrry allows you to use your own domain, which allows you to own your RSS feed.

- 🎙 **Podbean**—they offer 5 hours of total storage for free, forever. However, you will not own your RSS feed on the free plan. If you need more storage, you can try the $9 a month plan, which offers unlimited storage and the ability to own your RSS feed by hosting on your own domain. There are currently two higher plans, at $29 and $79 a month, which offer more advanced features.

- 🎙 **Podcastsecrets.app**—this is our own podcasting platform, which we've designed from the ground up to accommodate podcasters with guests. We offer a free plan with 1GB of lifetime storage, a maximum of 500 emails to your subscribers a month, a dedicated page for your show, and access to our unique Guest Workflow and Application Form modules, which make podcasting with guests a breeze. Our paid plans offer all of these features, in addition to the ability to Own Your RSS Feed with more storage and maximum emails per month. Our paid plans start at $29 a month.

Choosing a hosting platform is one of the first real steps toward bringing your podcast to life, so take the time to make it right. The platform you pick will be the backbone of your podcast—helping you reach listeners, understand your audience, and grow your show. From ensuring your RSS feed is accessible to handling episode distribution, your host will support every episode you release.

Remember, each feature matters differently depending on your vision and goals, so focus on what aligns best with your needs. This choice isn't just about hosting; it's about finding a home for your podcast where it can thrive and reach its full potential.

In the following chapters, we'll continue guiding you through the steps needed to create a successful podcast, from building your audience to monetizing effectively.

Let's make sure that every decision, starting with this one, sets you up for podcasting success.

To help you implement the strategies outlined in Podcasting Secrets for Entrepreneurs, we've put together a comprehensive Podcast Secrets Resource Kit, which is available for free.

This kit contains tools, templates, and guides to streamline your podcasting process, from the initial planning stages to audience growth and monetization.

https://podcastsecrets.biz/s/kit

CHAPTER 20

WHAT SOFTWARE DO YOU NEED?

"A tool is only as good as the hand that wields it." – **Anonymous**

O ne of the biggest challenges faced by the potential podcaster is "Tech Hell" where you can easily get overwhelmed by the sheer number of software and services available.

What software you need depends largely on the type of podcast you are creating. The simplest type involves only one host—you—talking into your microphone for the same period of time every episode.

For this type of podcast, all you really need is recording software, editing software, and a hosting platform. Audacity is a great option for podcasters using any operating system, whether that be Windows, macOS, Linux, or even FreeBSD. You can record your podcast with Audacity, edit it, and export the final file. At that point, you can use any platform you want to host your podcast, though we recommend picking one which puts you in control of your RSS Feed.

However, many podcasts are more complicated than that. They involve interviews with guests from across the globe. You'll need more than just Audacity and a basic hosting platform to accommodate these needs. There are some other considerations you should mull over.

Audio and Video

It's a great idea to record both video and audio—even if you have no intention of using the video recording. Creating a quality episode becomes much easier when you can see your guest. It's easier to connect if you can see the other human.

Meeting Software

For guest interviews,

Guest Workflow

Interviewing guests doesn't just mean jumping on a call and hitting the record button. You also need to consider the entire process, from interested people signing up to be guests for your show, providing you with the information and files you need, booking a time, communicating with your guests as the process progresses and when their episode releases, and providing resources for your guests to use.

Here's a full list of the needs we have for our own podcasts with guest workflows, for a real-world example:

1. Landing Page to send your guests to find out about the show and if they would like to apply. eg. https://evolvepreneur.app/page/guestapplication

2. Survey Software or a Google Form to handle the questions you want to ask.

3. Ability to review applications and approve or decline them and then email your response

4. Calendar Booking System to handle the guest booking and remind them to show up

5. Advise the guest on the show and prepare them for the episode

6. Link for the guest to click when the interview time has arrived

7. Meeting software to interview your guest

8. Platform to host the episodes and show page

9. The email system to advise the guest when the show

10. Let your subscribers know about the latest episode

11. Post on social media to attract listeners

As you might imagine, this is hard enough for one person to organize manually, let alone cobble together all kinds of software and services together to make this process fast and reliable. We thought so too, which is why we built our own podcast platform, which handles most of these things for us.

THERE IS A BETTER WAY

The main issue with podcasting with guests was the mess that some podcast hosts get into. They end up with various disjointed systems coupled together using a Virtual Assistant.

We decided that this was never going to work for us, so set off on a journey to build the ultimate "all-in-one" for podcasters.

The first goal was this setup process had to be quick and easy. Secondly, it had to be functional for the guest and lastly, the listener needed to get value from the show and be able to engage with you.

PodcastSecrets.App was designed to automate as much of the guest process and cut down the time spent by the Host.

Our app Includes:

- Create a Podcast Show page that includes your episodes, subscription and distribution links

- Ready-made Guest Landing Page and Guest Application

- Visual Applications Management automatically sends the guest to the next step once you decide to approve or decline them.

- Auto-create the episode and populate it with the guest details

- Guest Hub to help the guest prepare for their episode and post-interview as well as keep them informed of when their episode will be live.

- Host Hub to show the Guest details and make it a simple and easy process for the interview including the ability to record the episode on the same screen. We also host your audio files so no need for a podcast host platform

- 🎙 Once the episode is recorded simply clean up any episode details and schedule.

- 🎙 Our Subscriber system will automatically email your listeners when a new episode goes live, you can also collect email addresses to help build your audience list.

- 🎙 Once the episode is live, we will let the Guest know about it and send them a link

PodcastSecrets.App is always under active development. We plan to one day integrate a calendar booking system inside the app, along with any other features we identify a need for.

To help you implement the strategies outlined in Podcasting Secrets for Entrepreneurs, we've put together a comprehensive Podcast Secrets Resource Kit, which is available for free.

This kit contains tools, templates, and guides to streamline your podcasting process, from the initial planning stages to audience growth and monetization.

https://podcastsecrets.biz/s/kit

CHAPTER 21

CREATING YOUR EPISODE TRAILER: CAPTIVATE YOUR AUDIENCE AND SPARK CURIOSITY

"You never get a second chance to make a first impression." – **Will Rogers**

Think of your episode trailer as the movie preview for your podcast—a quick, punchy way to hook listeners and get them excited for what's to come.

A great trailer doesn't just tell people what your show's about; it gives them a taste of the personality, style, and unique vibe that makes your podcast worth hitting "subscribe" for.

In this chapter, we'll dive into the secrets of crafting a trailer that leaves listeners eager for more (without giving it all away!). Ready to make an unforgettable first impression? Lights, mic, action!

An episode trailer is a short, engaging audio or video clip that provides a sneak peek into your upcoming podcast episode. A well-crafted episode trailer can pique your audience's interest, generate excitement, and encourage them to listen to the full episode.

The Importance of Episode Trailers

Your episode trailer showcases what sets your show apart, offering a glimpse into what your episodes will provide listeners. It can quickly capture your audience's attention and create anticipation for your upcoming podcast episode, motivating them to tune in when the episode is released. You can easily share it on social media and use it for advertising to help you reach new listeners.

Elements of an Effective Episode Trailer

An effective episode trailer is concise, which means no longer than 2 minutes. Aim for between 30 seconds and 1 minute. It's meant to be consumed quickly by your audience and is easy to share on social media.

One way to create an episode trailer is to ask your guest to help you right after recording the episode. Re-introduce your guest and start with a hook that immediately grabs your listeners' attention. Whether this is a thought-provoking question, a surprising fact, or a compelling sound bite from your episode is up to you. Cover the highlights from the episode that are most interesting.

Lastly, end the trailer with a clear call-to-action (CTA) that encourages your audience to listen to the full episode. Tell your listeners where they can go to listen to the episode. If it hasn't been released yet, include information about the release date if you have it.

Steps to Create and Promote Your Episode Trailer

The best time to create an episode trailer with your guest is directly after you've finished recording your episode. Even if it isn't scripted, your memories of the episode will be fresh. It's a good idea to end the recording for the episode and start a new recording for the trailer; it will be easier to find it in the post-production stage.

Once you've recorded it, you need to edit the trailer. Consider what you might add to your trailer. Should you add background music, or include your podcast intro? Would it work better if the trailer opened 'cold', getting straight into the promotion? Should you add a lower third that introduces your guest to viewers watching without sound? These are the questions you need to answer during the post-production process.

When you're finished, you can share the trailer on social media. Be sure to link your followers to the episode on your website, or wherever the episode can be found.

You should also provide your guest with the episode trailer and encourage them to promote the episode.

CHAPTER 22

THE ART OF INTERVIEWING AND CONVERSATION

"Listening is an art that requires attention over talent." – **Anonymous**

Ever listened to a podcast interview and thought, "Wow, that just felt like a conversation between two friends"?

That's the art of interviewing—making your guest (and your listeners) feel at ease while still steering the conversation like a pro. In this chapter, we'll dive into the secrets of conducting interviews that are natural, engaging, and packed with value.

Whether you're chatting with a celebrity or the expert down the street, we'll help you bring out their best stories, insights, and unexpected laughs. Get ready to make every interview feel like one listeners won't want to end!

If you plan to have guests on your podcast or conduct interviews as part of your podcast, you should have a good understanding of the art of interviewing and conversation. This will help you connect with your guests and create a podcast that engages listeners.

Before you can connect with your guests, you need to know them. Whether you choose to do your research beforehand or get to know them just before you start, the interview is down to your preferences.

You may even get to know the guest while the episode is rolling, knowing nothing more than the short biography they've given you.

Nonetheless, it is essential to understand who the guest is, what they've done, and their ambitions. If you are looking to produce a focused interview, it makes sense to do your research and prepare a list of questions to guide the conversation. However, if you're interested in a more casual conversation, you can follow the conversation thread in exciting directions.

As mentioned in the previous chapter, it can be hard for some guests to get into the flow of conversation with just audio. Forming a connection will be much easier if you can see each other and make eye contact. That connection is important for creating engaging content.

Regarding etiquette, you need to know when to interrupt your guest. You should keep the conversation focused on the theme of your podcast where possible, though it's equally important to let your guest contribute to the conversation.

Sometimes, however, you need to correct the course of the interview gently. One of the best ways to do this is to ask another question about your guest. It shows them you're still interested in what they have to say, but that you want to focus on something more relevant.

One key aspect of creating a successful podcast is mastering the art of interviewing and conversation, particularly when it comes to engaging with guests. A well-conducted interview can captivate your audience, provide valuable insights, and help you forge strong connections with influential people in your niche.

This chapter will explore the essential skills and techniques for conducting compelling interviews and creating meaningful conversations with your podcast guests.

Conducting a Podcast Interview

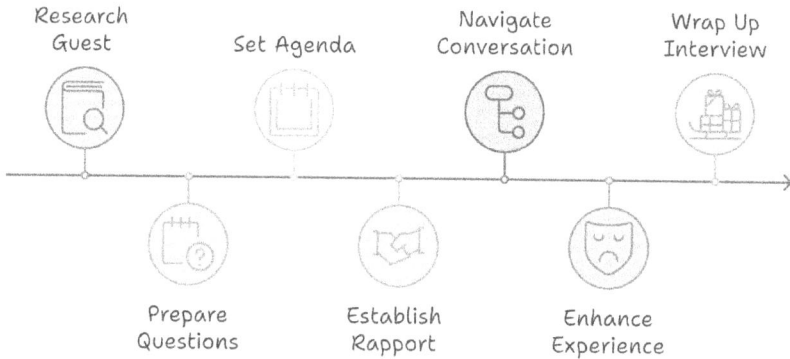

Research Guest   Set Agenda   Navigate Conversation   Wrap Up Interview

Prepare Questions   Establish Rapport   Enhance Experience

Preparing for the Interview

Before diving into the conversation, it is crucial to prepare for the interview. Proper preparation will not only make you feel more confident, but it will also help you conduct a smoother and more engaging discussion. Here are some steps to follow:

Research your guest: Get to know your guest's background, expertise, accomplishments, and current projects. Familiarize yourself with their work, and listen to any previous interviews they have done.

Prepare questions: Develop a list of open-ended questions to encourage your guest to share their thoughts and experiences. These questions should be relevant to their expertise and open to exploring new topics or ideas.

Set the agenda: Before the interview, share the objectives and format with your guest. This will help both of you feel more at ease and prepared for the conversation.

Establishing Rapport and Trust

Building rapport and trust with your guests is essential for creating a comfortable atmosphere where your guests feel at ease sharing their knowledge and experiences. Here are some tips to help you establish rapport and trust:

Start with small talk: Engage in casual conversation before the interview begins to help you and your guest feel more relaxed.

Be genuinely interested: Show your guest that you are genuinely interested in their story, expertise, and opinions. Active listening and empathetic responses can help you establish a strong connection.

Maintain eye contact: Eye contact is an essential aspect of effective communication. Maintaining eye contact demonstrates that you are fully present and attentive when conducting an in-person interview or a video call.

Navigating the Conversation

Once the interview begins, it is essential to guide the conversation while allowing your guest the freedom to share their thoughts and insights. Keep these points in mind as you navigate the conversation:

Follow a natural flow: Allow the conversation to flow naturally, and be ready to adapt your questions or explore new topics that arise during the discussion.

Be an active listener: Pay close attention to your guest's responses and follow up with relevant questions or comments. This will demonstrate your engagement and encourage your guest to open up further.

Be mindful of time: Track the interview's duration and manage the conversation accordingly. Ensure you cover all the essential topics without rushing or dragging the interview on too long.

Enhancing the Interview Experience

To make your interview stand out and keep your audience engaged, consider the following tips for enhancing the interview experience:

Use storytelling: Encourage your guest to share anecdotes, personal experiences, and stories that illustrate their points. This will make the conversation more engaging and relatable for your audience.

Create a conversational tone: Aim for a natural, conversational tone during the interview. This will make your podcast more enjoyable and help your audience feel like they are part of the conversation.

Encourage vulnerability: Create a safe space for your guest to be vulnerable and share their challenges, failures, and lessons learned. This can provide valuable insights and make your guest more relatable to your audience.

Wrapping Up the Interview

At the end of the interview, it is essential to thank your guest for their time and contributions. You may also want to:

- 🎤 **Summarize key takeaways:** Briefly summarize the main points and insights from the conversation. This will help reinforce the interview's value for your audience and provide a clear takeaway.

- 🎤 **Ask for final thoughts:** Allow your guests to share any final thoughts, advice, or insights they may have. This can be a valuable way to wrap up the conversation and provide additional value to your listeners.

🎙 **Promote your guest:** Make sure to mention your guest's website, social media accounts, or any projects they are working on. This shows your appreciation for their participation and allows your audience to connect with them further.

🎙 **Show gratitude:** Once again, thank your guest for their time and for sharing their expertise with your audience. A genuine expression of appreciation can leave a lasting positive impression on your guests and listeners.

Mastering the art of interviewing and conversation is crucial for creating engaging and valuable podcast content. By preparing for the interview, establishing rapport and trust, navigating the conversation, enhancing the interview experience, and wrapping up the interview effectively, you can provide your audience with insightful and memorable episodes.

As you hone your interviewing skills, you will create a more enjoyable podcast experience for your listeners and strengthen your connections with industry experts and leaders in your niche.

Here are some bonus tips for you...

Framing Questions for Control

Sometimes, your interview will go off track. Here are some scripts you can try to keep them on mission...

🎙 "With a potential recession... what are some things you are worried about when looking at your own business?"

🎙 "Those are all really great points… but I wanted to just go in a different direction… _____ "

🎙 "Before we dive into that… let me ask you this…

🎙 "Tell me, have you ever thought about writing a book?

🎙 Is there anything keeping you awake a night?

🎙 Tell me where do you see yourself in 5 years?

🎙 I was wondering ...

🎙 That's a very good question - to answer that, let me ask _____?

🎙 I appreciate where you're going, but based on what you said about _____,

🎙 I think we should explore _____

🎙 Thanks - we only have _____ (time) left, so let's finish on _____, then we can circle back on this if we have time, or I can address it in a follow-up email. Make sense?

🎙 Good point - you know, <name>, we set up this call to work on _____ for you - let's stick to that so we make sure we cover it well for you

🎙 I think we're getting a bit off the purpose of our call. I hope you don't mind, <name>, but can we get back to _____?

🎙 if they are rambling, like many do: I understand your passion - it's great! But we didn't finish covering _____, and then we can get back over to this if we have time. Sound like a plan?

🎤 I get it, there are many ways to address this. Our task today is to find the best solution for you. Can we get back to _____?

🎤 Yes, there are many challenges to running your business. Most coaches and authors I talk to have these same challenges with organizing their business. That's why we created the app. Here is how we can pull it all together....

🎤 If they ask too early about price: Thanks for your enthusiasm - we have several ways to help you, so I suggest we continue looking into what your needs are, then we can decide which of our packages will work best for you.

🎤 If they start to ramble about not committing: I understand your concerns for sure. It's a big step to commit to a solution to move your business to the next level. Here is one way to move ahead <mention the $500 deposit, then at least get the appointment.

Mastering the art of interviewing isn't just about asking questions; it's about creating a space where genuine conversation can unfold.

With each interview, you're building connections, drawing out stories, and delivering real value to your listeners.

As you hone these skills, you'll find that your interviews become not only engaging but also memorable—turning each episode into an experience that leaves listeners and guests wanting more.

So, keep refining your approach, embrace the unexpected, and let each conversation bring your podcast to life in ways you never imagined.

To help you implement the strategies outlined in Podcasting Secrets for Entrepreneurs, we've put together a comprehensive Podcast Secrets Resource Kit, which is available for free.

This kit contains tools, templates, and guides to streamline your podcasting process, from the initial planning stages to audience growth and monetization.

https://podcastsecrets.biz/s/kit

CHAPTER 23

MAXIMIZING YOUR PODCAST'S PRODUCTION VALUE

"Quality is not an act, it is a habit." – **Aristotle**

Great content deserves great production, and maximizing your podcast's production value is essential to making it sound polished and professional.

A well-produced podcast doesn't just engage listeners; it gives your show a sense of credibility and care that keeps people coming back for more.

In this chapter, we'll cover the essentials of high-quality audio, post-production techniques, and those final touches—like cover art and intros—that make a podcast truly shine.

Get ready to elevate your show from good to exceptional!

What does high-quality audio sound like?

High-quality audio has little reverb (no unmistakable echo); a consistent volume that is neither too loud nor too quiet; softened or altogether eliminated plosives and sibilants (hard 't', 'b', 'p' and 's' sounds that can be unpleasant to listen to); and no background noise.

Excessive reverb and background noise are difficult to fix in post-production, so it is important to get these right when recording.

Find a quiet location and record a few samples. If you can hear a lot of echoes, you must install sound dampeners.

Plosives can be softened by purchasing a pop filter for your microphone. Some professional microphones come with a pop filter already attached to the mount. These sounds can be further reduced in post-production.

If you want really high-quality audio, hire an audio engineer! These recommendations will take you far, but a professional best implements the minute technical details.

Post-Production

You can use a few basic techniques to shape your audio's quality.

1. Dynamic Range Compression

Dynamic Range is the difference between your audio's loudest and quietest parts. Audio with a high dynamic range (a large difference between the two) is generally much more unpleasant to listen to. To hear the episode properly, listeners must keep adjusting their volume up and down as they listen to it.

To reduce dynamic range, you need to use a compressor. This will take the parts of your audio that are too loud and smack them down so they are closer to the quieter parts of your audio. However, you can't leave it at that. Your audio will be much quieter after applying a compressor, which means you need to apply make-up gain or adjust the overall loudness of your audio.

2. Loudness Normalization

If you don't work in the broadcast industry, you are likely unaware of Loudness Standards. These standards dictate how loud the overall audio should be. With podcasts, however, most distribution platforms do not enforce loudness standards. However, you should still ensure your audio matches a reasonable level of loudness, if only to have mercy on your listeners.

In Audacity, you can apply Loudness Normalization by selecting your track, going to the top menu, clicking "Effect" and then "Loudness Normalization".

A reasonable level of loudness for a podcast is 16 LUFS.

3. Noise Reduction

Noise reduction, if required, is the first effect you should apply. There should not be much background noise if you've recorded your podcast in a quiet area. You should consider reducing the noise if consistent background noise is louder than -50dB. Too much noise will distract listeners. On the other hand, it can also be distracting if the background is completely dead. You need to find a careful balance between the two.

4. Preserving the Natural Flow of Conversation

When you're going over audio you've recorded, you might find awkward pauses or verbal slip-ups where you quickly corrected yourself. It can be very tempting to shorten these pauses and remove any mistakes, but there can be a cost. If you go too far, the conversation may no longer be delivered at a natural pace. When you are making edits, always go back and listen to how this small change fits into the rest of the sentence or surrounding sentences. It's easy to lose perspective when you're focusing on the small things.

Production Value

Beyond correcting and enhancing your audio, you can focus on other areas to improve your show's production value.

You should have professional cover art for your show. The title of your podcast should be clearly legible, but it should also be visually appealing. The easiest way to obtain professional cover art is to hire a professional to produce it. Your cover art is really important, because it's the first thing many potential listeners see. It needs to grab them.

Every show needs a good intro and outro. An intro should ideally be less than a minute long, and sum up the purpose of the show and the sort of content listeners should expect to be treated to. It is generally accompanied by music that captures the energy of the show.

Outros are the perfect place to direct your listeners to your other ventures. For example, if you've written a book related to the episode's theme or overall show, this is a great time to recommend it to readers. Or, if you have a website for your podcast, it makes sense to send listeners there for more content from you.

And if you don't have a website for your podcast, you need one!

Most distribution platforms do not give you any way to connect to your subscribers beyond producing another episode for your podcast.

If they go to your website to subscribe, you can connect with them via email. It's important to have a direct line of communication between you and the people most interested in your content.

With a focus on production value, you're setting your podcast up to stand out in a crowded field. From crisp audio and balanced volume to eye-catching cover art, these details may seem small, but together they create an experience that leaves a lasting impression.

So take the time to polish every episode, fine-tune the flow, and showcase your unique brand with professional touches.

Remember, your podcast is a reflection of you—and with top-notch production, you're showing listeners they're in for something special.

To help you implement the strategies outlined in Podcasting Secrets for Entrepreneurs, we've put together a comprehensive Podcast Secrets Resource Kit, which is available for free.

This kit contains tools, templates, and guides to streamline your podcasting process, from the initial planning stages to audience growth and monetization.

https://podcastsecrets.biz/s/kit

CHAPTER 24

TRANSCRIPTS AND CLOSED CAPTIONING

"Communication is key to personal and career success." – **Paul J. Meyer**

Imagine this: your amazing podcast episode, accessible to everyone—whether they're listening, reading, or watching.

That's the power of transcripts and closed captions!

Not only do they make your content available to a broader audience, but they also boost your SEO and help people find your show more easily.

In this chapter, we'll cover how to create high-quality transcripts and captions without turning it into a major headache.

Ready to make your podcast more inclusive and discoverable? Let's dive into the world of words-on-screen!

Why Are Transcripts Important?

The first, and most obvious reason transcripts are important is for accessibility. Providing transcripts and closed captioning ensures that your podcast is accessible to the deaf and hard-of-hearing community and individuals with auditory processing disorders or language barriers.

In addition to accessibility, transcripts improve the user experience. They cater to listeners who prefer to read content or are in a noisy environment. It also allows users to quickly find a section of the episode they want to listen to again; they can search for a sentence they remember in the transcript and find the right timecode.

Transcripts also provide SEO benefits. They create indexable text content which can be picked up by search engines that crawl your site, influencing your ranking. It may also appear in summary for the page when a user finds the page on Google or another search engine.

If you're looking to create more content, transcripts can be easily repurposed as a blog post, article, or social media update. You could also use portions of the transcript when promoting the episode with an episode trailer.

How Do You Create Transcripts?

The simplest way to create transcripts for your podcast episodes is to do it manually. Listen to the episode, note down the timecode, and write down what is said. This is quite time-consuming, so hiring a professional to do this for you makes sense. This way, you can ensure the transcripts are accurate and high-quality.

Another way to transcribe your episodes is to use a transcription service that uses text-to-speech technology. Many companies offer this service, such as Trint and Descript. While the resulting transcript often isn't perfect, it gives you a great place to start. These services also tend to be cheaper than professional transcriptions.

Whichever option you choose offers benefits over having no transcriptions.

How to Format Transcripts

If you're doing the transcripts yourself or cleaning up an auto-generated transcript, you need to format the final transcript properly. Ensure your transcripts are easy to read by using proper punctuation, paragraph breaks, and speaker identification. This helps listeners follow the conversation and understand the context more easily.

You should also ensure the time codes are accurate. Including timecodes alongside the text in your transcripts allows listeners to quickly navigate to specific audio sections or follow along with the podcast episode. The transcript should also be formatted to match the .srt file format so it can be used for closed captioning. Software such as Descript does this automatically for you.

How to Integrate Transcripts and Closed Captions With Your Podcast

Transcripts can be hosted on your website; on the episode page for your podcast. On podcastsecrets.app, you can add transcripts to the episode description. This allows listeners to read the transcript alongside the audio content.

If you've formatted you transcripts correctly, you can export a .srt file and use this for closed captioning on videos. This way, the lines will appear as they are spoken in the video. You'll need a video player that supports closed captioning to allow this.

Transcripts and closed captioning are essential components of an inclusive and accessible podcast. By investing time and resources into creating accurate and readable transcripts, you not only cater to a diverse audience but also enhance your podcast's online visibility and engagement.

As the podcasting landscape continues to evolve, prioritizing accessibility and inclusivity will set your podcast apart and contribute to a more inclusive digital ecosystem.

By following the best practices outlined in this chapter, you can ensure your podcast content reaches the widest possible audience and creates a positive user experience for all listeners.

Publish

Streamlining the publication process is essential for ensuring your podcast easily reaches your target audience. Choose the right hosting platform, considering factors such as pricing, features, storage, whether the platform lets you host the feed on your own domain, and analytics.

Consider how you might present your finished episode. Creating visually appealing cover art and writing compelling show notes will help you connect with more listeners.

To help you implement the strategies outlined in Podcasting Secrets for Entrepreneurs, we've put together a comprehensive Podcast Secrets Resource Kit, which is available for free.

This kit contains tools, templates, and guides to streamline your podcasting process, from the initial planning stages to audience growth and monetization.

https://podcastsecrets.biz/s/kit

CHAPTER 25

MAXIMIZING YOUR PODCAST'S VISIBILITY AND REACH

"Visibility without action is vanity." – **Bernard Kelvin Clive**

L aunching a podcast may start with a single episode and an RSS feed, but if you want to reach a bigger audience, that's just the beginning.

Simply publishing your show isn't enough to draw in listeners. To maximize your podcast's visibility, you need to distribute it across popular platforms, optimize it for search, and promote it through social media and email marketing.

In this chapter, we'll walk you through the key strategies for getting your podcast in front of more people and expanding your reach to connect with your ideal listeners.

Anyone who wants to listen to your podcast can copy your RSS feed and paste it into their podcast app, and they'll be alerted when you release new episodes.

That being said, you aren't going to reach a lot of people with your podcast that way. To really maximize your podcast's visibility and reach more people, you need to distribute your podcast on popular podcast distribution platforms. Reach your listeners where they are, rather than forcing them to come to you.

There are a lot of podcast distribution platforms out there, but these are some of the most popular:

- 🎤 **Apple Podcasts** features over 2 million podcast shows in its directory. It is available on all Apple devices, but not on Android devices. Apple Podcasts is one of the most popular podcast distribution platforms today.

- 🎤 **Spotify** is a popular music streaming service offering a wide selection of podcasts. Over 5 million podcasts are available on the service, and it is available on a variety of platforms, including iOS, Android, Windows, macOS, Linux, and the web. Submit your podcast's RSS feed to Spotify and take advantage of their promotional tools, such as custom playlist covers and shareable podcast badges, to enhance your show's visibility.

- 🎤 **TuneIn** is a streaming service that offers a wide selection of podcasts. It is available on various platforms, including iOS, Android, and the web.

- 🎤 **Amazon Music** is another platform that offers podcasts for its members to listen to. While the e-commerce giant is known more for books, it has recently invested more in podcasting. While it's not as popular as other platforms now, the company is clearly looking to grow the service.

Publish Your Podcast Everywhere

There is no reason to limit your podcast to one platform. Regardless of your chosen hosting platform, you can plug that RSS feed into Apple Podcasts, Spotify, and any other platforms you want to publish your podcast on. You only need to publish your show once—there is no ongoing maintenance. Each of these services pulls your show information and episodes from your platform.

Optimize your podcast metadata, including title, description, and cover art, to improve discoverability, and to comply with the platform's guidelines.

Publish your podcast show on as many platforms as possible, and reach a wider audience.

Promote Your Podcast

Getting your podcast published is only step one. That helps potential listeners find your show organically, but if you want to reach a much wider audience, you need to promote your show. There are a variety of channels through which you can promote your show—social media, email newsletters, and asking your guests to promote the episode to their audiences.

Show notes and a transcript can help to make your podcast more accessible and searchable, and can also be a valuable marketing tool. Create show notes summarising your episode and include links and resources mentioned in the episode, and consider creating a transcript for those who prefer to read rather than listen. Read the Transcripts and Closed Captioning chapter for more information on why it's important to have transcripts for your podcast.

Embed your podcast episodes on your website and share them across your social media channels to increase accessibility and reach. You can foster a loyal following and attract new listeners by making it easy for your audience to access your content from various sources.

Collaborate with other podcasters or industry experts by cross-promoting each other's podcasts or appearing as guests on other shows. This can help you reach new audiences and expand your podcast's presence across different platforms.

By publishing your podcast on multiple platforms and leveraging promotional opportunities, you can effectively reach a broader audience, increase your podcast's discoverability, and, ultimately, grow your listener base.

Optimize Your Podcast For Search

To increase your podcast's discoverability and attract more listeners, optimising your podcast for search is essential. Incorporating relevant keywords into your podcast's metadata can help your show rank higher in search results on podcast directories and search engines. Here are some tips for optimizing your podcast for search:

Enhancing Podcast Discoverability

- Reviews and Ratings
- Keyword Research
- Website Optimization
- Title Optimization
- Tags and Categories
- Description Optimization
- Episode Optimization

🎙 **Conduct keyword research:** Research popular keywords and phrases related to your podcast's niche or industry. Use keyword research tools like Google Keyword Planner, Ubersuggest, or Ahrefs to identify high-volume keywords with low competition. List these keywords to use strategically in your podcast's metadata.

🎙 **Optimize your podcast title:** Your podcast title is one of the most critical factors for search optimization. Incorporate one or two relevant keywords into your title while keeping it catchy, descriptive, and memorable. Avoid keyword stuffing, as this may appear spammy and deter potential listeners.

🎙 **Optimize your podcast show description:** Write a concise and informative description highlighting your show's unique value proposition, target audience, and topics or themes. Integrate relevant keywords naturally throughout the description to improve searchability, but be cautious not to overdo it. A well-written and keyword-optimized description can help your podcast rank higher in search results and attract more listeners.

🎙 **Use keywords in episode titles and descriptions:** When crafting episode titles and descriptions, include relevant keywords that accurately represent the content of each episode. Engaging and keyword-optimized titles can help individual episodes rank higher in search results, driving more traffic to your podcast.

🎙 **Add relevant tags and categories:** Many podcast directories, like Apple Podcasts and Spotify, allow you to add tags or categories to your podcast. Select relevant tags and categories representing your podcast's content and incorporate your target keywords. This can further improve your podcast's discoverability within the directories.

🎙 **Optimize your podcast website:** If you have a dedicated website for your podcast, ensure it is optimized for search engines by incorporating relevant keywords in your site's metadata, such as title tags, meta descriptions, and header tags. Also, ensure your website is mobile-friendly and has a fast loading time, as these factors can impact search engine rankings.

🎙 **Encourage reviews and ratings:** Positive reviews and high ratings on podcast directories can improve your podcast's search ranking and visibility. Ask your listeners to leave reviews and ratings for your show, and be sure to engage with them and express your gratitude for their support.

Promote Your Podcast on Social Media

Social media can be daunting, but here's the trick: focus on two key platforms where your audience hangs out. Instead of trying to be everywhere, invest time in building an audience on a couple of platforms to start with.

Social media is a powerful tool for promoting your podcast and engaging with your listeners. By leveraging various platforms, you can increase your podcast's visibility, drive traffic to your episodes, and foster a sense of community among your audience. Here are some more advanced tips for promoting your podcast on social media:

🎙 **Choose the right platforms:** Focus on social media platforms that are popular among your target audience and best suited to your content. For instance, Instagram and TikTok are ideal for sharing visually appealing content, while Twitter is more suited for sharing updates and engaging in conversations. Facebook and LinkedIn can be used to share longer-form content and establish industry connections.

🎙 **Create engaging content:** To capture your audience's attention, create visually appealing and engaging content that reflects your podcast's brand and theme. Share images, videos, quotes, or snippets from your episodes to pique your followers' interest and encourage them to listen to your podcast.

🎙 **Use relevant hashtags:** Incorporate relevant and popular hashtags in your social media posts to increase their visibility and reach. Research trending hashtags within your niche or industry and use them strategically to help your content get discovered by a wider audience.

🎙 **Schedule and share consistently:** Develop a consistent posting schedule to maintain your social media presence and keep your audience engaged. Use scheduling tools like Buffer, Hootsuite, or Later to plan and automate your social media posts, ensuring you consistently share fresh content.

🎙 **Engage with your audience:** Respond to your listeners' comments, messages, and mentions to foster a sense of community and demonstrate that you value their feedback. Engaging with your audience also helps build trust and loyalty, leading to increased word-of-mouth promotion

🎙 **Collaborate with influencers and other podcasters:** Partner with influencers or other podcasters within your niche to cross-promote each other's content on social media. This can help you reach new audiences and expand your podcast's presence on various platforms.

🎙 **Utilize paid advertising:** If you have a budget for marketing, consider using paid advertising options on social media platforms like Facebook, Instagram, or Twitter to reach a larger audience. Target your ads based on demographics, interests, or behaviors to ensure that they reach your ideal listeners.

🎙 **Monitor your performance:** Track your social media performance using analytics tools provided by each platform or third-party tools like Sprout Social or Socialbakers.

Analyze your data to identify trends, top-performing content, and areas for improvement. Adjust your strategy accordingly to maximize your social media efforts.

Connect With Your Listeners Through Email Marketing

Email marketing effectively promotes your podcast, stays in touch with your listeners, and builds a loyal audience. By sending regular newsletters and updates, you can keep your listeners engaged, share exclusive content, and encourage them to share your podcast with others. Here are some tips for using email marketing to promote your podcast:

- **Build your email list:** Start by encouraging your listeners to sign up for your email list. You can do this by promoting your newsletter on your podcast episodes, social media, and website. Offer incentives, such as exclusive content, discounts, or giveaways, to entice your audience to subscribe.

- **Choose an email marketing platform:** Select a user-friendly and reliable email marketing platform, such as Mailchimp, ConvertKit, or Sendinblue, to manage your email list and send newsletters. These platforms provide useful features like automation, segmentation, and analytics, which can help you optimize your email marketing efforts.

- **Craft engaging subject lines:** Your email subject line is crucial in determining whether your subscribers will open your email. Write attention-grabbing, curiosity-provoking subject lines that encourage your subscribers to open and read your emails.

- **Provide valuable content:** Your email content should be relevant, informative, and engaging to keep your subscribers interested. Share updates about your podcast, such as upcoming episodes, behind-the-scenes content, or exclusive interviews. You can also include industry news, tips, or resources that your audience might find valuable.

- **Promote new episodes:** Use your email list to announce new podcast episodes and provide direct links to the episodes on various platforms. Include a brief episode summary, highlighting key takeaways or interesting moments to pique your subscribers' interest.

- **Personalize your emails:** Personalize your emails by addressing your subscribers by their first name and offering different email campaigns based on their preferences or behaviors. This can help you establish a connection with your audience and make your emails more engaging.

- **Use clear calls-to-action (CTAs):** Encourage your subscribers to take specific actions, such as listening to your podcast, leaving a review, or sharing your content with their friends and followers. Make your CTAs prominent and easy to follow to increase engagement and conversions.

- **Test and optimize:** Regularly monitor your email marketing performance by tracking key metrics, such as open rates, click-through rates, and conversion rates. Use A/B

podcast collaboration   partnerships   guest appearances   cross-promotion   joint events

testing to experiment with different subject lines, content, and design elements to identify what resonates best with your audience. Adjust your email marketing strategy based on your findings to continuously improve your results.

Collaborate with other podcasts

Collaborating with other podcasts or bloggers within your niche can effectively cross-promote your podcast, expand your reach, and tap into a new audience. By joining forces with like-minded creators, you can share resources, knowledge, and exposure, ultimately benefiting both parties. Here are some tips for successful podcast collaborations:

- **Identify potential partners:** Research podcasts or blogs within your niche that share a similar target audience and values. Look for creators with a complementary style, content focus, and a comparable or larger audience size to ensure mutual benefits from the collaboration.

- **Establish relationships:** Reach out to your potential partners and express your interest in collaborating. Build rapport by engaging with their content, sharing their episodes, or mentioning them on your podcast. Genuine connections can lead to more successful collaborations and long-term partnerships.

- **Guest appearances:** Swap guest appearances on each other's podcasts to share your expertise and provide valuable content for both audiences. This exposes your podcast to a new audience and adds credibility to your brand by showcasing your knowledge and authority within your niche.

- **Co-hosted episodes or series:** Work together on co-hosted episodes or a series, where you combine your expertise and perspectives to create unique content for both of your audiences. This can result in engaging and dynamic episodes that attract new listeners and showcase the strengths of both podcasts.

- **Cross-promotion:** Promote each other's podcasts through social media, email newsletters, or website links. Share your collaboration episodes or recommend each other's shows to your respective audiences, helping to increase exposure and attract new listeners.

- **Joint giveaways or contests:** Partner with other podcasters or bloggers to organize joint giveaways or contests, which can generate buzz and engagement among your audiences. Offer podcast-related prizes, such as merchandise, exclusive content, or consultations, to encourage participation and grow your listener base.

- **Collaborative events:** Organize joint events, such as webinars, live podcast recordings, or panel discussions, to provide value to your audience and showcase your podcast collaboration. Promote these events across both of your platforms to attract a wider audience and strengthen your partnership.

- **Share knowledge and resources:** Collaborate behind the scenes by sharing knowledge, resources, and best practices related to podcasting. This can help both parties improve their podcast production, promotion, and overall success.

Collaborating with other podcasts or bloggers in your niche can effectively cross-promote your podcast, reach new audiences, and establish valuable connections within your industry. This strategy can increase your podcast's exposure, credibility, and growth.

Create Evergreen Content: Episodes That Keep Drawing Listeners

Some content is "evergreen," meaning it stays relevant long after it's published. Episodes that cover timeless topics or common challenges in your niche can continuously draw listeners. Here's how to make the most of this:

Repromote Old Episodes: Don't be afraid to reshare episodes that are still relevant. You can do this on social media, in your newsletter, or even as "throwback" content.Create Playlists: Group your episodes by theme or topic (e.g., "Best Episodes for New Entrepreneurs"), so listeners can easily find what's most relevant to them.

Power Tip: Compile an "Ultimate Guide" post on your website that links to your best episodes around a particular topic, making it easier for new listeners to find what they need.

By following these tips, you can maximize the visibility and reach of your podcast and grow your audience.

By putting your podcast on the right platforms, optimizing for search, and promoting it consistently, you'll give your show the best chance to reach new listeners and build a loyal audience.

Remember, the more visibility you create, the greater the impact your podcast can have. So take these steps, embrace creative ways to expand your reach, and watch your audience grow with each episode.

Your voice deserves to be heard—now let's make sure it reaches everyone who needs to hear it!

What if there was a better way?

PodcastSecrets.app automatically emails your subscribers, and you can use the RSS feed to schedule social media posts.

To help you implement the strategies outlined in Podcasting Secrets for Entrepreneurs, we've put together a comprehensive Podcast Secrets Resource Kit, which is available for free.

This kit contains tools, templates, and guides to streamline your podcasting process, from the initial planning stages to audience growth and monetization.

https://podcastsecrets.biz/s/kit

CHAPTER 26

BUILDING A WEBSITE AND SHOW PAGE FOR YOUR PODCAST

"Make it simple, but significant." – **Don Draper**

Creating a dedicated website and show page for your podcast is a crucial step in establishing your brand and attracting new listeners.

A well-designed show page serves as the hub for your podcast, showcasing episodes, providing valuable information for potential listeners, and connecting your audience with everything your brand has to offer.

In this chapter, we'll explore the steps to set up a strong online presence for your podcast, from selecting a domain to building an engaging show page that draws in listeners and keeps them coming back for more.

To establish your brand and create a professional platform for your podcast, it is important to consider building a show page on your website. A show page is a landing page for potential listeners to learn about your podcast, see the platforms it's available on, and see what episodes are popular. It should also include ways for your listeners to connect further with you, like signing up for your email list, blog, or course.

The first step is to acquire a domain name, if you don't have one already. You might wish to acquire a domain name that is directly related to your podcast. For example, if your podcast was called *Evolvepreneur Secrets For Entrepreneurs Show*, you might look to acquire the evolvepreneursecrets.show domain.

You can buy a domain name from a domain registrar like NameCheap, BlueHost, and GoDaddy. It's a good idea to purchase a domain name you think you want to use early, because if someone else buys the domain before you, they may not sell it to you—or if they do, it will be for a much higher price than from a domain registrar.

There exist several services that will help you build and host a website. WordPress is the single most popular choice for building websites, and you can use it to build a show page for your podcast. WordPress makes it easy to build simple static pages quickly. You can even download WordPress and install it on your own server. If you're really strapped for cash, you can choose the free plan on wordpress.com, but you won't be able to use your own domain. However, despite its popularity, it isn't without its drawbacks.

To properly secure WordPress, you need professional help. WordPress installations make up roughly 41% of the top 10 million sites on the web, making them an attractive target for the hooded denizens of the internet. And even if you do secure the base installation, you will likely find yourself reaching for custom themes and plug-ins for extra functionality.

This gives attackers more areas to target—if WordPress itself is secured, why not go after the WooCommerce plugin? Aside from this, plug-ins often do not result in a seamless experience for the user or the administrator because WordPress was not designed to accommodate this functionality from the start.

If you choose WordPress, you should consider these factors.

Wix and Squarespace are two other popular website builders. Because they are newer than WordPress, they haven't been struggling to modernize their service like WordPress. They make it similarly easy to build simple websites, and either would be a fine choice for creating a nicely-designed show page. Conversely, both services are more expensive than a basic WordPress plan, and may not offer the same level of customization you want from your website.

Your hosting platform may offer you the ability to host a show page. This is usually the best option, because they've focused on creating pages that are designed specifically for podcasting, rather than making you do all the work. Our own podcasting platform, podcastsecrets.app, allows you to create your podcast show page in minutes.

Once you've chosen a website builder, you must design your website. Consider your brand and target audience. Use colors, fonts, and images that are consistent with your brand, and that will appeal to your listeners. A powerful podcast show page is crucial for attracting and engaging your target audience.

Enhancing Your Podcast Show Page

Here are the key components that can make your show page stand out:

- 🎤 **Compelling tagline:** Choose a tagline that is catchy, memorable, and representative of your show's content. A short and impactful tagline can further convey your show's theme and help potential listeners understand what they can expect from your podcast.

- 🎤 **Detailed show description:** Write a concise yet informative description that highlights your podcast's unique value proposition, your target audience, and the topics or themes you cover. Include relevant keywords to improve searchability and ensure that your podcast is easily discoverable by potential listeners.

- 🎙 **Engaging episode titles and descriptions:** Craft compelling episode titles that pique potential listeners' curiosity and accurately represent each episode's content. Write informative episode descriptions that provide an overview of the episode's content, including key takeaways, guests, and any relevant timestamps.

- 🎙 **Clear call-to-action (CTA):** Encourage your listeners to engage with your podcast by including a clear call-to-action on your show page. This can involve subscribing to your podcast, leaving a review, signing up for your newsletter, or following you on social media.

- 🎙 **Links to relevant resources and social media profiles:** Make it easy for your listeners to connect with you and access additional content by providing links to your website, blog, or social media profiles. You can also include links to resources or articles mentioned in your episodes to offer further value to your audience.

- 🎙 **Reviews and testimonials:** Positive reviews and testimonials from your listeners can provide social proof and encourage new listeners to try your podcast. Highlight these reviews on your show page and encourage your audience to leave their feedback to help build credibility and trust.

By incorporating these key components into your podcast show page, you can create a powerful and engaging online presence that draws in potential listeners and fosters a loyal and engaged audience.

After you've created your website and show page, you need to promote it! Mention it at the end of your episodes and promote it on social media. It's no good if your listeners don't know about your website!

It's also a great idea to create a blog, giving listeners a reason to return to your website regularly. Not all hosting platforms offer this feature, in which case, you'll need to host it separately. You could host it on a subdomain, like blog.yourshowname.show.

Your podcast's website and show page are more than just places to host episodes—they're key tools for engaging your audience, boosting visibility, and building brand loyalty.

By creating an inviting, professional show page and promoting it across your channels, you make it easy for listeners to connect with your content and stay tuned for future episodes.

With a strong online presence, your podcast is positioned to grow, attract new fans, and create lasting impact.

So go ahead, make your mark online, and let your website work as an extension of your voice and vision.

What if there was an better way?

We offer the ability to host blogs, podcasts, support tickets, sell products and courses, and provide you a task management system with evolvepreneur.app. The platform is designed to accommodate the many needs of your business, while incorporating all of the features in our dedicated podcast hosting platform, PodcastSecrets.app.

PodcastSecrets.app lets you setup the whole platform in minutes, including a Show Page that is designed to convert listeners to subscribers.

To help you implement the strategies outlined in Podcasting Secrets for Entrepreneurs, we've put together a comprehensive Podcast Secrets Resource Kit, which is available for free.

This kit contains tools, templates, and guides to streamline your podcasting process, from the initial planning stages to audience growth and monetization.

https://podcastsecrets.biz/s/kit

CHAPTER 27

ETHICS AND RESPONSIBILITY IN PODCASTING

"Integrity is doing the right thing, even when no one is watching." – **C.S. Lewis**

A s podcasters, we hold a unique position of influence over our audience. Whether you're producing content for education, entertainment, or business, your listeners trust you to provide honest, accurate, and meaningful information.

With this power comes great responsibility—both to your audience and the wider community. Maintaining ethical standards in your podcast is not just about avoiding controversy or legal issues, but about fostering trust and integrity that will ultimately build a loyal and engaged audience.

This chapter will explore the core ethical principles and responsibilities that every podcaster should consider when producing content.

Transparency and Honesty

The principle of transparency is at the heart of ethical podcasting. Whether discussing your experiences, hosting guest interviews, or sharing advice, it's critical to be upfront and honest with your listeners.

Present Facts Accurately

Misleading your audience—intentionally or unintentionally—can damage your credibility. Always double-check your facts, especially when discussing data, research, or sensitive topics. If you make a mistake (and everyone does at some point), acknowledge it openly in your next episode. Honesty and humility will earn you far more respect than pretending an error didn't happen.

Disclose Sponsorships and Affiliations

If your podcast includes sponsored content or affiliate links, be clear and upfront with your audience. Transparency about paid partnerships is ethically sound and often legally required in many jurisdictions. Let your listeners know when you're being compensated to promote a product or service and, most importantly, ensure those promotions align with the values of your show.

For example, a simple disclosure might be: "This episode is sponsored by XYZ, a service we believe can truly benefit our audience. As always, we only recommend products we trust."

Stay Neutral When Necessary

While podcasts often feature personal opinions and viewpoints, be mindful of when neutrality is essential. If you're covering a highly polarizing or contentious topic, aim to present multiple perspectives. This ensures your audience gets a well-rounded understanding and doesn't feel like they're being swayed without adequate context.

Respecting Intellectual Property and Copyright

In the age of easily accessible online content, using music, images, or other materials is tempting without proper permission. However, doing so without the correct licenses can lead to serious legal and ethical issues.

🎤 **Credit Where It's Due:** Always give proper credit to creators whose work you feature in your podcast—whether it's a piece of music, an interview excerpt, or a reference from a book or article. Respecting intellectual property isn't just a legal obligation; it's a way of honouring the hard work of other creators.

🎤 **Use Licensed or Royalty-Free Materials:** If you're using music, sound effects, or images in your episodes, make sure you've secured the necessary rights. Many resources for royalty-free or Creative Commons-licensed materials allow for legal use under specific conditions. Always read and adhere to the terms of the license, and when in doubt, seek permission from the content owner.

🎤 **Create Your Own Content:** The most foolproof way to avoid copyright issues is to create your own content whenever possible. Originality protects you legally and enhances your brand's credibility and authenticity.

Handling Sensitive Topics

Podcasts often tackle challenging or controversial subjects, such as current events, political issues, or sensitive personal experiences. When addressing these topics, it's essential to approach them with care, respect, and responsibility.

🎤 **Be Mindful of Your Language.** Language matters, especially when discussing topics related to race, gender, mental health, or trauma. Ensure that your language is inclusive and respectful. Avoid terms or phrases that could be considered offensive, and if you're unsure, take the time to research appropriate language or consult experts.

🎤 **Balance Freedom of Speech with Responsibility.** While podcasting offers a platform for free expression, this doesn't mean anything goes. Be mindful of your words' impact on your audience and the wider community. If you're hosting guests with strong opinions or controversial views, consider providing context or clarification to ensure your audience understands your position. It's about finding the balance between allowing open conversation and avoiding harm.

🎤 **Provide a warning at the start of the episode:** Provide Trigger Warnings When Necessary if you're covering topics that could be triggering, such as violence, abuse, or mental health struggles. This allows your listeners to make an informed choice about whether they want to engage with the content.

Fair Treatment of Guests and Contributors

Your podcast guests and collaborators deserve to be treated with respect and fairness. Whether they're high-profile experts or listeners who've agreed to share personal stories, how you manage your relationship with them reflects your podcast's ethical standards.

- **Get Clear Consent:** Always get your guests' consent to record and broadcast their contributions. Explain the purpose of the interview, how it will be used, and where it will be distributed. If a guest requests that certain parts of their interview be edited or removed, respect that request whenever possible.

- **Represent Guests Accurately:** It's your responsibility to ensure that guests' opinions and statements are presented accurately and in context. Avoid editing interviews in a way that distorts their meaning or leads to misinterpretation. If a guest expresses views you strongly disagree with, consider including a respectful counterpoint rather than trying to silence or distort their message.

- **Credit Contributors:** Always credit contributors—whether it's a guest interview, someone who helped with research, or a behind-the-scenes editor. Proper acknowledgment fosters a culture of respect and professionalism within your podcasting community.

Avoiding Exploitation of Listeners

One less discussed ethical consideration is how podcasters manage their relationship with their audience, particularly when monetization is involved.

- **Respect Your Listeners' Trust:** Your audience trusts you to provide value, whether through information, entertainment, or guidance. Don't exploit that trust by bombarding them with constant ads, low-quality sponsorships, or paid content that doesn't align with their interests. Always put your listeners first, ensuring that any monetization strategy enhances rather than detracts from the podcast experience.

- **Avoid Manipulative Tactics:** Hard-selling tactics, scare-mongering, or clickbait-style promotions might drive short-term engagement, but they erode trust over time. Keep your audience engaged through authentic content, and avoid using manipulative tactics to increase downloads or push products.

Maintaining Editorial Independence

Whether running a small independent show or a larger podcast with corporate sponsorship, maintaining editorial independence is critical to preserving your podcast's integrity.

- **Don't Compromise Content for Sponsors.** Sponsors are valuable to podcast monetization, but they shouldn't dictate your content. Make it clear to sponsors that while you'll promote their products or services, your editorial control over the podcast remains non-negotiable. This ensures that your audience trusts your recommendations and knows that external interests do not bias your content.

- **Declare Conflicts of Interest.** If a sponsor, product, or topic presents a potential conflict of interest—such as when you're being paid to discuss a product or service—be upfront about it. Declaring conflicts of interest builds credibility with your audience and prevents any appearance of bias or manipulation.

Ethics in podcasting isn't just about following legal guidelines—it's about maintaining the trust and respect of your audience, guests, and collaborators. By prioritizing transparency, fairness, and integrity in everything you do, you'll create a podcast that resonates with listeners and stands the test of time.

Ethical practices build credibility, and credibility builds a loyal and engaged audience— ultimately setting you up for long-term success in the podcasting world.

CHAPTER 28

HANDLING NEGATIVE FEEDBACK AND MANAGING PODCAST CRISES

"Criticism, like rain, should be gentle enough to nourish a man's growth without destroying his roots." – **Frank A. Clark**

L et's face it: not every comment is going to be a glowing review.

At some point, you might encounter a critical listener, a technical glitch, or—worst-case scenario—a full-blown podcast crisis.

But don't worry! Handling negative feedback and occasional bumps in the road is all part of the podcasting journey.

In this chapter, we'll guide you through responding gracefully to critics, keeping cool under pressure, and turning mishaps into opportunities for growth. By the end, you'll be ready to handle anything that comes your way—without missing a beat!

While it can be disheartening, learning how to handle criticism and manage potential crises effectively is crucial for any podcaster.

The goal isn't to avoid negative feedback altogether—because that's impossible—but to respond thoughtfully and professionally, ensuring your podcast and brand emerge stronger.

This chapter will cover strategies for responding to negative feedback and managing crises that could impact your podcast's reputation.

Managing Negative Feedback and Crises in Podcasting

Receive Negative Feedback

Stay Calm and Professional

Use Feedback Constructively

Identify Crisis Early

Communicate Transparently

Acknowledge Feedback Promptly

Clarify or Apologize

Engage Positive Listeners

Assess Crisis Scope

Why Negative Feedback Happens

It's important to recognize that negative feedback is a normal part of the creative process. Podcast listeners have diverse expectations, opinions, and preferences, so, inevitably, some episodes, guests, or topics may not resonate with every listener.

Common reasons for negative feedback include:

- Some listeners may simply disagree with your viewpoint or your guests' perspectives.
- Poor audio quality, glitches, or inconsistent episode delivery can lead to frustration.
- Listeners may feel let down if an episode doesn't meet the expectations set by your podcast description, title, or promotions.

Whatever the reason, negative feedback can provide valuable insights if you know how to approach it correctly.

Responding to Negative Feedback

When negative feedback comes your way, your response matters. How you handle criticism can shape your relationship with your audience and affect how your podcast is perceived. Here are some approaches you can take to managing negative feedback:

- **Stay Calm and Professional:** It's easy to become defensive, especially if the feedback feels harsh or unfair. However, your goal is to defuse the situation, not escalate it. Take a breath, and respond in a calm, measured tone. Avoid getting into a back-and-forth argument, as this can quickly spiral out of control and damage your reputation.
- **Clarify or Apologize When Necessary:** If the negative feedback points to a genuine mistake—whether it's an audio issue, factual inaccuracy, or a misunderstanding— own it. Offering a sincere apology can go a long way in maintaining trust with your audience. For example, "We noticed the audio quality wasn't up to our usual standards on this episode. We're working to fix it and appreciate your patience." Alternatively, clarify any confusion without appearing dismissive.
- **Use Constructive Criticism to Improve:** Not all negative feedback is bad. Some criticisms can highlight areas for genuine improvement. Review the feedback objectively and assess whether it reveals something you hadn't considered. If multiple listeners are pointing out the same issue, it may be a signal that you need to adjust something about your content, format, or production process.
- **Engage with Positive Listeners:** Balance negative feedback by engaging more actively with positive listeners. Often, people who enjoy your show may not leave reviews or comments as frequently as those with criticisms. Encourage positive engagement by responding to positive feedback, sharing user testimonials, and fostering a supportive community.

Managing a Podcast Crisis

Occasionally, you may encounter a crisis that goes beyond the typical negative review or critical comment. Crises require a more structured approach to manage, whether it's a controversial episode, technical failure, or guest-related issue.

Here's how to handle podcast crises effectively:

- 🎙 **Identify the Problem Early.** The quicker you identify a brewing crisis, the easier it will be to control. Monitor feedback on all platforms—whether that's through your podcast's social media pages, comments on your website, or podcast review sites like Apple Podcasts. Set up alerts or designate a team member (if you have one) to watch for any emerging issues, so you can act swiftly.

- 🎙 **Assess the Scope of the Crisis.** Not all problems are created equal. Some may be minor—such as a technical glitch that can be easily fixed—while others may pose a more significant threat to your podcast's reputation. Evaluate the situation carefully. Is this feedback coming from a small portion of your audience, or is it something affecting the majority of your listeners?

- 🎙 **Communicate Transparently.** One of the most important actions during a crisis is communicating openly with your audience. If an episode contains factual errors or if a guest's remarks have sparked controversy, address the issue head-on. Craft a statement that is clear, honest, and non-defensive. Explain what happened, what steps you're taking to address it, and how you'll prevent similar issues in the future. Transparency builds trust.

- 🎙 **Take Corrective Action.** When necessary, take swift corrective action. For example, if an episode has technical issues, consider re-editing or re-releasing it with corrections. If there was an inaccuracy, issue a clarification or correction in the following episode. Depending on the severity of the situation, if a guest said something offensive, it might be worth editing out the comment in question and releasing a revised version of the episode. The key here is to demonstrate that you take your podcast's quality and integrity seriously.

- 🎙 **Manage Social Media Backlash.** If your podcast gains traction, you may face social media backlash, especially if your show covers controversial or sensitive topics. It's crucial not to fuel the fire. Stay composed, avoid inflammatory responses, and address concerns professionally. Sometimes, it's better to issue one comprehensive response rather than trying to respond individually to every comment, which can quickly escalate the situation.

- 🎙 **Learn from the Crisis.** Every crisis presents an opportunity to learn and grow. After the situation is resolved, review what went wrong and what could have been done differently. Are there gaps in your content review process? Did a technical issue arise due to outdated equipment or poor preparation? Reflect on these lessons and adjust your approach going forward.

Preventative Measures

The best way to handle crises is to prevent them in the first place. While you can't foresee every potential problem, you can put processes in place to minimize the likelihood of a major issue. Here are a few tips:

- 🎙 **Pre-screen Guests:** If you regularly interview guests, do your homework. Vet your guests thoroughly to ensure their views align with your podcast's tone and values. This can help you avoid unintentional controversies.

- 🎙 **Test Audio and Equipment:** Ensure your technical setup is reliable. Test your equipment and audio quality regularly to avoid echo, poor sound levels, or dropped recordings.

🎤 **Have a Backup Plan:** Keep backup copies of all your episode files, scripts, and editing versions in case something goes wrong. If a technical failure wipes out an episode, having a backup ready to go can save your schedule.

🎤 **Set Clear Guidelines:** If you have co-hosts, contributors, or sponsors, set clear guidelines for content. Make sure everyone is aligned on the podcast's tone, language, and content boundaries.

Handling negative feedback and managing podcast crises are part of the journey to building a successful show. By responding to criticism with professionalism and addressing crises quickly and transparently, you can turn challenging situations into opportunities for growth.

Most importantly, always remember that mistakes and setbacks are part of the learning process—what matters is how you respond and move forward. When handled correctly, these experiences can strengthen your podcast and foster a deeper connection with your audience.

CHAPTER 29

THE LEGALITIES OF PODCASTING: COPYRIGHTS, TRADEMARKS, AND MORE

"Obey the principles without being bound by them." – **Bruce Lee**

When it comes to podcasting, you don't want any legal surprises down the road. This chapter covers the basics of podcasting law—copyright, trademarks, licensing, and more—to help you protect your content and avoid common legal pitfalls.

We'll break down the essentials in plain language so you can focus on creating without worry.

As you put all the pieces together to create a successful podcast and attract high-profile guests, it's important to be aware of the legalities of podcasting.

Here are a few key legal issues to consider when podcasting:

- **Copyright:** If you use any copyrighted material in your episodes or webpages, such as music, images, or text, it is important to obtain permission from the copyright owner. Failure to do so can result in legal action and financial penalties. To avoid copyright infringement, you can either use royalty-free materials, material licensed with a compatible Creative Commons license, or obtain the necessary licenses for copyrighted content. A good place to get royalty-free images is Pixabay.

  It's also a good idea to register a copyright for your own content in the United States. Copyright laws in over 180 countries meet the same minimum standards because they have all signed the Berne Convention. One of these standards is that authors automatically own the copyrights to any works they create; in the past, this had to be registered at a government office for a small fee.

  This is true even in the United States, but it is still a good idea to register your copyrights in the United States, regardless of whether you are a citizen. This is because a lack of explicit registration makes it harder to defend yourself in court, even despite the conditions agreed upon by the Berne Convention. Registration is free, and you can do so here: *https://www.copyright.gov/registration/*

  There is a section on the website for foreigners: h*ttps://www.copyright.gov/help/faq/ faq-who.html#foreigners*

- 🎙 **Trademarks:** If you use any trademarks in your podcast, such as brand names or logos, it is important to use them correctly and to obtain permission if necessary. Using trademarks improperly can result in legal action and financial penalties.

  Likewise, you should seriously consider trademarking your show title. If you use a show title that has been trademarked by someone already, they can pursue you legally, or, at the very least, compel you to stop using their trademark without permission. Even if you've been using that title for a long time; since before another person registered it, you can still be pursued. Check here to start: *https://www.wipo.int/trademarks/en/*

- 🎙 **Privacy:** Respecting the privacy of guests or interviewees on your podcast is essential. Always obtain consent from participants before recording and publishing their comments or conversations. Inform them about the purpose of the recording and how it will be used to ensure transparency and compliance with privacy regulations.

- 🎙 **Disclaimer:** A disclaimer can state that the views and opinions expressed in your podcast are your own and are not necessarily those of your guests or sponsors. By understanding and following the legalities of podcasting, you can create a successful and sustainable podcast without putting yourself or your listeners at risk. This also applies to affiliations, sponsorships, or potential conflicts of interest related to your podcast. You may have a legal obligation to disclose these relationships, but regardless, you should disclose any financial relationships or promotional arrangements to maintain your listeners' trust.

- 🎙 **Libel and defamation:** Be cautious about making false or damaging statements about individuals or organizations in your podcast. Libel and defamation can result in legal action and financial penalties. Stick to facts and well-researched opinions, and avoid making derogatory or defamatory remarks.

By familiarizing yourself with the legalities of podcasting and adhering to the relevant regulations and best practices, you can create a successful, long-lasting podcast that maintains a positive reputation and avoids putting you or your listeners at risk.

Creating a Privacy Policy and GDPR Compliance

While we have already touched on privacy somewhat previously, this is an important topic that deserves its own section. You need a privacy policy for your podcast.

The internet has become an essential part of our lives, and with it, concerns about privacy and data protection have increased. Like all online content creators, podcasters must ensure that their activities comply with privacy laws and regulations, including the European Union's General Data Protection Regulation (GDPR). This chapter will guide you through creating a privacy policy and adhering to GDPR compliance, specifically for your podcast.

Understanding The GDPR and Its Implications

The GDPR is a comprehensive data protection law that took effect on May 25, 2018. It applies to any organization, regardless of location, that processes the personal data of people residing in the EU. In the context of podcasting, if you have listeners in the EU or market your podcast to European audiences, you need to comply with the GDPR; but the GDPR enforces good practices that benefit all your listeners.

Elements of a Privacy Policy for Podcasters

A privacy policy is a legal document that explains how you collect, use, and disclose personal information from your listeners. It should be easily accessible on your podcast website and include the following elements:

- 🎤 **Personal Data Collection:** Clearly state the types of personal data you collect from your listeners, such as names, email addresses, IP addresses, and any other information that can be used to identify an individual.

- 🎤 **Purpose of Data Collection:** Explain why you collect personal data and how you use it. This may include purposes like sending newsletters, providing personalized content, or analyzing listener behavior.

- 🎤 **Third-Party Sharing:** If you share personal data with third parties, such as podcast hosting providers or marketing services, disclose this information and explain the purpose of the data sharing. If possible, name these third parties.

- 🎤 **Data Storage and Security:** Describe the measures taken to protect your listeners' personal data and how long you retain the information.

- 🎤 **User Rights:** Explain the rights users have concerning their personal data, including the right to access, rectify, delete, or restrict the processing of their information.

- 🎤 **Contact Information:** Provide contact information for your designated Data Protection Officer or another representative responsible for privacy matters.

GDPR Compliance for Podcasters

To ensure GDPR compliance, podcasters should take the following steps:

- 🎤 **Obtain Consent:** When collecting personal data, obtain explicit consent from your listeners. This can be done through opt-in checkboxes or consent banners on your website. Consent should be freely given, specific, informed, and unambiguous.

- 🎤 **Limit Data Collection:** Collect only the personal data necessary for the purposes you've specified in your privacy policy. Avoid collecting excessive or irrelevant information.

- 🎤 **Data Processing Agreements:** If you work with third-party service providers that process personal data on your behalf, ensure you have GDPR-compliant data processing agreements in place.

- 🎤 **Data Breach Notification:** In the event of a data breach, you must notify the appropriate supervisory authority within 72 hours and inform affected individuals without undue delay.

- 🎤 **International Data Transfers:** If you transfer personal data outside the European Economic Area, ensure appropriate safeguards are in place, such as the EU-US Privacy Shield or Standard Contractual Clauses.

Additional Privacy Regulations

In addition to the GDPR, other privacy regulations may apply to your podcasts, such as the California Consumer Privacy Act (CCPA) or the Brazilian General Data Protection Law (LGPD). Familiarize yourself with the privacy laws that apply to your target audience and ensure your podcast is compliant with all relevant regulations.

Privacy policies and GDPR compliance are essential aspects of podcasting, particularly as the online landscape continues to evolve. By being transparent about your data collection practices and respecting the privacy rights of your listeners, you are protecting both yourself and your listeners.

Music Licensing for Podcasts

In relation to podcasting, music licensing plays a critical role in ensuring that creators are abiding by copyright laws when using music in their shows. Podcasters often use music to enhance the mood, add depth to their content, or to create a more engaging listening experience for their audience. However, using copyrighted music without proper licensing is copyright infringement and can lead to legal consequences. To put it in plainer terms, this is what rightsholders generally refer to as 'piracy'.

Here are some key points to consider when it comes to music licensing for podcasts:

1. Copyright and intellectual property

Music is protected by copyright, which means that creators (composers, lyricists, and performers) have the exclusive right to reproduce, distribute, and publicly perform their works. Using copyrighted music in a podcast without obtaining a proper license infringes on these rights and can lead to legal trouble.

2. Types of licenses

There are two main types of licenses that podcasters need to obtain in order to use music legally in their podcasts:

- 🎤 **Mechanical license:** This covers the right to reproduce and distribute a copyrighted musical work. In the context of podcasting, this license is required when you want to include a specific recording of a song in your podcast. The interesting thing about music licensing is that it is compulsory; this allows anyone to use a copyright holder's music without their consent so long as they pay a fee. This is in contrast to most copyrighted content (like books), which can only be licensed or used with the copyright holder's consent.

- 🎤 **Public performance license:** This covers the right to publicly perform a copyrighted musical work, which includes playing it on a podcast. Performance rights organizations (PROs) like ASCAP, BMI, and SESAC manage these licenses on behalf of songwriters and publishers.

3. Royalty-free and Creative Commons music: An alternative to licensing copyrighted music is using royalty-free or Creative Commons-licensed music. Royalty-free music requires a one-time fee for unlimited use, while Creative Commons music is often available for free with certain usage restrictions.

Visit the Creative Commons website to see the terms of their various licenses: https://creativecommons.org/licenses/

4. Fair use: In some cases, the use of copyrighted music in a podcast may be considered "fair use" and not require a license. However, fair use is a complex legal concept that depends on factors such as the purpose of the use, the nature of the copyrighted work, the amount of the work used, and the effect on the market value of the work. It's always best to consult with an attorney to determine whether your specific use of music may qualify as fair use.

5. Obtaining licenses: To obtain the necessary licenses for using copyrighted music in your podcast, you can either contact the copyright holders directly or go through a music licensing platform. Many online platforms, such as Soundstripe, Epidemic Sound, and Artlist, offer a variety of music tracks for podcasters with the required licenses included.

Navigating the legal side of podcasting may not be the most glamorous part of launching a show, but it's one of the most essential steps for creating something that lasts. By covering your bases with copyrights, trademarks, privacy policies, and licensing, you're setting up your podcast for long-term success—and peace of mind. This foundation lets you focus on the exciting work of creating, connecting, and sharing your unique voice with the world.

As you move forward, remember that protecting your content and respecting others' rights is all part of building a trustworthy brand. It's about giving your listeners a show they can rely on, free of hidden risks or legal surprises. Armed with this knowledge, you're ready to make smart, informed choices that will keep your podcast thriving.

In the chapters ahead, you'll find everything you need to grow your show, reach a wider audience, and take your podcasting journey to the next level.

Let's keep building a podcast that isn't just impactful, but truly sustainable.

To help you implement the strategies outlined in Podcasting Secrets for Entrepreneurs, we've put together a comprehensive Podcast Secrets Resource Kit, which is available for free.

This kit contains tools, templates, and guides to streamline your podcasting process, from the initial planning stages to audience growth and monetization.

https://podcastsecrets.biz/s/kit

CHAPTER 30

YOUR PODCAST LAUNCH

*"Start where you are. Use what you have. Do what you can." – **Arthur Ashe***

Congratulations—you're about to launch your podcast!

It's a thrilling journey filled with anticipation, creativity, and yes, a few nerves. But don't worry, with a solid plan in place, you'll be ready to turn your podcast from an idea into a live show that reaches eager listeners.

Think of launch week as a grand opening: it's your chance to set the stage, showcase what makes your podcast unique, and make a splash that will keep people tuning in.

In this chapter, we'll cover everything from crafting a launch strategy to getting your show in front of as many ears as possible.

So let's roll out the red carpet for your podcast and give it the debut it deserves!

Podcast Launch Process

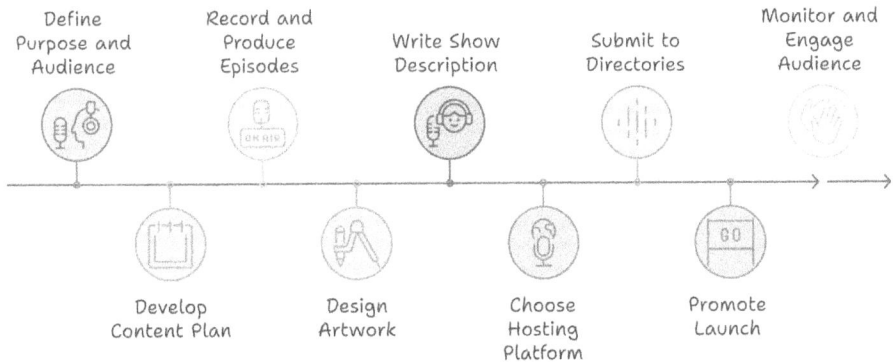

Define Purpose and Audience

Record and Produce Episodes

Write Show Description

Submit to Directories

Monitor and Engage Audience

Develop Content Plan

Design Artwork

Choose Hosting Platform

Promote Launch

Develop a content plan

Outline your first few episodes, including topics, guests, and any key takeaways you want to include. Aim for a mix of evergreen content (topics that will always be relevant) and timely discussions to keep your podcast fresh and engaging.

Design eye-catching artwork

Create attractive, professional-looking cover art for your podcast that stands out and captures the essence of your show. This artwork will be the first thing potential listeners see, so make sure it's visually appealing and accurately represents your podcast's theme.

Write a compelling show description

Craft a concise, engaging show description that explains your podcast's purpose, the topics you'll cover, and what makes your podcast unique. This description will help listeners understand what to expect from your show and entice them to subscribe.

Choose a podcast hosting platform

You've hopefully already done this following our advice in the Choosing Your Hosting Platform chapter, but if not, now is the time to make your final decision.

Submit your podcast to directories

Submit your podcast to popular podcast directories such as Apple Podcasts, Spotify, Google Podcasts, and others. This will help increase your podcast's visibility and make it easier for potential listeners to discover your show.

Promote your launch

Use social media, email marketing, and other channels to promote your podcast launch. Contact friends, family, and colleagues, and ask them to share your podcast with their networks. You can also collaborate with influencers, bloggers, or other podcasters in your niche to help spread the word.

Monitor and engage with your audience

Listen to listener feedback, and engage with your audience on social media and other platforms. Respond to comments and questions, and use this feedback to improve your podcast content and grow your listener base. Direct your listeners to your show page and website to maintain engagement on a platform you have direct control over.

Stay consistent and keep improving

Maintain a consistent release schedule and always strive to improve the quality of your content. Learn from your experiences and audience feedback and refine your podcasting skills.

Launch Week

An effective initial launch week is crucial for the long-term success of your podcast. Here are some tips and ideas to help you make the most of your launch week:

- 🎙 **Create a stockpile of episodes:** When you launch your podcast, have multiple episodes ready to publish a week apart. Remember, the most important thing your listeners demand from you is consistency.

- 🎙 **Host a launch event:** Organize a virtual or in-person launch event to celebrate your podcast's debut. Invite friends, family, colleagues, and experts in your niche. This event can include a live recording of an episode, a Q&A session, or a discussion panel related to your podcast's theme.

- 🎙 **Leverage your network:** Reach out to your personal and professional networks to spread the word about your podcast. Share your podcast on social media, email your list, and ask friends and family to help promote your show.

- 🎙 **Offer launch incentives:** Provide special incentives for early subscribers, such as exclusive bonus content, giveaways, or discounts on related products or services. This can help generate excitement around your podcast and encourage more people to subscribe.

- 🎙 **Collaborate with experts and other podcasters:** Partner with experts or other podcasters in your niche to cross-promote each other's shows. You can also invite them as guests on your podcast or appear as a guest on their show to reach new audiences.

- 🎙 **Run a social media campaign:** Create a social media campaign to promote your podcast during the launch week. Share teaser clips, behind-the-scenes content, and quotes from your episodes. Use relevant hashtags and engage with your audience to build excitement around your show.

- 🎙 **Publish a blog post or press release:** Write a blog post or press release announcing the launch of your podcast and publish it on your website. Share insights about your podcast's concept, the topics you'll cover, and any notable guests you've lined up. Distribute the press release to relevant media outlets and online platforms.

- 🎙 **Utilize email marketing:** If you have an existing email list, use it to promote your podcast launch. Send a series of emails leading up to the launch, sharing sneak peeks, episode highlights, and information about any special events or promotions.

- 🎙 **Ask for reviews and ratings:** Encourage listeners to leave reviews and ratings on podcast directories like Apple Podcasts. Positive reviews can boost your podcast's visibility and help attract more listeners.

- 🎙 **Track your performance:** During the launch week, monitor your podcast's analytics to see which episodes and promotional strategies resonate with your audience. Use this data to refine your marketing efforts and make adjustments as needed.

With a powerful launch under your belt, you're setting the tone for a successful podcasting journey. Remember, launch week is just the beginning—building your show and connecting with your audience is an ongoing adventure.

As you grow, keep refining, engaging, and having fun with the process. Each episode is a chance to make an impact, entertain, and inspire.

So keep the momentum going, and watch your podcast turn from a fresh launch into a lasting legacy. Here's to your podcast's debut—and the amazing journey ahead!

To help you implement the strategies outlined in Podcasting Secrets for Entrepreneurs, we've put together a comprehensive Podcast Secrets Resource Kit, which is available for free.

This kit contains tools, templates, and guides to streamline your podcasting process, from the initial planning stages to audience growth and monetization.

https://podcastsecrets.biz/s/kit

Cultivate

Cultivating meaningful connections with your best prospects is a strategic approach to both enriching your podcast content and selling your products or services. If your podcast involves a lot of interviews, carefully select guests who align with your show's theme and represent your target market.

During the conversation, foster an environment that encourages open dialogue, allowing your guests to share their expertise and experiences while subtly showcasing the benefits and relevance of your offerings.

Building rapport and establishing trust with these guests creates an organic pathway for potential business opportunities, turning your podcast into a powerful marketing tool.

CHAPTER 31

PROFITABLE PODCASTING

"Opportunities don't happen. You create them." – **Chris Grosser**

I n this chapter, "My Podcasting Journey", we explored how podcasting can be a powerful tool to connect, inspire, and build your brand.

But what if it could also fuel your business growth directly?

Podcasting offers unique paths to profitability, from traditional sponsorships and audience support to innovative strategies like curating guests who align with your ideal client profile.

In this chapter, we'll dive into these monetization methods, showing you how to turn your podcast into a profitable venture that not only engages listeners but also drives revenue.

Ready to make podcasting a key player in your business growth?

Let's get started!

Advertising and sponsorship

One of the most common ways to monetize a podcast is through advertising and sponsorship. This can involve placing ads within your podcast episodes, or partnering with brands or products for sponsored content. Of course, you need to build relationships with these sponsors over time, and the most successful method is creating a successful podcast. In essence, you need to be popular before you can attract sponsors.

Have Your Audience Sponsor You

Another way is to invite your audience to sponsor you. If they love your content, some listeners would happily sponsor you so you can produce more of it. There are various platforms you can use to do this. Patreon is the most popular one, although Liberapay takes no extra fees from donations. SubscribeStar is another option.

You may get some recurring revenue this way, but unless you have a large audience of adoring fans, don't expect to earn life-changing amounts of money this way.

Merchandise

Another way to monetize your podcast is through merchandise like t-shirts, mugs, and other branded items. By creating and promoting merchandise to your listeners, you can create a new revenue stream for your podcast.

Courses and coaching

If you have expertise in a particular area, you can create and sell courses or offer coaching services to your listeners. This can be a lucrative way to monetize your podcast, especially if you have a loyal and engaged audience.

Consulting and speaking

Another way to monetize your podcast is by offering consulting or speaking services to businesses or organizations. This can involve using your podcast as a platform to showcase your expertise and build your personal brand.

By implementing these strategies, you can create a profitable podcast that generates revenue and helps you to achieve your business goals. But there could be an even better and easier way than any of the above ideas.

What if you cultivated the best guests for your show who fit your dream customer profile as your strategic approach to not only enhance your podcast content, but also to attract and engage your target audience? Begin by identifying your dream customer's key characteristics, interests, and pain points.

Next, seek out potential guests who embody these qualities or have demonstrated success in addressing the challenges faced by your target market.

When inviting guests, look for knowledgeable, influential individuals who have a strong connection with your target audience. By featuring guests who reflect your dream customer, you create content that resonates with your listeners and effectively addresses their needs and aspirations.

During the interview, foster a welcoming atmosphere that encourages insightful conversation and allows your guests to share their expertise, experiences, and success stories. This not only positions your podcast as a valuable resource but also showcases your understanding of your target market, and your commitment to providing solutions that cater to their needs.

Establishing rapport with your guests can lead to long-lasting relationships that extend beyond the podcast, creating opportunities for collaboration, referrals, and word-of-mouth promotion.

By curating a roster of guests who personify your dream customer, you transform your podcast into a powerful platform for connecting with your target audience, attracting potential clients, and driving business growth.

Podcasting is more than a platform for sharing insights—it's a stage for building profitable connections and creating opportunities that directly support your business goals.

By focusing on strategic guest selection, audience engagement, and multiple monetization channels, you can shape a podcast that serves your brand and fuels your bottom line.

Remember, your journey with podcasting is just beginning, and the potential for profit grows with each carefully crafted episode.

So keep building, keep connecting, and watch as your podcast becomes a powerful asset for your business success!

Our Podcast Resource Kit includes an in-depth presentation on this concept, packed with practical insights and innovative ideas.

CHAPTER 32

GUEST INTERVIEWS FOR PROFITABLE PODCASTING

"The art of conversation is the art of hearing as well as of being heard." – **William Hazlitt**

The easiest way to turn your podcast into a revenue stream?

Invite the right guests. Not only do guest interviews provide engaging content, but they also open doors to profitable partnerships, collaborations, and even direct sales opportunities.

By carefully selecting guests who align with your audience—and who might be interested in your products or services—you can create an interview strategy that keeps your listeners hooked and boosts your business.

In this chapter, we'll explore how to find, connect, and engage with guests who add value to your show and might just become your next best customers.

- 🎤 **Identify your goals and objectives:** Before you start inviting guests to your podcast, it is important to identify your goals and objectives for having guests on your show. This can help you to choose guests that align with your goals and target audience.

- 🎤 **Consider your target audience:** To create a successful podcast guest interview strategy, it is important to have a clear understanding of your target audience, which is why we did this in the Defining Your Target Audience chapter. This can help you choose guests who are relevant and interesting to your listeners.

- 🎤 **Research potential guests:** Once you know what kind of guests you'll be interviewing, it is time to start researching potential guests. This can be done through social media, industry publications, and personal connections. One way is to look at podcasts similar to yours and see which guests appear.

- 🎤 **Create a list of potential guests:** As you research potential guests, create a list of those who align with your goals and target audience, and who have a unique perspective or expertise to offer your listeners.

- 🎤 **Reach out to potential guests:** Once you have a list of potential guests, it is time to start reaching out to them. This can be done through email, social media, or personal contact. Be sure to clearly explain the purpose of your podcast and the value that your guests can bring to your listeners.

- 🎤 **Set up interviews:** Once you have secured guests for your podcast, you need to set up the interviews in a professional and organized manner. This includes scheduling a time for the interview while considering differences in time zones, preparing any necessary materials or questions, and informing your guests throughout the process.

Guest Selection Process

Interview Setup

Identify Goals

Outreach Strategy

Target Audience

Research Guests

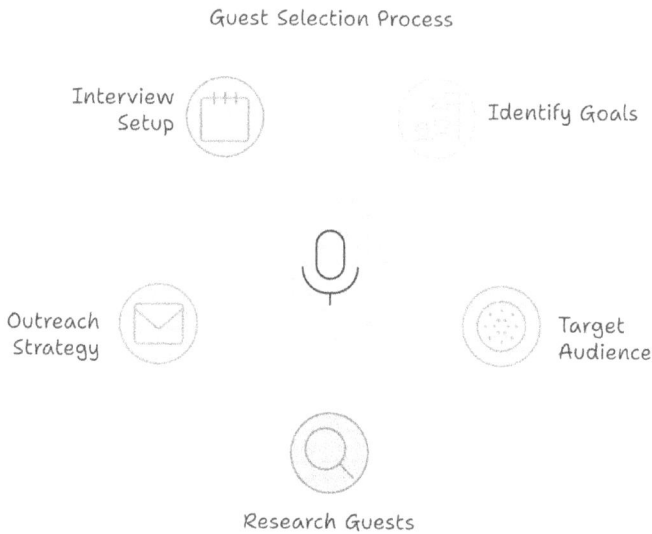

Why Guest Interviews?

Guest interviews are a valuable tool for profitable podcasting. They make for engaging and relevant content, while being simple to organize. Having a friendly chat with an interesting guest is easier than preparing an hour-long script. But how do you make money from guest interviews? Here are a few ways:

🎤 **Cross-promotion and collaboration:** By inviting guests to your podcast, you can create opportunities for cross-promotion and collaboration. This can involve promoting each other's content and working together on projects or initiatives. For example, your guest may be willing to offer your listeners a special offer for their products or services. This is a great way to bring value to your listeners while earning a commission.

🎤 **Selling to your guest:** Your guest may be interested in your services. After establishing a rapport with your guest over the course of the interview and finding out about their business and their needs, you can quickly identify whether they would benefit from your services. This is best done just after you have finished recording the episode. This is by far the more reliable method of profiting from podcasting, so we will cover it in more detail in the next section.

Figuring Out the Best Guest for Your Show Who Might Also Be Interested in Buying from You

Inviting guests to your podcast can provide valuable insights, fresh perspectives, and engaging content for your audience outside of what you can provide them yourself. However, selecting the right guests becomes even more critical when your podcast also serves as a platform for promoting your products or services. This section will guide you through the process of identifying the ideal guests for your show who might also be interested in purchasing from you.

Aligning Guests with Your Target Audience

🎤 Relevance to Audience: Ensure your potential guests have expertise, experience, or knowledge in a relevant subject matter to your target audience. This will help you create content that appeals to your listeners and adds value to the episode.

🎤 Shared Values and Interests: Look for guests with similar values and interests with your target audience. This will make establishing a connection between you and your guest, and your guest and your listeners easier, increasing the likelihood of successful promotion.

Identifying Potential Guests with Buying Intent or Promotion Opportunities

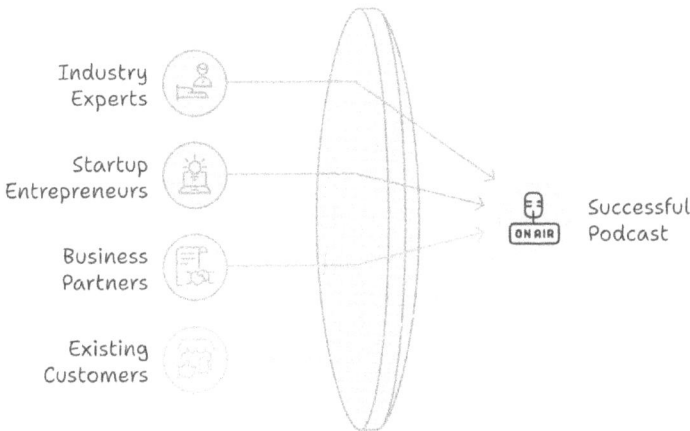

Podcast Guest Strategy

🎤 **Industry Experts:** Connect with industry experts who might be interested in your products or services. These individuals can provide valuable content and promote your offerings to their networks even if they don't end up buying from you.

🎤 **Startup Entrepreneurs:** These entrepreneurs most likely do not already have systems firmly in place, and are more open to change. They may be more excited about your services than industry experts. Their stories can also be inspiring for your listeners to hear.

🎤 **Business Partners and Collaborators:** Consider inviting business partners, collaborators, or suppliers with a vested interest in your success. These guests can help you promote your products or services while also sharing valuable insights and expertise.

🎤 **Existing Customers:** Reach out to customers who have already purchased from you and have a compelling story or valuable insights to share. These individuals can offer genuine testimonials and showcase the benefits of your product or service through their experiences.

Preparing for a Successful Guest Interview

There are three crucial steps you should follow for every guest interview you do:

🎙 **Pre-Interview Research:** Conduct thorough research on your potential guests to ensure they are a good fit for your podcast and your promotional goals. Learn about their background, expertise, and potential interest in your products or services using the advice above.

🎙 **Clear Communication:** Communicate your intentions and expectations with your guests before the interview. Discuss the topics you'll cover, the format of the interview, and how your products or services may be featured during the conversation.

🎙 **Prepare Engaging Questions:** Develop a list of engaging questions that will encourage your guests to share valuable insights while also highlighting the benefits of your products or services. Aim to create a natural, conversational flow that seamlessly incorporates promotional elements.

Leveraging Guest Appearances for Promotion

While your best customer is most likely your guest, you can use your guest interview as an opportunity to speak to your listeners about your services, too.

Here are some ways to do that:

🎙 **Call-to-Action:** Include a clear call-to-action (CTA) during your podcast episode, encouraging listeners to explore your products or services. This can be done through a special offer, discount code, or exclusive access related to your guest's appearance.

🎙 **Cross-Promotion:** As mentioned above, you can collaborate with your guest to promote the podcast episode through their social media channels, website, or email list. This can help you reach a broader audience and increase the likelihood of attracting potential customers.

🎙 **Post-Interview Follow-Up:** Maintain a relationship with your guest after the interview. Share updates on the episode's performance, thank them for their contribution, and explore potential collaboration opportunities in the future.

Profit From Guest Interviews!

Choosing the right guests for your podcast who are also likely to be interested in your products or services makes great content, but also allows you to have unguarded conversations with your best customers. By aligning your guests with your target audience, identifying individuals with potential buying intent, and making sure your interviews are successful, you will create engaging podcast episodes while also supporting your business objectives. This strategy can help you attract new customers, strengthen your brand, and grow your podcast in the long run.

With each carefully chosen guest, you're not only creating compelling content but also building pathways to new clients and lasting partnerships.

So go ahead—start curating your dream guest list, and watch your podcast become a profitable platform for growth and success!

CHAPTER 33

THE GUEST'S JOURNEY TO BECOMING A BUYER

"A sale is not something you pursue, it's what happens to you while you are immersed in serving your customer." – **Anonymous**

When inviting guests to your podcast, you're not just creating valuable content—you're potentially guiding them through their own buyer's journey.

Each conversation is a chance to build trust, establish your expertise, and introduce them to your services in a way that feels natural.

So, how can you lead your guests from initial awareness to becoming a buyer or valuable referral source?

Let's break down the key stages of the guest's journey, with a focus on how you can nurture each stage to turn guests into clients or allies.

Awareness: Building a Foundation

In the early stages, guests may not fully realize they need your services—they may only know that they've been invited to discuss their expertise on your podcast. Here, your job is to introduce them subtly to the value you offer by crafting insightful, relevant questions that highlight your own expertise and align with your services. Make sure your guests feel valued and understood; this is the first step in establishing a strong connection.

Consideration: Demonstrating Relevance

As the conversation progresses, your guests will start to see more clearly what you bring to the table. This is your opportunity to share specific insights, success stories, or experiences related to their pain points or challenges. By showing your knowledge in areas where they may need help, you spark curiosity and position yourself as someone they may want to work with.

Comparison: Addressing Pain Points Naturally

After recording, you'll often have an opportunity for post-interview discussions. Here, you can delve deeper, offering tailored advice or solutions based on what you've learned about their needs. Without a hard sell, talk about the unique ways you or your services can address their challenges compared to others. The goal is to offer solutions that feel relevant and beneficial to their specific business journey.

Decision: Solidifying Your Value

Finally, follow up with your guests post-episode. Share metrics, insights, or engagement stats from the episode to demonstrate the value they gained from the collaboration. If they're showing interest, this is an ideal time to explore how your services could further support their goals. Whether it's consulting, a specific offering, or a collaboration, make your next steps clear, concrete, and mutually beneficial.

Beyond the Interview: A Lasting Relationship

Even if a guest isn't ready to buy right away, keeping the relationship warm can lead to future referrals and introductions within their network. Send occasional updates, share resources, and let them know about relevant upcoming content. By nurturing these relationships, you're keeping the door open for new opportunities down the line.

Turning Conversations into Conversions

Guiding guests through their own buyer's journey is a powerful way to build a profitable podcast. With each conversation, you're not only creating compelling content but also fostering connections that can translate into direct business or high-value referrals.

By understanding your guests' needs, positioning your expertise naturally, and staying engaged post-interview, you can turn your podcast into a platform that does more than just entertain—it fuels growth, creates meaningful relationships, and brings real value to everyone involved.

CHAPTER 34

THE POTENTIAL OF PODCASTING AS A BUSINESS

"The best way to predict the future is to create it." – **Peter Drucker**

Podcasting isn't just for sharing stories or chatting about hobbies—it's a powerful business tool for entrepreneurs looking to drive growth and make meaningful connections.

For those skeptical of podcasting's potential, think of it as a marketing platform with endless reach, flexibility, and creative freedom.

When done right, a podcast can become a lead-generation machine, a networking tool, and a direct pathway to revenue.

In this chapter, we'll explore how podcasting can elevate your business, from building brand authority to attracting your ideal clients.

Let's dive into the true potential of podcasting and see why it's one of the smartest investments you can make.

Podcasting as a Lead Generation Powerhouse

Podcasting offers a unique and powerful business opportunity for entrepreneurs, allowing them to reach a targeted and engaged audience, to have control and flexibility over their content, and monetize their podcast in a variety of ways.

In today's digital landscape, businesses are constantly seeking innovative ways to generate leads and establish a strong presence in their industry. One such avenue that continues to gain prominence is podcasting. By creating a podcast focused on interviewing your best prospects, you can transform your show into a lead generation powerhouse, forging connections with potential clients and showcasing your expertise.

Identifying Your Best Prospects

Before launching your podcast, it's essential to identify your target audience and your ideal client profile. Consider factors such as demographics, interests, pain points, and goals to comprehensively understand your best prospects. This knowledge will guide you in selecting guests representing your target market and provide valuable insights to your audience. Read more about the types of guests who have buying intent in the Guest Interviews for Profitable Podcasting chapter.

Podcasting for Lead Generation

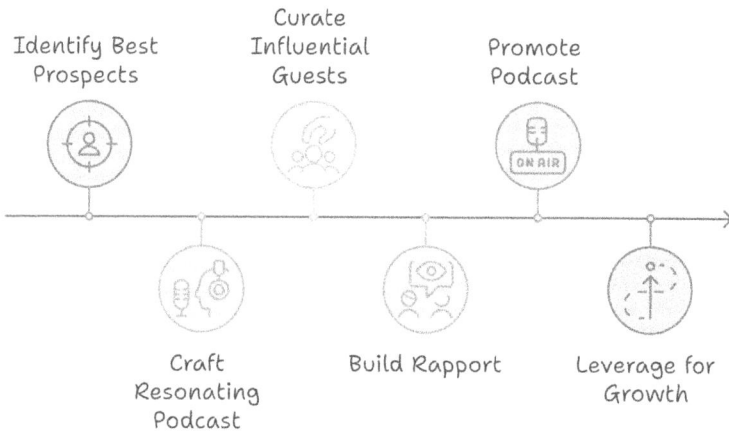

Identify Best
Prospects

Curate
Influential
Guests

Promote
Podcast

Craft
Resonating
Podcast

Build Rapport

Leverage for
Growth

Crafting a Podcast That Resonates with Your Dream Customer

With your ideal client profile in mind, develop a podcast that caters to the needs and aspirations of your target audience. Focus on creating content that addresses their challenges, explores industry trends, and provides practical advice. By crafting a podcast that genuinely resonates with your dream customer, you'll position yourself as an authoritative voice in your niche and foster loyalty among your listeners.

Curating a Roster of Influential Guests

Invite influential guests who embody the characteristics of your dream customer and have a strong connection with your target audience. Look for experts and success stories that align with your podcast's theme and can provide valuable insights to your listeners. By featuring these guests, you'll not only create engaging content but also establish credibility and trust with your prospects.

Building Rapport and Nurturing Relationships

During your podcast interviews, strive to build rapport with your guests by fostering an open and welcoming environment. Engage them in meaningful conversations, allowing them to share their knowledge and experiences while subtly showcasing the benefits of your product or service. As you nurture these relationships, you'll organically create opportunities for collaboration, referrals, and potential sales.

Promoting Your Podcast and Expanding Your Reach

To maximize the lead generation potential of your podcast, invest time and resources in promoting your show across various channels. Utilize social media, email marketing, and collaborations with other podcasters and experts to expand your reach. Actively engage with your audience, respond to feedback, and participate in industry events to further strengthen your presence and attract new prospects.

Leveraging Your Podcast for Business Growth

Your podcast will emerge as a powerful marketing tool by consistently producing valuable content and cultivating strong relationships with your guests. Use this platform to showcase your expertise, offer solutions to your target audience's challenges, and demonstrate your commitment to their success. As your podcast gains traction, you'll experience increased brand recognition, credibility, and ultimately, more leads and sales.

Podcasting as a Business Really Can Be Profitable

Creating a business around podcasting and interviewing your best prospects is a strategic approach to lead generation. You'll transform your show into a powerful marketing tool that drives business growth by crafting a podcast that resonates with your dream customer, inviting influential guests, and nurturing relationships. Embrace the potential of podcasting and witness your business flourish as you connect with your target audience in an authentic and engaging manner.

Podcasting offers entrepreneurs a unique way to connect, engage, and grow like no other platform. By turning each episode into a strategic opportunity—whether by inviting dream clients as guests, delivering targeted content, or promoting your expertise—you can transform your podcast into a true business asset.

As your show gains traction, the impact on your brand, credibility, and bottom line will be unmistakable.

Embrace podcasting's potential, and watch your business thrive as you harness the power of authentic conversations and lasting connections.

To help you implement the strategies outlined in Podcasting Secrets for Entrepreneurs, we've put together a comprehensive Podcast Secrets Resource Kit, which is available for free.

This kit contains tools, templates, and guides to streamline your podcasting process, from the initial planning stages to audience growth and monetization.

https://podcastsecrets.biz/s/kit

CREATING YOUR GUEST LANDING PAGE AND APPLICATION FORM: STREAMLINING YOUR GUEST MANAGEMENT PROCESS

"Your customer doesn't care how much you know until they know how much you care." – **Damon Richards**

Imagine this: your ideal guest stumbles upon your podcast and is intrigued enough to consider joining you for an episode.

But where do they go from there?

A guest landing page and application form can make this process seamless and professional, showcasing what your podcast is all about and inviting guests to take the next step. In this chapter, we'll walk you through designing a guest landing page that makes a strong impression and an application form that gathers everything you need.

Ready to make it easy for your dream guests to say "yes"?

Let's get started!

Managing guest appearances as a podcast host can be time-consuming and complex. Creating a guest landing page and application form can help you streamline your guest management process, saving you time and ensuring a seamless experience for your guests.

In this chapter, we will explore the benefits of a guest landing page and application form, the key elements of an effective page and form, and the questions you should ask on your form.

Benefits of a Guest Landing Page and Application Form

🎙 **Streamlined Guest Management:** Having a guest landing page and application form allows you to centralize guest communication, application, and scheduling, making it easier to manage your guest bookings.

🎙 **Improved Guest Experience:** A well-designed landing page and application form can give your guests a clear understanding of your podcast and what to expect during the recording process, increasing their comfort and confidence during their appearance.

🎙 **Time-Saving:** Automating your guest management process with a landing page and application form saves you time and lets you focus on other aspects of your podcast production.

Key Elements of an Effective Guest Landing Page and Application Form

🎙 **Landing Page:** Your landing page should include your podcast's branding, mission statement, and a brief overview of your show's format and style. Provide clear instructions on how to apply to be a guest, what to expect during the recording process, and any requirements or expectations you may have.

🎙 **Application Form:** Your application form should be simple, user-friendly, and easy to complete. It should include questions that help you determine the fit of the guest with your show's theme and objectives, as well as gather information such as contact details, social media handles, and headshots.

🎙 **Thank You Page:** Once the guest submits the application form, they should be directed to a thank-you page confirming their submission and providing details on the process's next steps.

Questions to Ask on Your Application Form

🎙 **Guest Information:** Collect information such as name, email, phone number, and social media handles.

🎙 **Topic Relevance:** Ask questions to determine the fit of the guest's expertise or experiences with your show's theme or specific episode topic.

🎙 **Previous Podcast Experience:** Inquire about the guest's previous podcasting experience, if any, and what topics they have covered in the past.

🎙 **Professional Background:** Ask about the guest's professional background, qualifications, or accomplishments that make them an ideal fit for your show.

🎙 **Personal Insights:** Gather personal insights or stories that can help you determine the guest's unique perspective or story that can add value to your show.

Creating a guest landing page and application form can help you streamline your guest management process, saving time and improving the guest experience.

By including key elements such as branding, clear instructions, and user-friendly application forms, you can create a seamless experience for your guests while gathering the necessary information to determine their fit with your show's theme and objectives.

By asking targeted questions on your form, you can ensure your guests are well-prepared and well-suited to deliver valuable content to your audience.

CHAPTER 36

SETTING GOALS AND OBJECTIVES FOR PROFITABLE PODCASTING

"Success is the sum of small efforts, repeated day in and day out." – **Robert Collier**

Launching a podcast without clear goals is like setting out on a journey without a map—you might reach your destination, but it will be much harder (and probably take longer).

To create a profitable podcast, it's essential to define your target audience, set clear goals, and outline specific objectives that guide each episode toward a greater purpose.

In this chapter, we'll break down how to set SMART goals, align your content with your business strategy, and create a solid roadmap for podcasting success.

With the right goals, your podcast can become more than a platform; it can be a powerful engine driving revenue, engagement, and growth.

Here are a few considerations for setting goals and objectives for profitable podcasting:

- Identify your target audience: To create a profitable podcast, it is important to understand your target audience clearly. This can help you to choose a topic and format that will be relevant and interesting to your listeners, and to select monetization strategies that align with your target audience.

- Define your goals: Once you have identified your target audience, defining your goals for your podcast is important. This can include generating revenue, building your personal brand, or creating a community of loyal listeners.

- Set specific, measurable, achievable, relevant, and time-bound (SMART) objectives: To effectively achieve your goals, it is important to set specific, measurable, achievable, relevant, and time-bound (SMART) objectives. This can help you to create a roadmap for your podcast and to track your progress towards your goals.

- Create a plan: Once you have defined your goals and objectives, creating a plan for achieving them is important. This can involve developing a content calendar, identifying monetization strategies, and creating a marketing plan.

A podcast plan could look something like this:

1. Approach 200 best prospects for your show to complete an application form
2. Aim to approve 80% of them to be on the show
3. Set a goal to convert 20% of them into a follow-up sales conversation
4. Then try to convert 10% of them to a sale

Let's do some Math:

- ▷ 200 x 80% = 160 Guests
- ▷ 20% x 160 = 32 Sales Conversations
- ▷ 32 x 10% = 3
- ▷ If your average sale price is $2,000, you just made $6,000!

Focus on tweaking your messaging and conversion rates, and you have created a low-cost lead generation machine. Not only that, remember that you have 200 email addresses to market to and 160 Guests eagerly promoting their episodes to their followers.

Setting meaningful goals for your podcast isn't just about increasing downloads or adding more followers; it's about creating a roadmap that brings tangible results to your business.

With clear objectives, a targeted audience, and a solid plan, you're building a podcast that works as a lead generator, community builder, and revenue source.

As you move forward, keep refining your approach, adjusting based on feedback, and tracking progress toward each goal.

By staying focused and intentional, you're well on your way to creating a profitable podcast that aligns with your business ambitions and resonates with your listeners.

CHAPTER 37

CLOSING THE INTERVIEW

"Endings are not always bad. Most times they're just beginnings in disguise."
– Kim Harrison

An interview is only as good as the way it ends!

This chapter will show you how to wrap up your podcast interviews smoothly, leaving both your guest and your audience with a positive impression.

From thank-you notes to post-interview follow-ups, you'll learn the art of closing with style, creating lasting connections, and leaving listeners eager for the next episode.

Here are some templates for closing the interview with your guest, which can be used at different points in the interview.

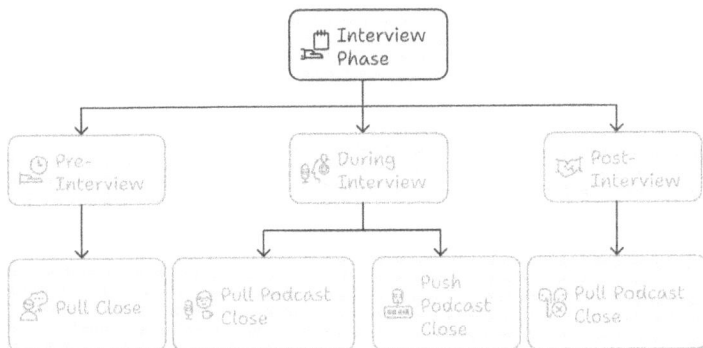

Pull Close: Pre-Interview

Opportunity #1: "Good morning. How was your day yesterday? What did you get up to?" — When they ask you the same in return, you can mention a crazy result or something you did for a client, or something you went through that demonstrates your value. E.g. "Yesterday was crazy. We heard from one of our clients that they closed $80k from their podcast in two months just from interviews. So we were all doing a little mini celebration in the office haha."

Pull Podcast Close (During-Interview)

You want to ask questions that get you talking about the topics surrounding your value. E.g. IF I want to talk about podcast closing... I'd ask questions like "Talk to me about how you're monetizing your podcast so far" or "Whats your favorite organic marketing strategy to get clients"

Pull Podcast Close (Post-Interview)

Bring the conversation back around to topics you discussed on the show, and give them the opportunity to ask you more about how you can help them or if they're curious. You can also make "statements" such as "Honestly, thanks so much for being so transparent on the podcast and talking about how lead gen has been tricky for you recently. I'm just so grateful that in our business we've got our podcast that brings us so many booked calls." --> That statement would give them an opportunity to ask you about it.

Push Podcast Close (During-Interview)

While rare, you can ask during the interview.

"Have you ever thought about doing _____?" This is often not a recommended approach as it's very direct and on air. But there are situations where this could happen... e.g. if the person is discussing doing something similar to what you help people to do.

E.g. If I was discussing on a podcast with someone "how to close high ticket sales with podcasts" that would be the perfect time to be direct and say "have you ever tried to directly close people who you interview onto a sales call?"

Push Podcast Close (Post-Interview)

The most popular push podcast close is:

"Hey... I meant to ask you. Have you ever thought about _____ (your cool awesome thing)? Well if you're open to it, I'd love to connect you with _____ to discuss a bit more about how we can help you in your business.

No worries if not, I just thought It'd be an awesome opportunity to see how we can help each other."

Every great interview deserves a memorable finish.

Wrapping up an interview smoothly isn't just about saying goodbye—it's about leaving your guest and audience feeling inspired, valued, and eager to return.

With a thoughtful closing, you turn a single conversation into a lasting connection, showing guests that they're more than just voices on an episode and giving your audience a strong reason to tune back in.

Remember, each interview is a step toward building a network, sharing insights, and strengthening your podcast's impact.

So, as you wrap up each episode, think of it as the start of something bigger. Keep building those connections, and let each closing bring a new opportunity for growth.

CHAPTER 38

PODCAST MONETIZATION STRATEGIES

"Do not go where the path may lead, go instead where there is no path and leave a trail."
– Ralph Waldo Emerson

Sure, podcasting may start as a labor of love (and yes, late-night editing marathons), but let's be real—at some point, you'll want it to bring in more than just the admiration of a few loyal listeners and your mom.

Thankfully, there are plenty of ways to turn your passion into profit, even if you're not topping the charts just yet.

From snagging sponsorships to creating premium content, this chapter will show you how to turn those hours behind the mic into something that pays. So, let's dive in—you've got bills, and your podcast could be the one to foot them.

Here are a few options:

Advertising and sponsorship

Advertising and sponsorship are among the most popular ways to monetize a podcast. By partnering with brands or products relevant to your show's theme and target audience, you can generate revenue through ad placements within your episodes or sponsored content.

When seeking advertisers and sponsors, build relationships with companies that share your values and resonate with your listeners. As your podcast grows in popularity, you may attract more significant sponsorship deals, which can lead to increased revenue. However, it's essential to maintain a balance between sponsored content and the value you provide to your audience to ensure you don't compromise the integrity of your show.

It will be difficult to get sponsors if your show isn't already popular, so this strategy is more likely to work after your podcast is already successful as an additional revenue stream.

Affiliate Marketing: Earn While You Recommend

Affiliate marketing is ideal for podcasters because it lets you earn a commission on products or services you already love and would naturally recommend. The key is to keep it authentic and only promote what you genuinely believe in.

Choose Products You Believe In: Select affiliates that align with your content. For example, if you're a health podcast, you might partner with a supplement brand or fitness gear company.Create Bonus Content: Make it even more valuable by creating bonus content around the product, like a how-to episode or a live demo that gives listeners added insight.

Example: One podcaster in the tech space regularly discusses his favorite software tools and includes his affiliate links in the episode notes. This strategy works because he's genuinely passionate about the tools, and listeners trust his recommendations.

Podcast Monetization Through Membership and Subscriptions

As your podcast grows, one of the most effective ways to generate consistent revenue is through a membership or subscription model. Unlike traditional advertising or sponsorship deals that fluctuate based on audience size, a well-established membership program can offer a steady income stream by directly engaging your most loyal listeners. This model helps monetise your podcast and strengthens the bond between you and your audience by offering exclusive content and perks in exchange for their support.

Power Tip: Rather than just quoting your total downloads, share engagement rates or listener loyalty stats. It's often more impressive to sponsors to know you have a smaller but highly engaged audience.

Why Membership and Subscriptions?

For many podcasters, relying solely on ad revenue or sponsorship deals can be unpredictable. Membership and subscription models, on the other hand, provide a recurring income that isn't dependent on listener numbers alone. It's about offering extra value your core audience is willing to pay for—bonus episodes, early access, or special behind-the-scenes content. Your dedicated listeners are often willing to invest in a deeper connection with your show, and a membership platform allows them to support you directly.

You can build a strong, loyal community around your podcast by creating a membership model. This not only generates revenue but also deepens audience engagement. When listeners subscribe to your premium content, they're more likely to stay invested in your show and spread the word, helping to grow your audience further.

Choosing the Right Platform

Several platforms make it easy for podcasters to implement a membership or subscription model. Depending on your audience size and content strategy, you might choose from options like:

Patreon: One of the most popular platforms for podcasters, Patreon allows you to set up tiered membership levels, offering different perks at different price points. From exclusive bonus content to Q&A sessions or even physical merchandise, Patreon gives you flexibility in rewarding your listeners.

Patreon is an excellent platform for podcasters looking to create a recurring revenue stream through monthly subscriptions. With Patreon, you can offer your listeners exclusive content, behind-the-scenes access, or other perks in exchange for their financial support.

This model is particularly effective for podcasters with a loyal and engaged audience, as it allows your most dedicated listeners to contribute to your show's ongoing success.

Additionally, Patreon can help foster a sense of community among your supporters, further enhancing their connection to your show.

The downside of creating and managing a community on Patreon is that you don't own the platform. It would be better to create a community on your own platform. It may also be difficult to earn a significant amount of money through audience-based sponsorship unless you're offering a particularly valuable reward to your audience.

Fun Idea: Host a "Supporter of the Month" feature, where you interview one of your patrons about their favorite episode or what they'd like to hear next. It's a fun way to show appreciation while adding value for the listener.

Supercast: Specifically designed for podcasters, Supercast integrates with your existing podcast and lets you offer premium content behind a paywall. It's a straightforward way to add subscription options without overhauling your current setup.

Apple Podcasts Subscriptions: If a large portion of your audience listens through Apple Podcasts, their subscription feature allows you to offer paid content directly within the platform. It's an easy way to monetise without needing to move your audience to another platform.

Other Ideas include:

Creating Exclusive Content

The key to successful membership monetization is offering something your free listeners don't get. This could be:

- **Bonus Episodes:** One of the most common perks for members. Bonus episodes allow you to dive deeper into topics, offer additional interviews, or provide special content only for paying subscribers.

- **Early Access:** Let your paying subscribers listen to episodes a few days before everyone else. This creates a sense of exclusivity and rewards your most loyal listeners for their support.

- **Behind-the-Scenes Content:** Share insights into how your podcast is made, your workflow, or even personal stories that you don't share on the main podcast feed.

- **Ad-Free Episodes:** Many listeners are willing to pay a small monthly fee to listen to episodes without interruptions. Offering an ad-free version of your podcast can be a simple yet effective perk.

- **Live Q&A or Private Community Access:** Create a private space for your subscribers where they can interact with you directly. Whether it's a live Q&A session or an exclusive online community, this adds value and fosters deeper connections.

Structuring Membership Tiers

Membership models work well when you offer tiered pricing. Each tier should offer increasing levels of value, enticing listeners to subscribe at a higher level for additional benefits. For example:

- **Tier 1 - Supporter Level ($5/month):** Subscribers get ad-free episodes and early access to new releases.

🎙 **Tier 2 - VIP Access ($10/month):** Includes everything in Tier 1, plus access to bonus episodes and behind-the-scenes content.

🎙 **Tier 3 - Inner Circle ($20/month):** Includes all previous benefits, plus access to monthly live Q&A sessions and exclusive community membership.

The key here is to provide a clear incentive for listeners to move up the tiers. You don't need to overcomplicate things—start simple and add value as your membership base grows.

Promoting Your Membership Program

Once you've set up your membership or subscription model, you'll need to promote it to your listeners consistently. Make sure to mention your program in your podcast episodes, in your show notes, and on your social media channels.

Call-to-Action in Episodes: A subtle but consistent reminder in each episode will help drive awareness. For example, a brief mention at the beginning or end of the show: "If you're enjoying the podcast and want to support the show, consider joining our Patreon community, where you'll get access to bonus episodes and other exclusive content."

Create a Dedicated Page: If you have a website or a podcast show page, include a section about your membership program. Highlight the benefits of joining, and make signing up as easy as possible.

Involve Your Community: Ask your existing listeners to spread the word about your membership. Word-of-mouth recommendations can be compelling, especially when coming from loyal supporters of your show.

Sustaining and Growing Your Membership

Keeping your members engaged is crucial once you've established a membership model. You'll need to deliver value to ensure that your listeners remain subscribed. Regular communication is key—keep them in the loop about upcoming episodes, new perks, and anything exciting happening behind the scenes.

You can also use surveys or direct feedback to learn what your audience values most and what they want to see more of. Continually refining your membership offerings based on feedback will help you retain and attract new members.

Monetizing your podcast through memberships and subscriptions is one of the most powerful ways to build a sustainable income while maintaining a solid connection with your audience. By offering exclusive content, structuring engaging membership tiers, and consistently promoting your program, you can transform your podcast into a thriving community of dedicated listeners who are eager to support your success.

It's a win-win: your listeners get access to more content they love, and you build a dependable revenue stream that grows alongside your podcast.

Live Events and Workshops: Take Your Show On the Road

Live events are a fantastic way to monetize and build deeper connections with your audience. Whether it's a virtual workshop, an online course, or an in-person meetup, live interactions are memorable for fans and profitable for you.

Start with Virtual Events: If in-person isn't feasible, begin with a virtual workshop where you teach on a topic your audience loves. You can charge for access or even create a series if it's popular.

Partner with Local Businesses: When planning in-person events, collaborate with local venues or sponsors. They often welcome the exposure, and it can make organizing the event easier (and cheaper) for you.

Example: *A popular true-crime podcaster held a virtual "behind-the-scenes" event where fans could ask questions and get a sneak peek of future content. The event was a hit and led to multiple spin-offs.*

Merchandise

Selling branded merchandise is another way to monetize your podcast while simultaneously promoting your show. This can include t-shirts, mugs, stickers, or other creative products representing your podcast's brand.

To make your merchandise appealing, focus on designing high-quality, visually attractive items that your listeners will proudly wear or display. When promoting your merchandise, ensure it's easily accessible through your website or other online channels, and consider offering special deals or promotions to incentivize purchases.

Courses and coaching

If you possess expertise in a specific area related to your podcast's theme, you can monetize your knowledge by creating and selling courses or offering coaching services. This can be a highly lucrative way to generate income, particularly if your podcast has cultivated a loyal and engaged audience that trusts your expertise.

When creating courses or coaching services, provide practical, actionable advice addressing your audience's needs and challenges. To promote these offerings, consider using your podcast as a platform to showcase your expertise, share success stories, or offer exclusive discounts to your listeners.

Consulting and speaking

Leveraging your podcast to position yourself as an expert in your niche can open up consulting or speaking engagement opportunities. These can involve offering your services to businesses or organizations seeking guidance in your area of expertise or speaking at industry events or conferences.

To maximize these opportunities, use your podcast as a platform to showcase your knowledge, build your personal brand, and demonstrate your ability to communicate effectively. As your reputation grows, consulting and speaking engagements may become a significant source of income, further contributing to your podcast's overall success.

By exploring these different monetization strategies, you can find the option that best fits your goals and target audience, and create a profitable podcast that generates revenue and helps you achieve your business goals.

One of the main reasons we developed our own podcast platform was so we could seamlessly add a Patreon-style donation option and even implemented e-commerce so you can sell your own products and services right off your show page, on the spot.

Monetizing your podcast is about more than just making money; it's about creating a sustainable platform that supports your business goals and lets you keep doing what you love.

By exploring these diverse revenue strategies—whether through memberships, sponsorships, or even live events—you're building a stronger connection with your audience and expanding the impact of your show.

Remember, each episode is an opportunity to grow your brand, engage your listeners, and build a dependable revenue stream.

So keep experimenting, stay true to your message, and watch as your podcast becomes a powerful driver of both passion and profit.

There is a better way:

Of course, you will also want to build your own subscriber list—we thought of that, too!

With *PodcastSecrets.app*, you have access to the email addresses of all your subscribers and can send them marketing emails.

CHAPTER 39

PODCASTING FOR LEAD GENERATION AND SALES FUNNELS

"People don't buy what you do; they buy why you do it." – **Simon Sinek**

For entrepreneurs, a podcast isn't just a platform for sharing ideas or engaging with an audience—it can also be a powerful tool for generating leads and nurturing potential customers through a well-structured sales funnel. With the right strategy, your podcast can become an integral part of your business's marketing system, driving prospects through your funnel and converting them into clients or customers.

In this chapter, we'll cover how to use podcasting strategically for lead generation and how to build an effective sales funnel around your show.

Why Podcasting is a Powerful Lead Generation Tool

Podcasts offer a unique opportunity to connect with your audience in a personal and engaging way. Unlike other forms of content, podcasting allows you to build trust and authority over time, giving listeners the chance to become familiar with your expertise, values, and brand. This trust-building is essential in moving prospects further down your sales funnel.

Here's why podcasting is particularly effective for lead generation:

- **Long-Form Content Builds Trust:** Podcasts are often longer than blog posts or social media updates, giving you more time to showcase your expertise and provide value. This deepens your relationship with listeners and establishes you as a trusted authority in your niche.

- **Niche Audiences are Highly Engaged:** Podcast listeners are typically more engaged because they choose to listen to your content for an extended period. This level of engagement makes them more likely to take the next step in your sales funnel.

- **Podcasts Foster Personal Connections:** Hearing your voice creates a more personal connection with your audience. This familiarity and authenticity often make listeners feel like they know you, increasing the likelihood that they'll trust your recommendations or consider your services.

How to Generate Leads Through Your Podcast

To turn your podcast into a lead generation machine, you'll need a clear plan for capturing listener information and moving them into your sales funnel. Here are some effective strategies to get started:

Podcast Lead Generation Funnel

🎙 **Offer a Lead Magnet:** A lead magnet is a valuable resource you offer to your listeners in exchange for their contact information (usually their email address). Your podcast provides the perfect opportunity to promote a lead magnet that is closely related to the episode's topic. This could be a downloadable guide, checklist, template, or access to exclusive content that listeners can't get elsewhere.

For example, if your podcast episode covers how to improve sales strategies, you could offer a free downloadable ebook titled "10 Sales Tactics You Can Implement Today" at the end of the episode. Listeners interested in taking action will be incentivized to provide their email address to access the resource.

🎙 **Use Strong Call-to-Actions (CTAs):** Each podcast episode should include a clear call-to-action (CTA) that encourages listeners to take the next step. Be direct and concise with your CTA. For example, you might say, "If you enjoyed today's episode and want more actionable strategies, visit [yourwebsite.com] to download our free guide on boosting your conversion rates." Your CTA could direct them to:

▷ Visit a landing page to download your lead magnet.

▷ Subscribe to your newsletter.

▷ Sign up for a free webinar or consultation.

▷ Join your private online community.

🎙 **Capture Listener Information:** Once you've directed listeners to your lead magnet or CTA, the next step is capturing their information. This is typically done through an opt-in form on a landing page. Ensure the process is simple and frictionless—ask for only essential details like their name and email address to maximize conversions.

🎙 **Leverage Guest Audiences:** If your podcast regularly features guest interviews, you can leverage your guests' audiences to generate more leads. Encourage guests to promote their episode to their followers, offering them a specific incentive (like your lead magnet) to tune in. You can also collaborate with guests on joint promotions or webinars, further expanding your reach and lead generation potential.

Building a Sales Funnel Around Your Podcast

Once you've captured your listeners' information, nurturing those leads through your sales funnel is the next step. Your podcast is at the top of the funnel, attracting potential customers with valuable content. But the real work begins after you've brought them into your ecosystem. Here's how to structure your podcast's sales funnel:

Top of the Funnel (Attract) The goal at the top of your funnel is to attract as many relevant listeners as possible. Your podcast episodes, lead magnets, and CTAs should all be tailored to your target audience. Use each episode to provide valuable information that solves a problem your audience is facing, building trust and positioning yourself as an expert.

At this stage, you should focus on growing your email list by offering value-rich content and compelling lead magnets.

Middle of the Funnel (Engage) Once a listener has joined your email list, the middle of your sales funnel is where you nurture that relationship. This is done through email marketing, where you provide additional resources, exclusive podcast content, and deeper insights to keep your audience engaged.

Consider creating an email sequence that delivers:

- A welcome email that thanks the listener for subscribing and provides a valuable resource.
- A follow-up series that highlights your most popular podcast episodes or blog posts, positioning them as must-listen content.
- Case studies or testimonials that demonstrate the success others have had by using your services or products.

The key here is to keep your leads warm and build on the relationship you've established through the podcast.

Bottom of the Funnel (Convert) At the bottom of your funnel is where you encourage your leads to take action—whether that's booking a consultation, purchasing your product, or enrolling in a course. At this stage, your listeners have already gotten to know you through your podcast and have been nurtured through your email marketing efforts, so they're much more likely to convert.

You can offer:

- A limited-time discount or special offer exclusively for podcast listeners.
- A free trial or demo of your product or service.
- A personal consultation or strategy session to help listeners solve their specific problems.

Be sure to include a strong, clear CTA in your emails, podcast episodes, and on your landing pages that drives leads toward this final conversion point.

Examples of Lead Generation Funnels for Podcasters

Let's look at a couple of practical examples of how podcasters can structure their lead generation and sales funnels.

Example 1: A Business Coach

- 🎙 **Podcast Content:** Episodes focus on topics like entrepreneurship, productivity, and scaling a business.

- 🎙 **Lead Magnet:** A free "Business Growth Checklist" offered to listeners at the end of each episode.

- 🎙 **Email Funnel:** A 5-part email series that dives deeper into the principles discussed on the podcast, offering actionable tips and highlighting success stories.

- 🎙 **Conversion Offer:** A free 30-minute consultation call to discuss how the coach can help listeners grow their business.

Example 2: An Online Course Creator

- 🎙 **Podcast Content:** Episodes provide educational content on digital marketing strategies.

- 🎙 **Lead Magnet:** A free webinar titled "How to Build a Profitable Online Course in 30 Days."

- 🎙 **Email Funnel:** A series of emails providing more in-depth strategies and insights, building anticipation for an upcoming course launch.

- 🎙 **Conversion Offer:** An early-bird discount for enrolling in the new online course, exclusive to podcast listeners.Tracking and Optimizing Your Funnel

To maximize the effectiveness of your podcast for lead generation, it's important to track how well your funnel is performing. Here are a few key metrics to monitor:

- 🎙 **Podcast Listener Growth:** Track how many new listeners tune in to each episode, and whether those numbers are increasing over time.

- 🎙 **Email Sign-ups:** Monitor how many listeners are converting to email subscribers via your lead magnets and CTAs.

- 🎙 **Engagement:** Pay attention to open rates, click-through rates, and engagement with your email content. This will help you gauge how well your audience is responding to your nurturing efforts.

- 🎙 **Conversion Rate:** Measure how many email subscribers convert into paying customers, clients, or members of your program.

Based on these metrics, you can adjust your strategy to improve performance. For example, if your CTA isn't driving enough sign-ups, try offering a different lead magnet or refining your messaging. If conversion rates are low, consider reworking your email sequence to provide more value or clarity around your offers.

Podcasting is an incredibly effective tool for generating leads and moving prospects through your sales funnel.

You can turn listeners into loyal customers by offering value-rich content, strong CTAs, and nurturing your audience with targeted email marketing.

Remember, the key to success is consistency—by continually providing value and engaging your audience, your podcast will become a powerful driver of business growth.

Amplify

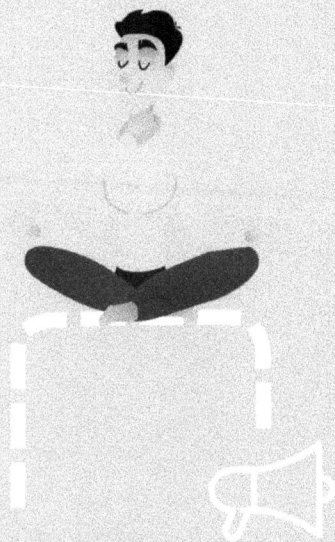

To ensure your podcast's success, it is crucial to amplify your brand. Promote your show across various channels, including social media, email marketing, and networking with other podcasters.

Engage with your audience by encouraging them to write reviews, and start discussions in your community. Collaborating with high-profile people in your niche and participating in podcast communities can also help expand your reach, captivating new listeners and solidifying your presence in the podcasting world.

CHAPTER 40

CREATING YOUR PODCAST ASSETS

"The details are not the details. They make the design." – **Charles Eames**

Every great podcast needs a few solid assets to amplify its presence and make it stand out to sponsors, guests, and listeners alike. From a polished media kit to eye-catching visuals, these assets are the building blocks of your podcast's professional identity.

One essential tool in your arsenal is the podcast one-sheet—a single-page document that showcases your show's unique selling points in a clean, visually appealing format.

In this chapter, we'll cover the steps for creating all the assets you need to elevate your podcast's brand, grab attention, and make a lasting impression on anyone who comes across your show.

Media Kits

A podcast one-sheet is a promotional document summarising your podcast and its key selling points in a concise, visually appealing format. It can be used when pitching your podcast to potential sponsors, advertisers, guests, or media outlets.

Creating an effective podcast one-sheet involves the following steps:

- **Start with design software:** You can either use a design template from a platform like Canva or create your own layout using design software like Adobe InDesign, Illustrator, Scribus, Affinity Designer, or even PowerPoint. Choose a design that aligns with your podcast's branding and style.

- **Choose the right format:** A one-sheet should ideally be a single-page PDF document, which can be easily shared via email, on a webpage, or printed for physical distribution.

- **Include your podcast logo and branding:** Make sure your podcast logo is prominently displayed on the one-sheet, along with any other relevant branding elements, such as color schemes or typography. Consistent branding makes your podcast easily recognizable and memorable.

- **Write a compelling podcast description:** Create a brief, engaging description of your podcast that highlights its unique value proposition, target audience, and overall theme. Be concise and focus on what sets your podcast apart from others in your niche.

- **Showcase your host(s):** Include a professional, high-quality photo of the host(s) and a brief bio, highlighting their expertise, achievements, and any relevant credentials. This helps establish credibility and build trust with potential sponsors or guests.

- **Highlight key podcast statistics:** Include important metrics like average episode downloads, total downloads, listener demographics, and growth rates to demonstrate your podcast's success and reach. Use the most recent and accurate data available.

- **List top episodes and notable guests:** Mention some of your most popular episodes or notable guests to showcase the quality of your content and attract potential collaborators.

- **Include testimonials or press mentions:** If you have received positive feedback from listeners, industry experts, or press outlets, include a few quotes to add credibility and social proof to your one-sheet.

- **Display your podcast's availability:** List the podcast platforms and directories where your podcast can be found (e.g., Apple Podcasts, Spotify, Google Podcasts), along with any relevant links or QR codes.

- **Provide clear contact information:** Make it easy for potential sponsors, guests, or media outlets to contact you by including your email address, phone number, social media handles, and website URL.

- **Proofread and optimize:** Before finalizing your one-sheet, proofread it for errors and ensure the design is clean, visually appealing, and easy to read. Optimize the file size to ensure it can be easily emailed without consuming too much bandwidth.

Once your podcast one-sheet is complete, save it as a high-quality PDF file and use it as a marketing tool to attract sponsors, secure guest appearances, and promote your podcast to a wider audience.

With a compelling one-sheet, professional images, and a cohesive brand, you're setting your podcast up for success. These assets don't just make your show look polished; they make it memorable, build credibility, and open doors to sponsorships, guest appearances, and wider promotion.

Remember, every visual and every word in your media kit represents the quality and personality of your show. So take the time to perfect these assets, and watch as your podcast gains traction and attracts the attention it deserves.

Branding and Images: Crafting a Visual Identity for Your Podcast

Branding is essential for establishing your podcast's identity and making it recognizable among a sea of other shows. Your brand isn't just about a logo—it's the entire visual language of your podcast, from color schemes and fonts to imagery that captures the essence of your content. These elements should work together to create a cohesive look and feel that aligns with the tone and purpose of your podcast, instantly conveying what your show is about to potential listeners.

Key Elements of Podcast Branding:

Logo

Your logo is the face of your podcast and one of the first things new listeners will notice. Aim for a design that is simple, memorable, and true to the essence of your show. Use a color palette that fits your theme, and choose fonts that complement your podcast's vibe, whether it's professional, playful, or edgy.

Cover Art

Cover art is crucial for attracting listeners on platforms like Apple Podcasts and Spotify. The best cover art stands out in a small thumbnail view, so focus on clarity and bold design. Consider adding your show's title in large, readable fonts, and choose high-contrast colors that are visually appealing.

Color Scheme and Fonts

Consistency is key in branding, so choose a color scheme and font set that can be applied across all your podcast's assets—from social media posts to website elements. For instance, using the same colors in your cover art, website, and episode graphics reinforces your brand identity and makes it easy for listeners to recognize your show.

Imagery

High-quality images help capture your podcast's personality and give listeners a visual sense of what to expect. Whether you're using stock photos, custom graphics, or personal photos, ensure they align with your brand's style and message. If your show covers a specific niche, such as business or wellness, choose imagery that reflects those themes.

Host and Guest Photos

Photos of you and your guests help add a personal touch to your brand. Use professional-quality images whenever possible, as these will be featured in media kits, your website, and social media posts. Consistent use of host and guest photos across episodes can build familiarity with your audience, making your show feel more personal and relatable.

Tips for Using Images Effectively:

🎙 **Consistency is Key:** Use your color palette and fonts in all image assets to maintain brand recognition.

🎙 **High-Resolution Photos:** Low-quality images can make your brand look less professional. Always opt for high-resolution photos that look sharp on any platform.

🎙 **Image Templates for Social Media:** Create templates for episode announcements, quotes, and guest features. This saves time and ensures that all posts align visually with your brand.

By putting thought into your podcast's branding and images, you're creating a recognizable and professional visual identity that draws listeners in and keeps them engaged. These elements not only communicate the tone and value of your show but also reinforce its credibility.

Every visual choice you make—from your logo and cover art to social media graphics—should tell a part of your podcast's story and make it easier for listeners to identify and connect with your brand.

You've done the work to create great content—now let your assets speak for your brand!

CHAPTER 41

GETTING SEEN AND FOUND

"True visibility is about being seen by the right people, not by everyone." – **Anonymous**

A ctive promotion is key to building your podcast, but what about growing your reach organically?

Getting your podcast seen and found by new listeners who haven't heard of you yet can be a powerful way to expand your audience without paid ads.

By optimizing for search engines, leveraging metadata, and making content easily shareable, you create pathways for listeners to discover your show naturally.

In this chapter, we'll explore the tactics that help your podcast get seen, found, and recommended—even by those who might not know they're looking for it yet!

We've already touched on some of the ways you can do this, like transcripts, but that's far from everything at you're disposal. Here are some ways to position your podcast:

- 🎤 **Search engine optimization (SEO)** is a crucial aspect of digital marketing that helps improve the visibility of your content on search engines, leading to increased organic traffic and engagement. Podcasts, despite being an audio-based format, can significantly contribute to your SEO efforts in several ways.

- 🎤 **Indexable content:** By transcribing your podcast episodes and publishing the transcripts on your website, you create indexable content search engines can crawl and rank. This increases the likelihood of your content showing up in search results and drives more traffic to your website.

- 🎤 **Keyword targeting:** Podcast transcripts allow you to target specific keywords related to your podcast topic, niche, or industry. This helps search engines understand the context of your content and increases the chances of ranking for relevant search queries.

- 🎤 **Episode Metadata:** Make sure your episodes have accurate, indexable metadata like titles, descriptions and tags. This will make it easier for search engines to find your episodes.

- 🎤 **Enhanced user experience:** Offering transcripts and show notes not only caters to a wider audience, including those who are hearing-impaired or prefer to read, but also improves the overall user experience on your website. Search engines like Google consider user experience a significant ranking factor, making it essential to offer your visitors a variety of content formats.

- 🎤 **Increased dwell time:** By providing transcripts, show notes, and other supplementary content, you encourage visitors to spend more time on your website, exploring and

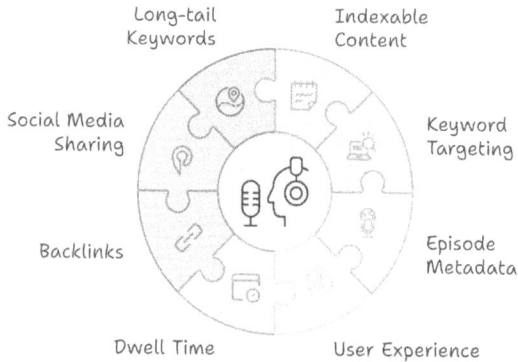

Enhancing Podcast SEO

engaging with your content. Search engines interpret this increased dwell time as a signal of high-quality content, which can lead to better search rankings.

🎙 **Backlinks and authority:** Podcasts offer opportunities to collaborate with experts and influencers in your industry, which can result in valuable backlinks to your website. As other websites and blogs reference your podcast, your site's authority improves, further boosting your SEO efforts.

🎙 **Social media sharing:** Podcasts are easily shareable across social media platforms, helping you reach a wider audience and drive more traffic to your website. Search engines use social signals as one of the many factors to determine the popularity and relevance of your content.

🎙 **Long-tail keywords:** Podcasts tend to cover niche topics and discussions, which can naturally include long-tail keywords in the transcripts. These long-tail keywords are less competitive and can help you rank higher for specific search queries.

To maximize your podcast's SEO benefits, it's essential to optimize your podcast's metadata, such as titles, descriptions, and tags, and to create a dedicated website or landing page for your podcast that includes transcripts, show notes, and other relevant content.

Google Knowledge Panel

The Google Knowledge Panel is a visual summary of information displayed on Google Search results pages when users search for entities, such as people, places, organizations, or things. It appears on the right-hand side of the search results (or at the top on mobile devices) and aims to provide users with a quick, authoritative overview of the searched entity.

The information displayed in the Knowledge Panel is extracted from various sources, including Google's Knowledge Graph, which is a vast database of interconnected information about entities and their relationships.

Key features of Google Knowledge Panels include:

🎙 **Basic information:** The Knowledge Panel displays an entity's basic information, such as name, image, profession (for people), or a brief description. For organizations, it may show the logo, founding date, founders, headquarters location, and more.

- **Relevant links:** Knowledge Panels often include links to official websites, social media profiles, and other relevant resources, making it easier for users to find and engage with the entity's online presence.
- **Related searches:** The panel often suggests related searches or entities, allowing users to explore similar topics or discover connections between entities.
- **Key facts and figures:** The Knowledge Panel presents key facts and figures about the searched entity, such as awards, notable works, or statistics, depending on the entity type. For example, the panel for a movie might show the cast, director, release date, and box office revenue, while the panel for an author could include their bibliography and literary awards.
- **Images and videos:** The panel may display relevant images and videos associated with the entity, providing users with a more engaging and visual understanding of the subject matter.
- **Reviews and ratings:** For businesses, products, or services, the Knowledge Panel may display reviews and ratings from various sources, giving users a snapshot of the entity's overall reputation and user satisfaction.
- **Events and updates:** In some cases, the Knowledge Panel may also display recent news, events, or updates related to the searched entity.

Businesses and individuals with an online presence need to have an accurate and up-to-date Google Knowledge Panel. To manage or claim your Knowledge Panel, follow these steps:

- Perform a Google search for your entity (e.g., your name or your business name).
- Locate the Knowledge Panel in the search results.
- Click the "Claim this knowledge panel" link at the bottom of the panel.
- Sign in to your Google account and follow the instructions to verify your identity and claim the panel.
- Once you've claimed your Knowledge Panel, you can request edits or updates to the information displayed. This ensures that users find accurate and relevant information about your entity in Google Search results.

To get yourself on a Google Knowledge Panel, you need to establish a notable online presence and have verifiable information about yourself available on the web. Google's algorithms and the Knowledge Graph will then recognize you as a notable entity and may generate a Knowledge Panel for you.

Follow these steps to improve your chances of getting a **Knowledge Panel:**

- **Create a personal website:** Build a professional website that showcases your work, achievements, and expertise. Include your full name, a high-quality photo, a brief bio, and relevant information about your accomplishments.
- **Optimize your website for SEO:** Ensure that your website is optimized for search engines. Use appropriate metadata, such as title tags and meta descriptions, and include relevant keywords related to your expertise or niche.
- **Build a strong online presence:** Create profiles on major social media platforms, such as LinkedIn, Twitter, Facebook, and Instagram. Ensure your profiles are consistent, and up-to-date, and feature your full name, photo, and a brief bio.

🎙 **Publish quality content:** Regularly create and share high-quality content related to your field, such as blog posts, articles, videos, or podcasts. This will help establish your authority and expertise, making it more likely that Google will recognize you as a notable entity.

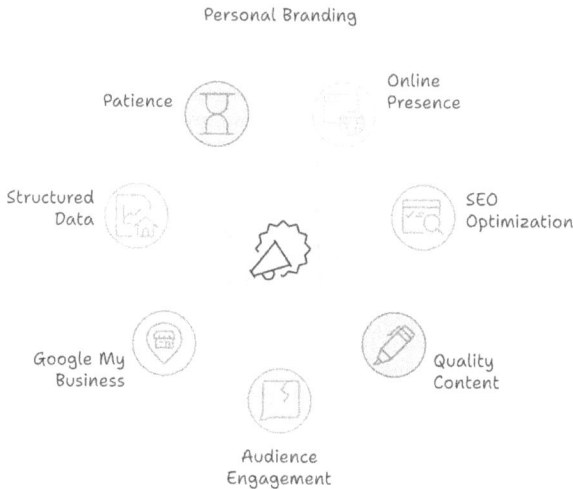

Personal Branding

Patience

Online Presence

Structured Data

SEO Optimization

Google My Business

Quality Content

Audience Engagement

🎙 **Get featured on reputable websites:** Contribute to well-known publications, blogs, or websites in your industry. Guest posts, interviews, or expert quotes can help increase your online visibility and credibility.

🎙 **Engage with your audience:** Actively engage with your audience on social media and your website, responding to comments and participating in relevant discussions. This helps build your reputation and increases your chances of being recognized as an authoritative figure in your field.

🎙 **Claim or create a Google My Business profile:** If you have a business associated with your personal brand, claim or create a Google My Business profile. This can help improve your visibility on Google Maps and local search results.

🎙 **Use structured data:** If you have authored articles or books, make sure the websites hosting these works use structured data markup (such as Schema.org) to help Google understand your authorship and the relationship between your content and your personal brand.

🎙 **Be patient:** It takes time for Google to recognize your online presence and determine your notability. Keep building your online presence and sharing valuable content.

There is no guaranteed method to get a Knowledge Panel, as it ultimately depends on Google's algorithms and the Knowledge Graph, but following the steps above will increase your chances of being recognized by Google and appearing in a Knowledge Panel. Building organic visibility for your podcast isn't just about ranking higher; it's about positioning your show as a valuable, easy-to-find resource for listeners who are ready to tune in. By optimizing your SEO, using strategic keywords, and enhancing user experience, you're making it easier for new fans to stumble upon—and stick with—your podcast.

Each small step in optimizing your content brings you closer to an audience that grows on its own, driven by quality, engagement, and discoverability. So go ahead—put these tactics into practice and watch as your podcast finds its way into more earbuds, naturally!

CHAPTER 42

HOW DOES PODCAST RANKINGS WORK?

"It's not who you are that holds you back, it's who you think you're not." – **Hanoch McCarty**

D ream of seeing your podcast in the top charts? This chapter is all about podcast rankings—what they are, why they matter, and the steps you can take to improve your ranking.

We'll cover algorithms, listener engagement, and tips to increase visibility so you can reach new listeners and climb the charts.

Podcast rankings serve as a measure of a podcast's popularity and visibility within a certain podcast distribution platform. The most coveted rankings are in the Apple Podcasts platform.

Understanding the factors influencing these rankings can help entrepreneurs design their podcasts for success and reach a broader, more engaged audience. While there is no way for us to know for certain what factors are taken into account on Apple Podcasts' closed ranking algorithm or any other platform, we can make some educated assumptions based on past history.

Here is an expanded overview of the key factors we believe affect podcast rankings:

- 🎙 **Downloads and streams:** The number of downloads and streams a podcast receives is the primary factor affecting its ranking. As a podcast gains popularity, the increased downloads and streams propel it higher in the rankings. To boost this metric, focus on creating engaging and valuable content and encouraging listeners to download, stream, and share your podcast with others at the end of each episode.

- 🎙 **Ratings and reviews:** Listener ratings and reviews play a crucial role in determining a podcast's ranking. Positive ratings and reviews can improve a podcast's visibility, while negative ones can hinder its progress. Encourage your listeners to leave ratings and reviews, and be sure to respond to feedback and make improvements as needed.

- 🎙 **Engagement and social media activity:** A podcast's ranking can also be influenced by the level of engagement and social media activity surrounding it. This includes the number of comments, shares, likes, and mentions it receives on social media or its website. Increase engagement by actively participating in conversations with your audience, promoting your podcast on various platforms, and leveraging social media algorithms to boost visibility.

🎙 **Consistency and release frequency:** Regularly releasing new episodes can help maintain or improve your podcast's ranking. Consistency signals to podcast platforms and listeners that your podcast is active and reliable, which can contribute to better rankings. Develop a consistent release schedule and stick to it, ensuring your audience always has fresh content to enjoy.

As mentioned in Getting Seen and Found and Maximizing Your Podcast's Visibility and Reach, your podcast metadata is a determining factor in how visible your podcast is. Optimizing your podcast's metadata, such as the title, description, and tags, can improve its discoverability and ranking. Use relevant keywords and phrases that accurately describe your podcast and appeal to your target audience.

Podcast metadata refers to the information associated with your podcast and its episodes, which helps listeners and podcast platforms understand what your podcast is about. Metadata plays a crucial role in podcast discoverability, as it impacts how search engines and podcast directories index and display your podcast. By optimizing your podcast's metadata, you can improve its visibility, reach a larger audience, and rank higher in search results and recommendations.

POWER TIP:

To edit metadata on an audio file, you'll need to use audio editing software or a dedicated metadata editor.

There are several options available to you, depending on the operating system you're using. We've written short guides below for several software:

Option 1: Using Audacity (free, open-source audio editing software)

Download and install Audacity from the official website (https://www.audacityteam.org/).

Open Audacity and go to **File > Open** to import your audio file.

After the audio file has been imported, go to **File > Export > Export as MP3** or another desired audio format. Save it with a new name and the "Edit Metadata Tags" window will appear.

Enter or edit the metadata fields, such as title, artist, album, track number, genre, and year.

Click 'OK' to export the file with the updated metadata.4

Option 2: Using iTunes (for macOS and Windows users)

Open iTunes and import your audio file by clicking on **File > Add to Library.**

Locate and select the audio file in your iTunes library.

Right-click the selected audio file and choose 'Song Info' or 'Get Info' from the context menu.

In the Info tab, you can edit metadata fields like title, artist, album, track number, genre, and year.

After making the necessary changes, click 'OK' to save the updated metadata.

Option 3: Using VLC (for Windows, macOS, and Linux users)

Open the file in VLC and then hit Command+I or CTRL+I depending on your operating system, or go to **Window > Media Information** to bring up the relevant window.

Enter the relevant metadata and click **"Save Metadata".**

Option 4: Using id3v2 (for advanced users on Unix-like operating systems)

This is a command-line utility available for Unix-like operating systems like macOS and Linux intended to be used by advanced users. It can be used in scripts to automate metadata tagging. It can be installed on macOS using homebrew, and likely through your package manager on Linux.

Go here for information about the frames you can use that the id3 standard supports: https://id3.org/id3v2.3.0#Declared_ID3v2_frames

Note that these steps may vary slightly depending on your software version or operating system. If you encounter any issues, always refer to the official documentation for your chosen software.

Various podcast ranking systems, such as those implemented by Apple Podcasts, Spotify, and other platforms, can offer valuable insights into your podcast's performance.

Introduction to Prefixes in Podcast Analytics

In the world of podcast analytics, prefix URLs play a unique role by tracking specific data points before an episode reaches the listener. Essentially, a prefix URL is an extra bit of code that podcast publishers insert at the start of their episode file links, allowing analytics providers to track and analyze download data.

For example, rather than linking directly to your audio file, a prefix URL might look like this:

https://chtbl.com/track/87369E/https://media.whooshkaa.com/show/13119/episode/805615.mp3

This means that before the audio file is delivered, the request first hits the prefix partner (such as Podtrac, Blubrry, or Podsights), allowing them to gather data on listener activity. After gathering the needed information, the prefix provider redirects the request to the original file URL, allowing the episode to play as usual.

Key Benefits of Using a Prefix URL

Consistent Tracking Across Platforms

Prefixes standardize data tracking, especially helpful when switching between podcast hosts. While hosting providers vary in data interpretation, a prefix remains constant, providing consistent tracking across hosts.

Third-Party Verification

As podcast advertising grows, ad buyers increasingly want reliable third-party analytics. Prefix providers are typically IAB-certified and can deliver verifiable numbers that buyers trust.

Ad Attribution and Impression Counting

Prefixes can help track ad impressions and measure listener engagement with specific ads, especially useful for baked-in ads without dynamic ad insertion. They also act as conversion tags, giving publishers insights into listener actions across other platforms, such as social media or other podcasts.

How Prefix URLs Work

When a listener clicks play, the request goes through the prefix provider first, which collects information on the listener's IP address, device, and session details. The provider then redirects the listener to the original file URL, counting the activity as a valid download according to industry standards. By gathering data at this initial point of contact, prefixes allow providers to filter and analyze engagement accurately, contributing to comprehensive insights on listener behavior.

Challenges with Prefixes

While prefix URLs provide valuable analytics, they are not without limitations. For instance, some ad blockers may prevent episodes from loading if they detect certain prefix URLs, which could affect data accuracy. However, for most podcasters, prefix URLs offer a powerful and accessible way to start understanding their audience's habits and improve engagement. As publishers grow, more direct data integrations, like CDN log sharing, may offer even more precise insights.

Prefixes are a great starting point for podcasters of all sizes to track performance metrics, understand audience behavior, and attract ad buyers. They may not be the final frontier of analytics, but they're a solid foundation that helps you grow with confidence.

OP3.dev: Open Podcast Prefix Project

OP3.dev, the Open Podcast Prefix Project, is a free, open-source analytics tool for podcasters. Unlike paid services, OP3 is community-driven and prioritizes privacy by anonymizing listener data. By adding an OP3 prefix to your episode URLs, you can track reliable, IAB-standard metrics—like downloads and device types—without sacrificing user privacy. OP3's transparency and adherence to industry standards make it a great choice for podcasters seeking accurate insights without a price tag. It's built by and for the podcasting community, providing valuable data to creators and advertisers alike, all while respecting listener trust and privacy.

Climbing the podcast charts can feel like a mysterious, elusive goal—kind of like trying to get a good seat at a sold-out concert. But by focusing on the factors you can control, like listener engagement, consistency, and quality, you're setting yourself up to make real progress in the rankings.

Remember, it's not about obsessing over algorithms but creating episodes that keep listeners coming back and eager to share. With each episode, you're building momentum and attracting an audience that loves what you do. So, keep refining, stay consistent, and don't forget to celebrate every milestone on the way up.

Who knows?

One day, you might just see your show up there in the top charts!

CHAPTER 43

ADVANCED ANALYTICS AND METRICS

"If you torture the data long enough, it will confess." – **Ronald Coase**

Podcasting offers a unique way to connect with an audience, but as with any other medium, understanding how well your content performs requires data.

Analysing your podcast's performance goes beyond simply counting downloads—you need to track a range of metrics to truly understand your listeners, optimize your content, and measure the effectiveness of your promotional strategies.

In this chapter, we'll dive into advanced podcast analytics and metrics, giving you a clearer picture of how your episodes are performing and how to use that data to make informed decisions.

Whether your goal is to grow your audience, increase engagement, or improve your monetization efforts, mastering your metrics is essential.

The Importance of Podcast Analytics

While podcasting is an excellent platform for building an audience, it doesn't have the same granular analytics tools that video or social media platforms offer. However, with the right approach, you can still track crucial data points that will help you understand your audience's behaviour and the overall success of your show.

Podcast Analytics Process

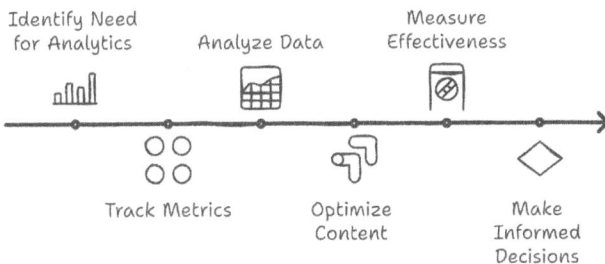

Effective use of analytics can help you:

🎤 Identify trends in audience growth.

🎙 Understand listener retention and engagement.

🎙 Optimize your content based on performance.

🎙 Track the success of marketing campaigns.

🎙 Improve monetization through targeted strategies.

By analyzing your podcast's data, you can make data-driven decisions that refine your content, improve listener satisfaction, and, ultimately, grow your podcast.

Key Podcast Metrics to Track

Here are the key metrics every podcaster should track to assess performance:

1. Downloads

Downloads are the industry-standard metric for tracking podcast audience size. A "download" occurs when a listener's device requests your episode's media file from your hosting platform. Downloads are often used as the benchmark for audience size, as they provide clear, server-side evidence of how often your episodes are requested.

However, it's important to understand that a download does not necessarily equal a listen. Many podcast apps automatically download new episodes when they're released, even if the listener doesn't actually play them. While downloads are a useful metric for tracking demand and reach, you should also focus on other data points for a clearer picture of listener engagement.

Download Calculation

Downloads are calculated through server logs of incoming HTTP requests for podcast media files. Here's how OP3, an example of an auditable infrastructure platform, calculates downloads:

🎙 **Non-GET requests are ignored:** Only GET requests are relevant since they represent actual file requests.

🎙 **Range requests are filtered:** Only meaningful range requests (more than two bytes) are considered downloads. This excludes requests that don't represent an actual attempt to access the file.

🎙 **Duplicate requests:** If the same listener (based on IP hash + User-Agent) requests the file multiple times within the same 24-hour UTC period, only the first request counts as a download. This ensures that listeners replaying an episode or downloading it again do not skew your metrics.

🎙 **Bot and crawler detection:** Requests from bots, spiders, or non-human user agents are excluded to prevent artificially inflating download numbers.

OP3 aims to provide accurate download counts by filtering out noise and irrelevant data, ensuring download numbers closely reflect unique human listeners.

2. Listener Retention

Listener retention measures how much of each episode your audience listens to. This is one of the most important metrics for gauging engagement. Are your listeners staying with you throughout the episode, or do they drop off midway? Tracking retention can help you identify which sections of your episodes hold the most attention and which need improvement.

Podcast platforms like Apple Podcasts, Spotify, and Google Podcasts provide insights into listener retention.

These metrics can show you:

- 🎙 The average percentage of each episode that listeners play.
- 🎙 The points at which most listeners drop off.
- 🎙 Episodes that maintain high retention versus those with lower engagement.

3. Unique Listeners

Unique listeners are the individual users who download or stream your podcast. Unlike download counts, which might be inflated by automatic downloads, tracking unique listeners gives you a more accurate picture of your actual audience size.

Hosting platforms and analytics services often aggregate data from IP addresses, device IDs, or user profiles to calculate unique listeners. This metric helps you understand how many different people are engaging with your content, giving you a clearer measure of your podcast's reach.

4. Engagement Metrics

Engagement metrics provide insights into how your audience interacts with your content across platforms.

These include:

- 🎙 Likes, shares, and comments on social media.
- 🎙 Reviews and ratings on podcast platforms like Apple Podcasts.
- 🎙 Email responses or feedback from your audience.

These metrics indicate how deeply your listeners are connecting with your podcast. High engagement often correlates with strong loyalty and can help you build a community around your content.

Key Metrics for Podcast Success

Geographic and Demographic Data

Completion Rates

Episode Performance

Subscriber Growth

🎙 **Geographic and Demographic Data:** Understanding where your listeners are located and their demographic profile (age, gender, interests) can help you tailor your content to meet their preferences. Most hosting platforms provide this data, which can also inform your marketing efforts and sponsorships by highlighting who your core audience is.

🎙 **Completion Rates:** Completion rates measure how often listeners finish an episode. If your episodes regularly have high completion rates, it's a sign that your content is resonating well with your audience. However, if many listeners drop off halfway through, it could indicate that your episodes are too long, lose focus, or aren't engaging enough.

🎙 **Episode Performance Over Time:** Some episodes will naturally perform better than others, depending on the topic, guest, or timing. Analyzing which episodes consistently perform well—and which don't—can help you fine-tune your content strategy. Look for patterns in what resonates with your audience, such as specific topics, formats (interviews vs. solo episodes), or episode lengths.

🎙 **Subscriber Growth:** Your subscriber count shows how many people are following your podcast and receiving updates when you publish new episodes. Steady growth in subscribers suggests your content is attracting new listeners and keeping your existing audience engaged.

Using Analytics to Optimize Your Podcast

Once you're tracking these metrics, the next step is using the data to optimize your podcast. Here are a few ways to leverage analytics effectively:

🎙 **Content Optimization:** If you notice that listener retention drops at certain points during your episodes, analyze those segments to understand why. Are they less engaging, too long, or unrelated to the main theme? Use this data to streamline your content and maintain higher engagement throughout your episodes.

🎙 **Episode Length:** Analytics can help you determine the ideal length for your episodes. If listeners consistently drop off after 30 minutes, you might experiment with shorter episodes to see if engagement improves. Alternatively, if you see high retention even in longer episodes, it may be worth exploring more in-depth content.

🎙 **Tailoring Marketing Efforts:** Geographic and demographic data can inform your marketing strategy. For example, if you notice a significant portion of your audience is from a particular region, you might tailor your content to be more relevant to that location or focus your advertising efforts there.

🎙 **Refining Your Call-to-Actions:** Engagement metrics, such as how often listeners act on your calls-to-action (CTAs), can help you refine your approach. If certain CTAs are consistently ignored, consider rephrasing them, simplifying the action required, or offering more compelling incentives for listeners to engage.

🎙 **Improving Listener Retention:** Listener retention data allows you to experiment with different formats, content structures, and pacing. If retention is low, consider reordering your content, offering more engaging openings, or cutting out non-essential segments.

Advanced Analytics Tools for Podcasters

While most podcast hosting platforms provide basic analytics, several advanced tools can offer deeper insights and help you make more data-driven decisions:

- 🎤 **Podtrac:** Provides audience measurement services that go beyond basic download stats, offering insights into demographics, unique audience metrics, and audience engagement.

- 🎤 **OP3:** Focuses on auditable infrastructure and download analytics, ensuring that your data is accurate, transparent, and filtered from non-human interactions. It's a reliable tool for accurate download tracking and filtering non-human requests like bots and crawlers. And it's free!

- 🎤 **Spotify for Podcasters:** Offers detailed analytics for podcasts published on Spotify, including listener demographics, episode performance, and audience retention rates. It's especially useful if Spotify is a major platform for your audience.

- 🎤 **Google Podcasts Manager:** Gives podcasters insights into listener habits, including the number of plays, retention rates, and the devices used to access your podcast.

- 🎤 **Apple Podcasts Connect:** Provides valuable insights into listener behavior on Apple Podcasts, such as average consumption rate, episode duration, and geographic data.

Advanced analytics and metrics are essential for podcasters who want to grow their audience, optimize content, and monetize effectively.

By tracking and interpreting key metrics such as downloads, retention, and listener engagement, you can make informed decisions that enhance the success of your podcast.

With a data-driven approach, you'll be better equipped to meet your audience's needs and take your podcast to the next level.

To help you implement the strategies outlined in Podcasting Secrets for Entrepreneurs, we've put together a comprehensive Podcast Secrets Resource Kit, which is available for free.

This kit contains tools, templates, and guides to streamline your podcasting process, from the initial planning stages to audience growth and monetization.

https://podcastsecrets.biz/s/kit

CHAPTER 44

BUILDING A LOYAL AUDIENCE AND ENGAGING WITH YOUR COMMUNITY

"The currency of real networking is not greed but generosity." – **Keith Ferrazzi**

Creating a podcast is one thing; building a dedicated, can't-wait-for-your-next-episode kind of audience? That's where the magic happens—and where the real work begins. Your listeners are out there, but keeping them hooked takes more than just a great voice and catchy intro music.

It's about crafting content they can't get enough of, connecting with them personally, and giving them a reason to hit "subscribe" (and maybe even tell a friend or two).

In this chapter, we'll dive into the secrets of building a fanbase that sticks around, shares your show, and treats each episode like the release of a new season of Stranger Things. Ready to turn casual listeners into lifelong fans? Let's go!

To create a successful podcast, you need to build a loyal audience and engage with your community. This means connecting with your listeners, creating interesting content, and building a real community around your podcast.

Building a community around your podcast is all about offering a unique experience that keeps listeners coming back.

But what makes a listener into a "fan"?

Here's where it pays to think about what your ideal listener wants most, whether it's inspiring stories, practical advice, or just a good laugh.

Once you know this, tailor your episodes and engagement to reflect those desires.

Creating Interesting Content

Focus on Relevant Topics
Deliver Content Professionally
Use Storytelling

Building a Loyal Podcast Audience

Building a Community

Encourage Listener Interaction
Provide Support Forums
Examples like Reddit

Here are a few tips for building a loyal audience and engaging with your community:

Create Interesting Content

To build a loyal audience, you should focus on topics that are interesting and relevant to your target audience and deliver your content professionally. If your podcast involves a lot of guest interviews, what better way to cover a topic than to interview an expert in the field?

If you're the only one speaking in your podcast, introduce the topic with your own story. Listeners love stories; they allow your audience to feel more connected to you while providing a frame of reference for the concepts covered in the episode.

Building a Community

There is nothing more powerful than the human collective. When we are able to come together and focus on one thing, great things happen. Some of the most amazing projects in the world are the product of human collaboration.

Podcast distribution platforms like Apple Podcasts do not generally encourage community participation. They focus on delivering content from a creator to an interested listener and little else. But what about the relationship between listeners? Listeners who enjoy a podcast are likely to share it with their friends, and for many platforms, that is where the 'community' begins and ends.

While you should encourage your listeners to share your podcast with those they think will find it worthwhile, you can do so much more. Encourage your listeners to share their thoughts and opinions publicly on a social media post, or preferably your own community platform. Spur them on by responding to their feedback in a genuine, authentic way.

Depending on the topics your podcast covers, your listeners might need help. You should provide a forum where they can ask for that help from you or other, more knowledgeable listeners. Never underestimate the members of your community willing to dedicate their time to helping other members. Your role is to provide a place for these valuable members and help them out when needed.

Think of platforms like Reddit—the site owners are referred to as the 'admins', but 'subreddits' (Reddit's term for communities within the huge platform) are managed by community members who have stepped up to take responsibility themselves and nominated themselves as Moderators. Reddit Admins are responsible for high-level moderation, but trust their Moderators to enforce the platform's standards, and provide them with the tools to do so.

A self-managing community is a powerful thing, and while it's not easy to build, you should take some of the lessons we've learned from Reddit in building our own self-sustaining community.

Give Your Audience a Reason to Spread the Word

One of the most powerful forms of marketing is word-of-mouth, especially when it comes from enthusiastic listeners. But to encourage this, you need to give people a reason to talk about your show. This could be through memorable content, standout interviews, or practical takeaways they can't help but share. Think about what makes your podcast different—then amplify it.

Power Move: Create an "insider's club" experience by giving your audience access to exclusive content, like behind-the-scenes episodes or first dibs on new episodes. Make your listeners feel like they're part of something unique, and they'll want to tell others.

Encourage and Respond to Feedback Regularly

Asking for feedback not only helps you improve but also shows your audience you're listening. Keep an open invitation for listeners to share what they love or what they'd like to see more of. Whether it's via social media, email, or in the comments, make it easy for them to reach out. And remember, the key is to respond when they do—acknowledge their input, ask follow-up questions, or simply thank them for reaching out. This level of responsiveness is rare and can set your podcast apart.

Example: One host set up a "listener hotline" where fans could call in with thoughts on recent episodes. Not only did it make listeners feel valued, but it also provided the host with real-time insights that shaped future content.

Creating a loyal audience for your podcast isn't just about gaining followers—it's about building genuine connections and a community that feels like family.

When you prioritize engagement, respond to feedback, and give your listeners a reason to keep coming back, you're creating more than just a show; you're creating a shared experience.

Remember, each interaction with your audience strengthens their loyalty and commitment to your podcast. Keep the conversations going, stay true to what makes your show unique, and watch as your listeners become lifelong fans who eagerly spread the word.

Your community is out there—nurture it, and let it grow into something extraordinary.

To help you implement the strategies outlined in Podcasting Secrets for Entrepreneurs, we've put together a comprehensive Podcast Secrets Resource Kit, which is available for free.

This kit contains tools, templates, and guides to streamline your podcasting process, from the initial planning stages to audience growth and monetization.

https://podcastsecrets.biz/s/kit

CHAPTER 45

INTERACTIVE AUDIENCE ENGAGEMENT

"People don't care how much you know until they know how much you care." –
Theodore Roosevelt

One of the most powerful aspects of podcasting is its ability to create a close connection between the host and the audience. While many podcasts operate as a one-way street—where the host shares insights or interviews guests without much listener involvement—those that actively engage their audience can foster a deeper sense of community.

Interactive audience engagement involves creating opportunities for your listeners to participate in your podcast and influence its content. By opening up channels for feedback, discussion, and interaction, you can strengthen relationships with your audience and turn passive listeners into active participants. This engagement drives listener retention and offers valuable insights into what your audience values most.

In this chapter, we'll explore strategies for cultivating an interactive audience, leveraging engagement tools, and using listener involvement to enhance your podcast.

Enhancing Podcast Success through Engagement

Listener Polls and Surveys

Increased Loyalty

Listener Q&A Sessions

Valuable Feedback

Monetization Opportunities

Community Building

Why Audience Engagement Matters

Podcasting inherently offers an intimate format—listeners feel connected to the hosts because they spend extended periods hearing their voices and ideas. Engaging with your audience takes this connection to the next level by making them feel like an integral part of the podcast's journey.

Here's why audience engagement is crucial for long-term success:

🎙 **Increased Loyalty:** Engaged listeners are more likely to become loyal fans who regularly tune in to new episodes, share your content with others, and support your podcast's growth.

🎙 **Valuable Feedback:** Active engagement provides you with direct feedback on what's resonating with your listeners and what isn't. This helps you refine your content and make episodes that speak directly to their interests.

🎙 **Community Building:** Interactive elements encourage your listeners to connect with each other, fostering a sense of community around your podcast.

🎙 **More Opportunities for Monetization:** A highly engaged audience is more likely to invest in paid content, such as memberships, courses, or merchandise, and they may be more receptive to sponsored content if they feel like active participants rather than passive listeners.

Strategies for Interactive Audience Engagement

There are many ways to engage with your podcast audience beyond just asking them to subscribe or leave a review. Below are proven strategies to create deeper interaction and foster a thriving community around your show.

1. Listener Q&A Sessions

Hosting regular listener Q&A sessions allows your audience to directly ask questions and share their thoughts. You can invite listeners to submit questions through social media, email, or a dedicated voicemail line, and then dedicate part of an episode to answering them. This makes listeners feel heard and provides fresh content ideas based on what your audience is curious about.

For example, you could end each episode with, "Got a question you'd like us to answer on the show? Send it to [email] or drop us a message on social media, and we'll feature it in an upcoming episode."

2. Listener Polls and Surveys

Polls and surveys are excellent tools for gauging your audience's preferences, gathering episode ideas, or even deciding future guests or topics. You can easily create polls using social media platforms, your podcast's website, or through email newsletters.

Examples include:

🎙 Polling listeners on what topic they'd like to hear next.

🎙 Asking for feedback on episode formats, such as whether they prefer interviews or solo episodes.

🎙 Conducting surveys to learn more about their interests, which can guide your content strategy.

By involving your listeners in decision-making, you increase their investment in your podcast and create content tailored to their preferences.

3. Live Episodes or Events

Hosting live episodes or virtual events is an effective way to engage with your audience in real-time. Whether it's a live recording of your podcast, a webinar, or a virtual meet-up, these events allow for direct interaction through Q&A sessions, live chats, and feedback. Live events create a sense of excitement and exclusivity, giving your audience a unique experience beyond your standard episodes. Platforms like YouTube, Facebook Live enable you to host live events where listeners can engage in real-time. For example, you might promote an upcoming live Q&A session: "Join us next Thursday for a live episode where we'll be answering your questions and taking live feedback—don't miss it!"

4. Listener-Generated Content

Another great way to engage your audience is by inviting them to contribute to your podcast in more meaningful ways. Listener-generated content can take several forms:

- 🎙 **Voice Messages:** Invite listeners to submit short voice messages or clips, which you can feature in future episodes. Services like SpeakPipe allow listeners to record and submit audio directly to you, giving your show a more interactive feel.

- 🎙 **Listener Stories:** If your podcast focuses on personal experiences or storytelling, invite your audience to share their own stories related to the episode's theme. You can either read their submissions or invite them to join you as guests.

- 🎙 **Fan Shoutouts:** Dedicate part of an episode to giving shoutouts to listeners who've engaged with your content, left reviews, or supported your show in other ways.

5. Interactive Social Media Campaigns

Social media platforms are perfect for sparking conversations and creating ongoing engagement between episodes. Use your podcast's social media accounts to interact directly with listeners:

- 🎙 **Ask Questions:** Pose questions related to your latest episode to encourage listener responses and start discussions.

- 🎙 **Host Contests or Giveaways:** Create incentives for engagement, such as offering a giveaway to listeners who share your podcast or leave a review. This can increase your visibility while also rewarding your most loyal listeners.

- 🎙 **Weekly Hashtags:** Use a recurring hashtag to build a community. For example, you could start a hashtag like #PodcastQuestionOfTheWeek, where you ask your audience a new question each week and feature the best responses on your show.

6. Private Listener Communities

Consider creating a private space where your listeners can interact with each other and with you. This could be a Facebook group, a community in PodcastSecrets.app, or a paid membership community. These communities allow your audience to discuss episodes, share their thoughts, and feel part of something exclusive. Private groups also give you a space to share behind-the-scenes content, host exclusive Q&A sessions, and gather direct feedback. PodcastSecrets.app has the ability to create private podcasts.

For example, you might promote a listener group with: "Want to join our private podcast community? Head over to [platform] to chat with fellow listeners, get exclusive content, and take part in special live events!"

Building an Engaged Community

Engagement doesn't stop at interactive content—you'll also need to build and maintain a sense of community around your podcast. Here are some tips for fostering that sense of belonging:

- **Be Consistent:** Consistency is key to building trust with your audience. Whether it's replying to social media comments, answering listener questions, or running regular live events, make sure to engage with your audience regularly and reliably. Inconsistency can cause your audience to lose interest or feel disconnected.

- **Show Authenticity:** Your audience values authenticity, so be genuine in your interactions. Whether you're replying to comments, featuring listener-generated content, or hosting live Q&As, showing your personality and staying true to your brand fosters stronger connections.

- **Reward Loyalty:** Recognizing your loyal listeners is a powerful way to maintain engagement. Consider creating special perks or rewards for your most dedicated fans—whether that's giving them early access to episodes, exclusive content, or simply acknowledging their support on your show.

- **Ask for Feedback:** Your audience is your most valuable resource for improving your podcast. Ask for their feedback regularly—whether through surveys, direct questions, or social media polls. This helps you improve your content and reinforces that you value their input.

Measuring Engagement Success

To gauge how well your audience engagement strategies are working, track key metrics such as:

- **Listener participation:** Are you getting more listener questions, comments, or stories with each episode?

- **Social media interactions:** Track engagement on platforms like Instagram, Twitter, or Facebook to see if your followers are responding to your posts and participating in discussions.

- **Podcast reviews and ratings:** A spike in positive reviews or ratings can indicate that your audience feels connected to your show and is enjoying the content.

- **Audience growth:** Engaged listeners are more likely to share your podcast with others, leading to organic growth in your subscriber base.

Regularly assessing these metrics will help you fine-tune your engagement strategies and continue to build a thriving, interactive community. Interactive audience engagement is a powerful way to build loyalty, foster community, and enhance the value of your podcast. By actively involving your listeners—through Q&A sessions, listener-generated content, live events, and social media campaigns—you create a two-way relationship that strengthens your podcast's impact and grows your audience.

Engagement is a long-term investment, but the rewards in terms of listener retention, community building, and monetization opportunities are well worth the effort.

CHAPTER 46

THE POWER OF VIDEO PODCASTING

"Seeing is believing." – **Anonymous**

Ready to take your podcast to the next level—and give listeners a front-row seat? Enter: video podcasting!

Adding a visual element to your show isn't just about putting a face to the voice; it's about expanding your reach, deepening audience connection, and, let's be honest, giving your podcast that extra "wow" factor.

In this chapter, we'll break down how to get started with video, from setting up a simple studio to engaging your viewers without feeling like you're on a movie set.

Lights, camera… podcast!

While podcasts are traditionally audio-only, video podcasts are an easy way to connect more deeply with an audience interested in video content.

The Benefits of Video Podcasting

Enhanced Engagement

Video podcasts provide a visual element that captivates your audience, creates a more personal connection, and makes your content more memorable and engaging. Most people listen to podcasts while they're doing something else; while driving to work, or cooking dinner, or just before they sleep.

However, there is another audience contingent which engages singularly with your content, carving out time in their schedule to pay attention only to your podcast. For these people, video podcasting gives them something more interesting to look at.

Connect with Guests

Video also helps you connect more deeply with your guests, as it's easier to have a conversation when you can see the other person's face. There's more energy with video.

Broader Reach

By offering your podcast as a traditional audio-only podcast, and as a video podcast, you can appeal to more listeners.

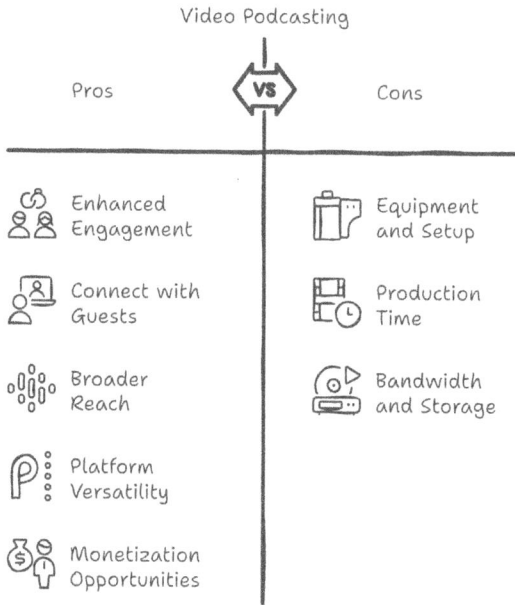

Platform Versatility

Video podcasts can be distributed on popular video-sharing platforms, such as YouTube and Vimeo, in addition to traditional podcast directories like Apple Podcasts.

Monetization Opportunities

Video podcasts can provide additional monetization options, such as access to Google's advertising network on YouTube with video ads, and sponsorships for a wider range of products, offering potential revenue streams beyond those available with audio podcasts.

Video podcasts give sponsors more freedom to advertise their products and services so they can draw in a wider pool of sponsors.

Considerations for Video Podcasting

Equipment and Setup

Video podcasting requires more equipment in addition to what is covered in the *Essential Podcasting Equipment* chapter, such as a video camera, a good lighting setup, and video editing software. You'll need to invest in quality equipment and learn to use them properly to create professional video.

There are several non-linear editors (NLEs), which are used for video editing, available to you. You can use Adobe Premiere Pro, DaVinci Resolve, or Lightworks. All of these editors are available on Windows and macOS, but Lightworks is available on Linux, as well. DaVinci Resolve has powerful color grading capabilities, better than any other NLE, and also a dedicated digital audio workstation tab for editing your audio.

DaVinci Resolve has a free version with most of the functionality you'll ever need, and a lifetime license at a modest cost if you really need the extra features, which is why we recommend it to new podcasters.

Production Time and Effort

Video podcasting can be more time-consuming and labor-intensive than audio podcasting, as it involves recording, editing, and optimizing audio and video content. Be prepared to allocate additional time and resources for video production.

Bandwidth and Storage

Video files are typically larger than audio files, which can impact your podcast hosting costs and data usage for both you and your audience. Consider these factors when choosing a hosting provider and distributing your video podcast.

You should choose a video hosting provider like YouTube or Vimeo; these companies are well-equipped to serving video to all manner of audiences. It's complex and costly to setup video hosting on a platform not designed for it like AWS, because you will need to replicate all of the optimizations these platforms make for audiences with slower network connections and less powerful devices. YouTube will automatically transcode and adjust the video bitrate for the user without you having to do anything aside from upload the video, for example.

However, neither YouTube nor Vimeo is a storage solution. You should not delete your local video files after uploading them to their servers. You should choose a real cloud storage solution to store your files, like Dropbox or Box.com.

Tips for Creating a Successful Video Podcast

Plan Your Content

Develop a content plan that takes advantage of the visual element of video podcasting. Consider incorporating visual aids, demonstrations, or on-screen graphics to enhance your message and provide additional value to your audience.

Maintain Audio Quality

While video is a crucial component, don't neglect the importance of high-quality audio. Ensure your audio is high-quality and free from distractions using the suggestions outlined in the *Setting Up a Recording Space and Maximizing Your Podcast's Production Value* chapters.

Optimize for Different Platforms

Edit and optimize your video podcast for various platforms, such as YouTube, Vimeo, and social media sites like Facebook to ensure the best viewing experience for your audience. This may involve adjusting aspect ratios, video quality, and file formats.

For example, most social media sites are being browsed on a phone, which means the standard 16:9 ratio requires users to flip their phones to landscape to watch the video comfortably. Many creators choose to use an aspect ratio more appropriate for phones in portrait mode, like 9:16.

Promote Your Video Podcast

Leverage social media, email marketing, and collaborations with other content creators to promote your video podcast and attract new viewers. Share teasers, highlights, or short clips to entice potential viewers to watch your full episodes.

Our promotional advice for audio-only podcasts remains the same as in the *Maximizing Your Podcast's Visibility and Reach* chapter, but video podcasting allows for more interesting teasers to share on social media sites.

Ready to turn your podcast into a full-blown multimedia experience?

Video podcasting is your ticket to more engaging content, wider reach, and a stronger connection with your audience.

Sure, it might mean investing in a bit more gear (and maybe learning to love the camera), but the payoff is worth it.

Plus, who knows?

Your next episode could be the one that has listeners—and viewers—coming back for more.

So, lights, camera… podcast!

Let's show the world what you've got.

CHAPTER 47

REPURPOSING PODCAST CONTENT ACROSS MULTIPLE PLATFORMS

"Adaptability is not imitation. It means power of resistance and assimilation."
– Mahatma Gandhi

Creating a podcast episode requires significant time and effort, from planning and recording to editing and promoting. There are more ways to take advantage of a finished episode after it's published. Repurposing your podcast content across multiple platforms is an easy way to reach more people.

In this chapter, we'll explore how to strategically repurpose your podcast content into different formats and distribute it across various platforms.

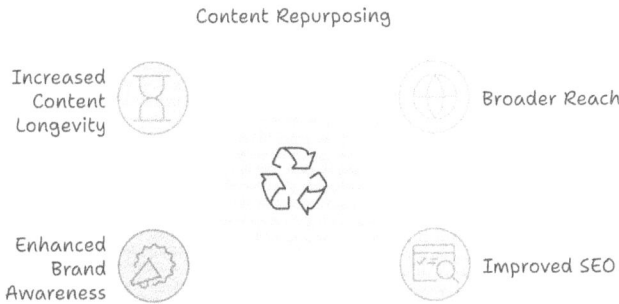

Content Repurposing

Increased Content Longevity

Broader Reach

Enhanced Brand Awareness

Improved SEO

Why Repurpose Content?

Repurposing podcast content helps you reach people who prefer consuming information in formats other than audio. Not everyone listens to podcasts, but many might read a blog post, watch a video, or engage with short clips on social media. Repurposing enables you to meet your audience where they are, using your existing content as the foundation for new materials. This means:

- **Broader Reach:** By adapting your content into different formats, you attract people who may not typically listen to podcasts.
- **Improved SEO:** Written content, such as blog posts or articles, enhances your search engine optimization (SEO) efforts, helping your podcast appear in more online searches.

🎙 **Enhanced Brand Awareness:** Consistently showing up on multiple platforms strengthens your brand presence and keeps your podcast top of mind for your audience.

Starting with Transcriptions

A simple yet powerful way to begin repurposing your podcast content is by creating transcripts of each episode. Transcriptions serve as the foundation for various content formats, including blog posts, social media updates, and articles.

🎙 **SEO Benefits of Transcriptions:** Search engines can't "listen" to podcast audio, but they can read text. By publishing transcripts of your episodes on your website or blog, you create keyword-rich content that boosts your SEO, making it easier for potential listeners to discover your show through search engines.

🎙 **Creating Accessible Content:** Transcriptions make your podcast more accessible to a wider audience, including those who are hard of hearing or prefer reading over listening. Accessibility is an important consideration for ethical content creators and helps grow your audience.

🎙 **Tools for Transcribing:** Several tools can help automate the transcription process, such as Otter.ai, Rev, or Sonix. These services generate transcriptions quickly, though it's a good idea to proofread them for accuracy before publishing.

Turning Episodes into Blog Posts

One of the easiest ways to repurpose a podcast episode is by transforming it into a blog post. This doesn't mean simply copying the transcript word for word but rather summarizing key points and adding some structure to make it readable and engaging.

1. Episode Recaps: Write a concise blog post that summarizes the episode, highlighting the key takeaways or insights. You can include bullet points or headings to make it easy for readers to skim. Be sure to link to the full episode so readers can listen if they want more details.

For example, if you've done an interview with a successful entrepreneur, your blog post might outline the top three lessons they shared about scaling a business, with a call to action encouraging readers to listen to the full episode.

2. Deep Dives into Specific Topics: Some podcast episodes cover several topics in one go. You can break these down into individual blog posts that take a deeper dive into each topic. This gives you multiple pieces of content from a single episode and allows you to explore specific subjects in more detail.

3. Answer Common Questions: If your podcast frequently answers questions from listeners or addresses common industry challenges, you can turn those answers into standalone blog posts. This helps position you as an authority in your niche and adds additional value for your audience.

Creating Social Media Content

Social media is a powerful tool for promoting your podcast, and repurposing content for these platforms is an excellent way to maintain a steady presence. Here are some ideas for turning your podcast into engaging social media content:

- 🎙 **Audiograms:** An audiogram is a short, visually engaging clip that combines audio from your podcast with a waveform graphic or static image. These are ideal for sharing key quotes, interesting soundbites, or exciting moments from your episode. Tools like Headliner or Wave.video can help you create these easily. Keep the clips brief—30 to 60 seconds is usually enough to capture attention.

- 🎙 **Quote Cards:** Pull compelling or thought-provoking quotes from your episodes and turn them into visual graphics for platforms like Instagram, Facebook, or Twitter. Quote cards are highly shareable and can spark interest in the full episode. Be sure to include a link to the episode in your post caption.

- 🎙 **Highlight Reels:** For social media platforms that expect long-form content like YouTube or LinkedIn, consider creating a highlight reel from your episode. This could be a 2-3 minute video that covers the most exciting parts of the conversation. Add captions to increase accessibility and engagement, especially for viewers who may watch without sound.

- 🎙 **Polls and Discussions:** Encourage audience interaction by asking questions or starting a conversation based on the themes of your latest episode. For example, if your podcast episode was about overcoming business challenges, you might ask your social media followers to share their own challenges and how they've overcome them.

Turning Episodes into Videos

Repurposing your podcast content into video format can dramatically extend your reach. Many people prefer watching video content over listening to audio alone, and video platforms like YouTube offer great potential for discoverability.

- 🎙 **Upload Episodes to YouTube:** One of the simplest ways to repurpose your content is to upload your full podcast episodes to YouTube. You don't need to create complex visuals—just a static image or a simple animation with your podcast branding and episode title. Add timestamps and a detailed description to optimize it for search.

- 🎙 **Create Short, Topic-Based Videos:** Rather than uploading the entire episode, you could create shorter videos that focus on specific topics discussed in the podcast. This is especially useful for educational podcasts, where breaking down complex subjects into bite-sized videos makes the content more digestible for viewers.

- 🎙 **Record Video Versions of Your Podcast:** If you have the resources, consider recording a video version of your podcast. Even if the video is just you and your guest talking, this adds a new dimension to your content. Many listeners enjoy seeing the faces behind the voices. You can upload these video versions to YouTube and share clips on social media.

Turning Episodes into Email Newsletters

Email marketing remains one of the most effective tools for building a loyal audience. Repurposing podcast content into email newsletters is a great way to keep your subscribers engaged while promoting new episodes. There are a few ways to do it:

- 🎙 **Episode Highlights in a Weekly Newsletter:** Use your email newsletter to recap the highlights of each new episode, similar to a blog post. Include a brief summary of the key takeaways, a quote or two, and a link to listen to the full episode. Adding personal commentary or insights can make the newsletter feel more intimate and engaging.

- 🎙 **Exclusive Content for Subscribers:** Offer your email subscribers something extra—such as behind-the-scenes insights, uncut versions of interviews, or bonus content related to the episode. This helps drive engagement and builds a stronger connection with your audience.

- 🎙 **Share Repurposed Blog Posts or Videos:** If you've already repurposed a podcast episode into a blog post or video, share that content with your email subscribers. This ensures that even if they miss the podcast, they still have access to the core message in a different format.

Creating a Book or Course

For podcasters with a wealth of content, repurposing podcast episodes into a book, eBook, or online course is a fantastic way to deliver even more value to your audience.

- 🎙 **Turn Your Podcast into a Book:** If you've covered a series of connected topics on your podcast, you may have enough material to create a book. Organize the episodes into chapters and expand on key points. Publishing a book gives you another revenue stream and positions you as an expert in your niche.

- 🎙 **Create an Online Course:** If your podcast delivers educational content, consider turning your episodes into a structured online course. For example, if your podcast is about business development, you could create modules around specific themes covered in your episodes—adding additional resources, video lessons, and workbooks to create a comprehensive learning experience.

Repurposing your podcast content across multiple platforms is a smart way to extend your reach, engage with new audiences, and maximize the value of every episode you produce.

Whether you're turning your podcast into blog posts, videos, or social media content, the key is to adapt the material to fit the format of each platform without losing your unique voice.

By embracing repurposing, you can significantly increase your podcast's impact without constantly reinventing the wheel.

CHAPTER 48

BUILDING A PODCAST NETWORK YOU CONTROL AND OWN

"Control your own destiny or someone else will." – **Jack Welch**

The podcasting industry has grown rapidly in recent years, with countless creators launching their own shows across various platforms.

However, as podcasters and entrepreneurs alike are beginning to realize, relying on external platforms for hosting and distribution—whether it's Spotify, Apple Podcasts, or YouTube—can come with limitations.

You're always playing by someone else's rules, subject to their algorithms, policies, and revenue models. This is why more podcasters are exploring the idea of building their own podcast network—where they control the platform, the audience, and the revenue.

In this chapter, we'll explore how you can build and grow your own podcast network. A network where you not only host your own shows but also provide a platform for others to create their podcasts.

This isn't just about running a few shows; it's about creating a media empire that you fully control, much like owning your own version of Spotify or Apple Podcasts, but built around your vision and brand.

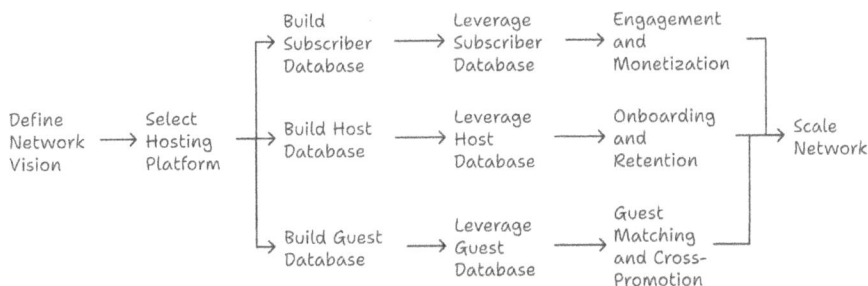

Why Own Your Platform?

In a world dominated by external media platforms, the idea of owning your content and distribution channels has never been more appealing—or more important. Here's why building and owning your podcast network makes sense:

Control Over Content and Policies

When you own the platform, you make the rules. There's no need to worry about ever-changing algorithms, platform bans, or restrictive content policies. Whether you want to talk about niche topics or experiment with new formats, owning your platform gives you the freedom to create content without limitations.

Revenue Ownership

Many creators rely on third-party platforms that take a cut of their revenue or limit their monetization options. Owning your platform means owning the revenue. Whether it's through ad placements, subscriptions, or premium content, all the income generated stays within your ecosystem.

Building a Community

Having your own podcast network creates a sense of community. You're not just broadcasting content; you're building a home for creators and listeners alike. With full control over user interaction, you can foster deeper connections, promote collaboration between hosts, and engage directly with your audience on your terms.

Monetization Flexibility

On your platform, you can implement various monetization strategies, from selling hosting services to offering premium memberships, advertising space, or even exclusive content. This flexibility enables you to create new revenue streams that third-party platforms might not allow.

Databases to Power Growth

One of the most powerful assets of owning a podcast network is the ability to build and leverage three key databases: your subscribers, your hosts, and their guests. Each database opens up unique opportunities to grow your network and monetize in multiple ways.

Three Types of Databases to Build and Leverage

When you own your podcast network, you're not just hosting content—you're collecting valuable data that can fuel your growth. By building three distinct databases, you can create a system where each group (subscribers, hosts, and guests) interacts with and benefits from the others. Here's how you can build and leverage each database:

1. Subscriber Database

Your subscribers are the listeners who regularly engage with your network's podcasts. They follow shows, download episodes, sign up for newsletters, and even become paid members. This database is a goldmine for both audience growth and monetization.

Here are some ways you can use your subscriber database:

🎙 **Monetization Opportunities:** Once you have a growing base of subscribers, you can offer premium content or memberships, sell products and services from your hosts, or run targeted ads and sponsorships. By understanding your subscribers' preferences, you can introduce them to relevant content and offers.

- 🎙 **Engagement Tools:** Use email campaigns, SMS notifications, or exclusive community groups to keep subscribers engaged. Offer special perks like early access to new episodes, live Q&A sessions, or behind-the-scenes content.

- 🎙 **Cross-Promotion:** Leverage your subscriber database by promoting new podcasts or episodes across your network. When a new show launches, send out targeted promotions to subscribers who may be interested based on their listening habits.

2. Host Database

Your host database includes the podcasters who use your network to distribute and manage their shows. These individuals are more than content creators; they are partners in growing the network.

Here are some ways you can use your host database:

- 🎙 **Onboarding and Retention:** Offer various hosting packages that cater to different needs—whether it's beginner podcasters looking for basic tools or advanced creators who need robust analytics and premium features. Keep your hosts engaged by offering value-added services like editing, guest management, or marketing tools.

- 🎙 **Monetization Opportunities:** You can charge hosts a subscription fee for using your platform, but the real opportunity lies in upselling premium services. For example, hosts can pay for better analytics, additional storage, podcast editing services, or even access to guest directories to improve their content.

- 🎙 **Cross-Promotion and Collaboration:** Encourage collaboration between your hosts. By facilitating cross-promotion, you help each host grow their audience, which in turn benefits the entire network. Hosts can guest on each other's shows, or promote episodes to their own listeners.

3. Guest Database

The guest database consists of individuals who appear on podcasts across your network. These guests are often experts, influencers, or thought leaders with their own audiences. Properly leveraging this database can significantly increase the reach of your network.

Here are some ways you can use your guest database:

- 🎙 **Guest Matching for Hosts:** One of the services you can offer your hosts is a guest-matching feature. By building a directory of potential guests, you can help your hosts find experts, influencers, or niche leaders who would be great fits for their shows. This adds immense value for hosts, as finding high-quality guests is often one of the biggest challenges podcasters face.

- 🎙 **Expand Audience Reach:** When a guest appears on a show, they often promote the episode to their own audience. By building a solid guest database, you encourage this cross-promotion, which helps your network grow organically.

- 🎙 **Monetization Opportunities:** You can offer additional services to both guests and hosts. For example, guests might pay to appear on certain high-profile shows, or you could charge hosts for access to premium guests from the directory.

Steps to Building Your Own Podcast Network

Building a podcast network you control isn't as complex as it might sound. By following a few key steps, you can create a platform where not only your shows thrive but where others can join and build their own successful podcasts under your umbrella.

1. Define Your Network's Vision

Before you dive into the technical aspects, it's essential to have a clear vision for your podcast network. Consider the following questions:

- 🎤 What type of content will your network focus on?
- 🎤 Are you targeting a specific niche or a broad audience?
- 🎤 Will you focus on hosting your own shows, or will you also provide space for other podcasters to join?

Defining your vision helps set the foundation for your network's brand and guides how you attract creators and listeners alike. For example, if your niche is business podcasts, you can position yourself as the go-to network for entrepreneurs and business leaders looking for valuable content.

2. Select a Podcast Hosting Platform That Gives You Control

You don't need to build everything from scratch. There are platforms available that offer white-label solutions, allowing you to create a fully branded podcast network that feels uniquely yours. A platform like Evolvepreneur.app provides an easy way to create and manage your own podcast network without worrying about the technical setup. It allows you to focus on content and growth while ensuring you maintain full control over the infrastructure.

The key is to choose a platform that:

- 🎤 Allows full customization and branding so that your network feels like your own.
- 🎤 Offers tools for managing multiple hosts and podcasts seamlessly.
- 🎤 Includes monetization options like subscription billing, advertising management, and premium content offerings.
- 🎤 Provides analytics to help you optimize content and track growth.

With the right platform, you can be up and running quickly, managing everything from guest and subscriber interactions to billing and payment processing without getting bogged down by technical details.

Monetizing Your Podcast Network

One of the main advantages of owning your network is the flexibility to monetize in multiple ways:

- 🎤 **Subscription Hosting:** Charge hosts a monthly fee for using your platform to distribute their content. You can offer tiered plans with advanced features like detailed analytics or monetization tools available at higher levels.
- 🎤 **Premium Content and Memberships:** Offer exclusive content or bonus episodes to listeners who pay a subscription fee. You can also create membership programs where fans gain access to behind-the-scenes content, live streams, or early access to new episodes.

🎙 **Sponsorship and Advertising:** As your network grows, you can sell advertising space within episodes or across the network. You could also partner with sponsors who align with your audience's interests.

🎙 **Selling Services to Subscribers:** You can go beyond podcast content and offer services or products to your subscriber base. Whether it's merchandise, online courses, or special promotions from your hosts and sponsors, your subscriber database represents a powerful asset for generating revenue.

Monetizing and Scaling a Podcast Network

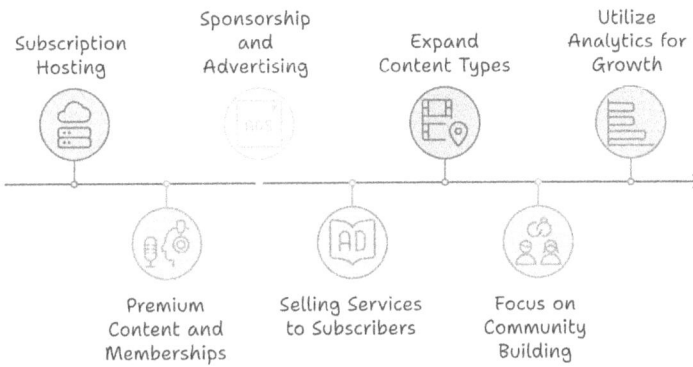

Subscription Hosting	Sponsorship and Advertising	Expand Content Types	Utilize Analytics for Growth

Premium Content and Memberships	Selling Services to Subscribers	Focus on Community Building

Scaling Your Network and Becoming Your Own Media Platform

The ultimate goal of building a podcast network is to scale it into a self-sustaining media platform—your own version of Spotify or Apple Podcasts but under your control. Here are some key strategies for scaling:

🎙 **Expand Content Types:** Consider expanding your network beyond audio to include video podcasts, live events, or e-learning modules. This diversification allows you to tap into new audiences and create more opportunities for engagement.

🎙 **Focus on Community Building:** Use tools like forums, chat rooms, or exclusive groups to foster a community around your network. Encouraging listeners to engage with both you and the hosts strengthens loyalty and can increase retention.

🎙 **Utilize Analytics for Growth:** Regularly track listener data, engagement rates, and subscription metrics to optimize your network. Use these insights to refine content, introduce new features, or scale successful podcasts across the platform.

Building your own podcast network is about more than just hosting podcasts—it's about creating a media platform that gives you full control over your content, your audience, and your revenue.

By focusing on building and leveraging three key databases—subscribers, hosts, and guests—you can create a thriving ecosystem that drives growth and monetization.

With the right vision and platform, your podcast network can evolve into a powerful, scalable business.

To help you implement the strategies outlined in Podcasting Secrets for Entrepreneurs, we've put together a comprehensive Podcast Secrets Resource Kit, which is available for free.

This kit contains tools, templates, and guides to streamline your podcasting process, from the initial planning stages to audience growth and monetization.

https://podcastsecrets.biz/s/kit

CHAPTER 49

PODCAST GROWTH STRATEGIES

"Growth is never by mere chance; it is the result of forces working together." – **James Cash Penney**

Growing your podcast is essential if you want to reach more listeners, increase engagement, and monetize effectively. While creating high-quality content is crucial, it's only part of the equation. A strategic approach to growth will help you build a loyal listener base and establish your podcast as a leader in your niche.

In this chapter, we'll cover proven strategies for growing your podcast audience, from organic tactics to paid promotion methods.

Whether you're just starting or looking to take your podcast to the next level, these strategies will help you build momentum and grow sustainably.

Podcast Growth Strategies

Leverage Guest Audiences — Utilize Social Media — Cross-Promotion and Partnerships — Encourage Reviews and Ratings

Optimize for SEO — Build a Podcast Network — Paid Advertising

Why Growth Matters

Growth is essential not only for expanding your listener base but also for sustaining your podcast over the long term. With a larger audience, you can:

- 🎙 **Attract sponsorships and partnerships:** A bigger audience means more opportunities for monetization.
- 🎙 **Increase brand awareness:** The more listeners you have, the more widely recognized your brand becomes.
- 🎙 **Build a community:** An engaged audience creates opportunities for deeper connections, feedback, and collaboration.

1. Leverage Guest Audiences

One of the most effective ways to grow your podcast is by featuring guests on your show. Guest interviews provide valuable content for your audience and allow you to tap into your guest's audience as well.

🎙 **Collaborate with Industry Experts:** Invite experts, influencers, or thought leaders from your industry to be guests on your podcast. This exposes your podcast to their followers, increasing your reach.

🎙 **Encourage Guests to Share the Episode:** Make it easy for guests to share the episode with their audience by providing them with shareable graphics, audiograms, or direct links to the episode.

By featuring notable guests and encouraging them to promote the episode, you can significantly expand your reach and attract new listeners.

2. Optimize Your Podcast for SEO

Search engine optimization (SEO) isn't just for websites—it's also crucial for growing your podcast. Optimizing your podcast episodes and show notes can help you attract more listeners organically.

🎙 **Use Descriptive Titles and Show Notes:** Your episode titles and show notes should include keywords that are relevant to your content and industry. These keywords help search engines index your podcast, making it easier for people to find when searching for related topics.

🎙 **Transcribe Your Episodes:** As mentioned in an earlier chapter, adding transcriptions to your podcast's website not only improves accessibility but also boosts SEO. Search engines can crawl the text of your transcript, increasing the chances of your podcast appearing in search results.

The goal is to ensure your podcast is easily discoverable by people searching for related content. Optimizing your metadata, episode descriptions, and website content will help drive organic traffic to your show.

3. Leverage Social Media

Social media is one of the most powerful tools for promoting your podcast and growing your audience. It allows you to share your episodes, engage with listeners, and build a community around your show.

🎙 **Create Shareable Content:** Repurpose your podcast episodes into bite-sized pieces of content for social media. You can create audiograms, short video clips, or quote graphics that highlight key moments from your episodes.

🎙 **Engage with Your Audience:** Social media platforms like Instagram, Twitter, and LinkedIn allow you to interact with your listeners directly. Reply to comments, ask for feedback, and encourage listeners to share your content with their networks.

🎙 **Use Hashtags and Communities:** Join podcasting communities and use relevant hashtags to increase your podcast's visibility. For example, using industry-specific hashtags on Twitter or Instagram can help attract listeners interested in your niche.

A consistent and interactive social media presence can increase awareness of your podcast, foster a sense of community, and encourage listeners to spread the word.

4. Build a Podcast Network

If you've established a strong podcast with a growing listener base, consider expanding by building a podcast network. A podcast network allows you to partner with other shows, cross-promote each other's content, and tap into shared audiences.

- 🎙 **Partner with Similar Shows:** Look for other podcasts in your niche that have a complementary audience. By forming a network, you can collaborate on episodes, share guests, and cross-promote each other's shows.

- 🎙 **Offer Value to New Podcasters:** If you've built up experience, you can help new podcasters by offering resources, promotion, or guest spots on your show. In return, they'll introduce you to their audience.

Building a podcast network not only grows your audience but also positions you as a leader in your niche. It helps you create a stronger sense of community while expanding your reach.

5. Cross-Promotion and Partnerships

Cross-promotion with other podcasters, influencers, or brands can help grow your audience by introducing your show to new listeners who are already interested in similar content.

- 🎙 **Swap Ads or Mentions:** Collaborate with other podcasters to swap promotional ads or mentions in each other's episodes. This mutually beneficial strategy exposes your podcast to a new audience.

- 🎙 **Collaborate on Joint Ventures:** Partner with brands, businesses, or influencers in your industry to co-create content, host events, or collaborate on a series of episodes. These partnerships help attract new listeners and build credibility for your podcast.

Cross-promotion works best when you partner with podcasters or brands that share your target audience. The goal is to create authentic collaborations that provide value to both parties.

6. Paid Advertising

While organic growth is important, paid advertising can help accelerate your podcast's growth by reaching new audiences quickly.

- 🎙 **Run Ads on Podcast Platforms:** Many podcast directories, such as Spotify, allow you to run targeted ads that promote your show to users interested in your niche.

- 🎙 **Use Social Media Advertising:** Platforms like Facebook, Instagram, and LinkedIn allow you to create targeted ad campaigns that promote your episodes or your podcast's brand. You can target listeners based on their interests, behaviors, and demographics.

Paid advertising can give your podcast an initial boost or help grow your audience during specific promotions or events.

7. Encourage Reviews and Ratings

Podcast reviews and ratings play a significant role in attracting new listeners. When potential listeners come across your show, they often check the reviews to gauge whether it's worth their time. Positive reviews help build social proof and credibility.

🎙 **Ask for Reviews:** Don't be afraid to ask your audience to leave reviews and ratings on platforms like Apple Podcasts. Mention it at the end of each episode and explain how reviews help the show grow.

🎙 **Run a Giveaway or Contest:** To incentivize reviews, you can run a contest or giveaway for your listeners. Offer a prize for listeners who leave a review, and feature some of your favorite reviews in your episodes.

The more positive reviews and ratings your podcast has, the more likely it is to attract new listeners.

Growing your podcast requires a mix of organic strategies, audience engagement, and sometimes paid promotion. By leveraging guest audiences, optimizing your podcast for SEO, harnessing the power of social media, and exploring partnerships and paid advertising, you can significantly expand your reach and grow your listener base.

Growth takes time and consistent effort, but by implementing these strategies, you'll be well on your way to building a thriving, engaged podcast audience.

CHAPTER 50

TURNING YOUR PODCAST INTO A BOOK

"There is no greater agony than bearing an untold story inside you." – **Maya Angelou**

Ever thought your podcast episodes were so good they deserved to be… well, immortalized?

Good news: turning your podcast into a book is not just possible—it's a brilliant way to extend your reach, reinforce your expertise, and create something tangible from all those hours behind the mic.

In this chapter, we'll show you how to repurpose your best episodes, organize them into a compelling read, and maybe even get that shiny "author" title next to your name. Ready to see your podcast on paper? Let's make it happen—one page (or episode) at a time!

Turning your podcast into a book can be an excellent way to expand your reach, monetize your content, and establish yourself as an authority in your niche. A book based on your podcast can offer your existing audience a new way to consume your content while attracting new readers who may not have discovered your podcast yet.

This chapter will explore the benefits, strategies, and steps for transforming your podcast into a book.

Benefits of Turning Your Podcast Into a Book

- 🎙 **Reach a Wider Audience:** By repurposing your podcast content into a book, you can reach a completely different audience to podcast listeners, but who can benefit all the same from your content.

- 🎙 **Establish Expertise:** Publishing a book can help you establish yourself as an authority in your field, leading to new opportunities such as speaking engagements, collaborations, and partnerships.

- 🎙 **Monetization:** A book can serve as an additional revenue stream, allowing you to monetize your podcast content through book sales. It's also something you can market to your current listeners.

- 🎙 **Long-lived Content:** Books have a longer shelf life and serve as an evergreen resource for your audience, offering value and insights long after your podcast episodes have been released. If it's a paper book, it won't be taken off the internet, or updated to have parts of it removed. Readers could even pass the book down to their children.

Transforming a Podcast into a Book

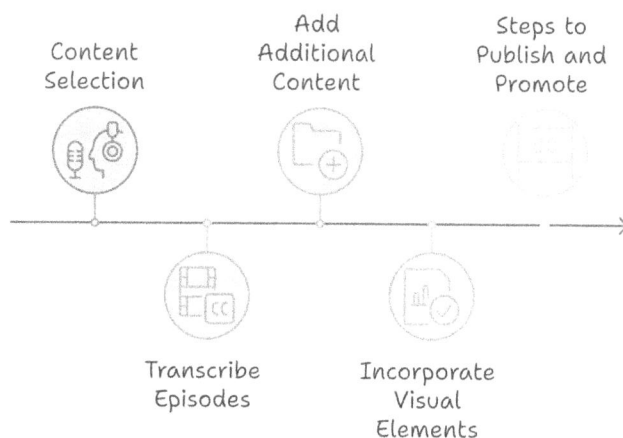

Content Selection

Add Additional Content

Steps to Publish and Promote

Transcribe Episodes

Incorporate Visual Elements

Strategies for Transforming Your Podcast Into a Book

Content Selection

Review your podcast episodes and select the most relevant, informative, and engaging content to be included in your book. What remains is to arrange them in a logical order, and add a few book-exclusive chapters to serve as connective tissue. You could organize the chapters by themes.

Transcribe Your Episodes

Transcribe your selected podcast episodes and edit the transcriptions into a reader-friendly format. This will involve reorganizing content, removing superfluous dialogue, and refining the language for a written format. Treat these transcripts as a strong base that will eventually coalesce into a final chapter, as you consider what is appropriate for this new audience. You may want to enlist the help of an editor to expedite this process.

Additional Content

Consider adding new content, such as case studies or personal anecdotes to enhance the value of your book and provide readers with fresh insights not found in your podcast episodes. This will make your book an easier sell to those who are already listeners and are looking for more from you. You can add exclusive chapters as suggested above, but you can also add to each chapter created from one of your podcast episodes.

Visual Elements

Incorporate visual elements, such as charts, graphs, or illustrations, to support your content and make your book more engaging and visually appealing. Keep in mind that the more images you have, the higher the cost of printing the book will be. You should also consider whether color is an important element to images, as printing your book in color is significantly more expensive than black and white.

Steps to Publish and Promote Your Podcast-Based Book

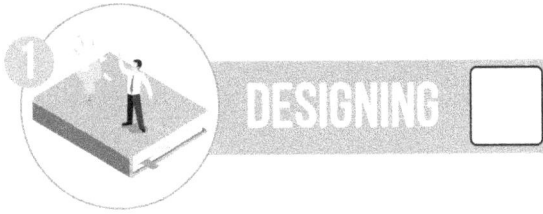

1. Designing Your Book

Before jumping into the process, brainstorm all the benefits of what a book can do for you. How will it enhance your life? What will it do for others? You need to lay the groundwork before you can start getting your book written.

In this stage, you'll answer questions like:

- Deciding the type of book you should write: legacy-oriented or logic-oriented
- Setting expectations for what you want your book to accomplish for you
- Basing your book around a blueprint or framework
- Defining the customer journey
- Determining how to tell your story
- Creating a good title and subtitle
- Creating an awesome cover for your book (and how to avoid creating a bad one)
- Learning how to write a real and effective bio

2. Creating Your Book

It's time to set out on your journey to create your book. This is the step which will take the longest to complete, and while it is important, it is not the most important step in the process. That comes after Publishing. Nonetheless, you should dedicate your full attention to this process, because this is the best time to change things.

Before you get going, let's take a look at everything you'll accomplish in this step:

- Setting expectations
- Determining the number of pages your book should be
- Deciding how many images you should have
- Deciding whether to print in colour or black and white
- Including a glossary
- Pinning down what to write about

- 🎤 Creating chapter outlines and planning
- 🎤 Creating content rapidly
- 🎤 Figuring out the actual content
- 🎤 Drafting and editing

Work with professional editors and designers to ensure your book is polished and well-formatted. This includes editing for grammar, style, and making sure your writing is appropriate for your audience. It's a good idea to finalize your book's content to the best of your ability, because it will be much harder (and more expensive) to make changes once you enter the Publishing stage.

3. Publishing Your Book

You have several options available to you, as an author, when getting your book published. Your choice will depend primarily on whether you are willing to sell the rights to your book—primarily your copyright. If you don't wish to sell your rights, you can self-publish, or enlist the help of a hybrid publisher who will help you publish the book for a fee. Self-publishers can publish their books on sites like Amazon and Smashwords.

If you are willing to sell your rights, and can convince a publisher to do so, you can contact a traditional publisher. Traditional publishers are notoriously picky on which authors they will publish, and they may want to alter the content of your book. It also takes a long time (usually longer than 12 months) for the traditional publisher to finally publish the book, even after finalizing the contract. Additionally, the publisher may take your book off stores if it doesn't sell as well as they hope.

If you are chasing a traditional publisher, you should do it for the money, because you lose a lot of control over the book in the transaction.

Before you can get your book published, however, there's still some work to do if you're choosing self-publishing or a hybrid publisher. You need a polished, nicely-designed interior for print and digital editions. If you're self-publishing, you'll need to work with designers directly to transfer your manuscript into these interiors. You'll also need to get various versions of your book cover done to satisfy the demands of both print and digital.

A hybrid publisher will deal with these parties on your behalf, while also getting your input to the designers. Which option you choose depends on whether you want maximum control or minimum fuss.

4. Promoting Your Book

This is the most important step in the process, but many authors spend minimal time on promoting their book, if any at all. This is an ongoing process you need to dedicate energy to in terms of months, not weeks.

How can your readers know about your book if you don't make it known? It's time to get your marketing hat on and start working on getting your message out to your market.

Here are some things you should consider doing throughout this stage:

- 🎙 Creating a best seller campaign
- 🎙 Generating Leads
- 🎙 Getting Reviews
- 🎙 Harnessing Social media
- 🎙 Creating an author website
- 🎙 Creating a book marketing plan

Leverage your podcast platform, social media channels, email marketing, and collaborations with other content creators to promote your book. Offer exclusive content or promotions to entice your podcast listeners and new readers to purchase your book.

5. Evolving Your Book

One of the most common questions we get asked by authors is: "What's next?"

Writing your book is the beginning, not the end. It's the start of your journey as an author to convince your audience of your credibility and what you can offer them.

Your book is one of the foundations for your business. Once it's published, there are numerous ways to leverage it.

A lot of authors will think that once they have published their book, they can relax, forget about it, and move onto the next project on their "to-do" list.

But now is the time to get moving!

You need to promote the book until you are sick of hearing about it. At that point, you may think that you have done enough, but the reality is virtually no one knows about it.

This stage is about:

- 🎤 Going from being an author to being an authority
- 🎤 How you can expand from your book
- 🎤 The bookselling system
- 🎤 The "Dream Sell 100"

This stage is about revealing the secrets to the next stage of your book journey. This is where the real money is made, and more often than not, it is criminally overlooked and under-appreciated by most authors.

Turning your podcast into a book is a powerful way to repurpose your content, reach a broader audience, and create new opportunities for monetization and professional growth. By carefully selecting and adapting your podcast content, enhancing it with additional insights and visual elements, and navigating the publishing process, you can successfully transform your podcast into a valuable resource for your audience.

Embrace the challenge of crafting a book that captures the essence of your podcast while providing readers with a unique and engaging experience. With a strategic approach, dedication, and effective promotion, your podcast-based book can help you establish your expertise, grow your brand, and open doors to new opportunities in your niche.

Check out our book, *Book Publishing Secrets for Entrepreneurs*, for all of our book-related advice, available from *www.evolveinstantauthor.com*

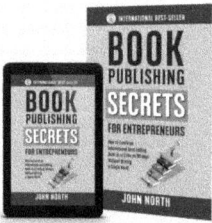

BOOK PUBLISHING SECRETS FOR ENTREPRENEURS: HOW TO CREATE AN INTERNATIONAL BEST-SELLING BOOK IN AS LITTLE AS 90 DAYS WITHOUT WRITING A SINGLE WORD!

194 Pages / $14.95 / 978-1979285773 / Paperback / eBook / Hardcover

Available from: https://getmybook.store/s/publish

Having a published book is one of the most powerful ways to gain authority in your industry. It's the ultimate marketing strategy that sells itself!

And with these 5 Book Publishing Secrets, getting your book written, published, and into the hands of as many people as possible has never been easier!

We speak to many entrepreneurs every day, and this question eventually comes up…"What's the fastest and easiest way to boost my marketing and get more customers?"

Almost without exception, we say, "a book! "You can base your book around your business or use it to start a whole new business. The great thing about writing a book is that it not only ensures that you get crystal clear on what you do, but also how you do it.

Check out www.evolveglobalpublishing.com for more information.

CHAPTER 51

RECRUITING JOINT VENTURE PARTNERS

"Alone we can do so little; together we can do so much." – **Helen Keller**

Joint venture (JV) partners are a great way to significantly grow and expand your business. By forming strategic partnerships, you can leverage the strengths and resources of your partners to achieve common goals. This chapter will guide you through identifying and recruiting the right JV partners, and provide strategies to ensure a successful partnership.

Identifying Potential JV Partners

The first step in recruiting JV partners is identifying businesses or individuals that complement your own. Consider the following factors when evaluating potential partners:

- **Synergy:** Look for partners with a similar target audience, complementary products or services, and share the same values and goals.

- **Expertise:** Choose partners who can bring unique skills, knowledge, or resources to the table that your business may lack.

- **Reputation:** Partner with businesses or individuals with a strong, positive reputation in their industry, as this will boost the credibility of your joint venture.

- **Commitment:** Your partner should be ready to commit to this relationship at the same level you are. A partnership only works if every partner is excited about what they can do together and willing to put in the work.

Building Relationships

Before approaching potential JV partners, it's essential to establish a connection and build a relationship. This can be done through the following:

- **Networking:** Attend industry events, conferences, and workshops where you can meet potential partners and begin building rapport. Use the tips in the previous sections to determine who would make a good JV partner.

- **Online interactions:** Engage with potential partners on social media, comment on their blog posts, or share their content to show your interest and appreciation for their work. Contact business people you think would be receptive to working together through the contact methods they list on their website.

- **Personal introductions:** Leverage your existing network to get introduced to potential partners who may be interested in a joint venture. You could join a group of business people interested in the same topic you are and ask them if they or someone they know would want to work together.

Crafting Your JV Proposal

When approaching potential JV partners, you'll need to present a compelling proposal outlining the partnership's benefits and objectives. Your proposal should include the following:

- A clear explanation of your business and its strengths, goals, and objectives of the joint venture
- The specific roles and responsibilities of each partner
- The resources and expertise of each partner will contribute
- A detailed plan of action and timeline for the joint venture
- The expected outcomes and benefits for both parties

Negotiating the Partnership

Once you've presented your JV proposal, be prepared to negotiate the terms and conditions of the partnership. This may involve discussing:

- **Profit sharing:** Agree on how profits will be divided between partners and ensure the **arrangement is fair and mutually beneficial.**
- **Decision-making:** Establish a clear decision-making process and determine how conflicts or disagreements will be resolved.
- **Intellectual property:** Discuss the ownership of any intellectual property created during the joint venture and ensure that each partner's rights are protected.
- **Exit strategy:** Outline the circumstances under which the partnership can be terminated and the process for dissolving the joint venture.

Nurturing Your Partnership

A successful JV partnership requires ongoing communication, collaboration, and trust. To maintain a strong relationship with your JV partner:

- **Set regular check-ins:** Schedule meetings or calls to discuss progress, challenges, and opportunities, and ensure that both parties are aligned and working toward the same goals.
- **Foster open communication:** Encourage transparency and open dialogue to address any issues or concerns as they arise. Issues should be resolved before they have time to fester and result in bitterness.
- **Celebrate successes:** Acknowledge and celebrate your joint venture's accomplishments to reinforce the partnership's value and maintain motivation.
- **Be adaptable:** Be prepared to adjust your plans and strategies as needed to accommodate changes in the market, industry, or partner circumstances.

Recruiting joint venture partners can be a powerful way to grow your business and achieve your goals. By carefully selecting partners, building relationships, and fostering a collaborative partnership, you can create a joint venture that benefits both parties significantly. Remember that nurturing and maintaining the partnership is key to ensuring long-term success and mutual growth.

CHAPTER 52

HASHTAG FOR YOUR PODCAST: BOOSTING VISIBILITY AND FOSTERING ENGAGEMENT

"Content is fire; social media is gasoline." – **Jay Baer**

Want to make your podcast easier to discover and spark more conversations around it?

A simple hashtag can do wonders! Adding a hashtag to your podcast's social media strategy not only boosts visibility but helps build a community that talks about your show, even when you're offline.

In this chapter, we'll dive into the power of creating a unique and relevant hashtag, tips for promoting it, and ways to encourage listeners to get involved. With the right hashtag, you'll turn your podcast into a social media magnet that keeps listeners engaged and new fans tuning in! A hashtag is a keyword or phrase preceded by the "#" symbol, used on social media platforms to categorize and group content.

But why should you use a hashtag. Well, there are a lot of reasons:

- **It helps with discovery.** When people search for relevant hashtags on social media, your posts showing that hashtag will appear. This can help new listeners discover your podcast.

- **It helps you build a community around your show.** Listeners can use your podcast hashtag when discussing your show. This can help you build a community that wants to discuss your podcast on social media without you having to prime them with a post yourself.

- **It makes your posts more searchable.** Social media platforms index posts with hashtags, making those posts more discoverable through search. This can help more people find your posts about your podcast.

- **It can be used for marketing.** You can promote your podcast hashtag in your show notes, website, and other marketing materials. Encouraging listeners to use it can help spread the **word about your podcast.**

- **It provides analytics.** Some social platforms provide insights into how popular different hashtags are. You can see how effective your podcast hashtag is at reaching an audience.

Here are some tips and strategies for creating and using an effective hashtag for your podcast.

Choose a Unique and Relevant Hashtag

- 🎙 **Branding:** Ensure that your hashtag aligns with your podcast's brand, making it easy for your audience to associate it with your show. You can use the name of your podcast or a recognizable abbreviation as the basis for your hashtag.

- 🎙 **Simplicity:** Keep your hashtag simple and easy to spell and remember. Avoid using overly long or complicated words, and avoid special characters or numbers that may confuse others.

- 🎙 **Relevance:** Your hashtag should be relevant to your podcast's theme, subject matter, and target audience. This will make it more likely that users searching for content related to your podcast's niche will discover your hashtag and, subsequently, your show.

Promote and Use Your Hashtag Consistently

- 🎙 **Incorporate in Social Media Bios:** Include your podcast's hashtag in your social media profiles and bios, making it easy for your audience to find and use the hashtag when engaging with your content.

- 🎙 **Use in Social Media Posts:** Consistently use your podcast's hashtag in your social media posts, encouraging your followers to adopt and share the hashtag. This can help to increase visibility and create a sense of community among your listeners.

- 🎙 **Engage with Your Hashtag:** Monitor and engage with posts that use your podcast's hashtag. Respond to comments, like or share relevant content, and thank your listeners for their support. This helps to foster a sense of community and encourages more users to use your hashtag.

Encourage Listener Participation

Here are a few ideas for how you can leverage the hashtag to get listeners participating in discussion on social media:

- 🎙 **Call-to-Action:** Use call-to-action (CTA) prompts in your podcast episodes, social media posts, and email marketing to encourage your listeners to use your hashtag when sharing their thoughts, questions, or feedback about your show.

- 🎙 **Host Contests or Giveaways:** Organize social media contests or giveaways that require participants to use your podcast's hashtag as part of their entry. This can help to increase engagement and generate buzz around your show.

- 🎙 **Feature Listener Content:** Share or feature listener-generated content that uses your podcast's hashtag. This can include fan art, testimonials, or questions submitted via social media—whatever makes sense for your show! By showcasing your listeners' content, you can encourage more users to engage with your hashtag and feel connected to your podcast community.

With the right hashtag, your podcast can reach new audiences, foster community, and keep the conversation going long after each episode airs. By promoting your hashtag consistently and encouraging listeners to use it, you're giving your audience a simple way to connect with your show—and each other. Remember, a strong hashtag is more than just a symbol; it's a way to bring your podcast brand to life on social media.

So get out there, spark conversations, and watch your hashtag help your podcast grow and thrive!

The Future of Podcasting

To help you implement the strategies outlined in Podcasting Secrets for Entrepreneurs, we've put together a comprehensive Podcast Secrets Resource Kit, which is available for free.

This kit contains tools, templates, and guides to streamline your podcasting process, from the initial planning stages to audience growth and monetization.

https://podcastsecrets.biz/s/kit

CHAPTER 53

EMERGING TRENDS AND OPPORTUNITIES

The only limit to our realisation of tomorrow is our doubts of today." – **Franklin D. Roosevelt**

Just when you thought you'd mastered podcasting, new trends keep popping up, bringing fresh challenges—and plenty of opportunities.

From video podcasts to AI-driven content creation, the podcasting world is evolving faster than ever. In this chapter, we're diving into the latest developments shaping the industry and how you can leverage them to grow your audience, improve your content, and maybe even add a few revenue streams.

So, buckle up—podcasting in the future is going to be a wild (and rewarding) ride!

Exploring Podcasting Trends

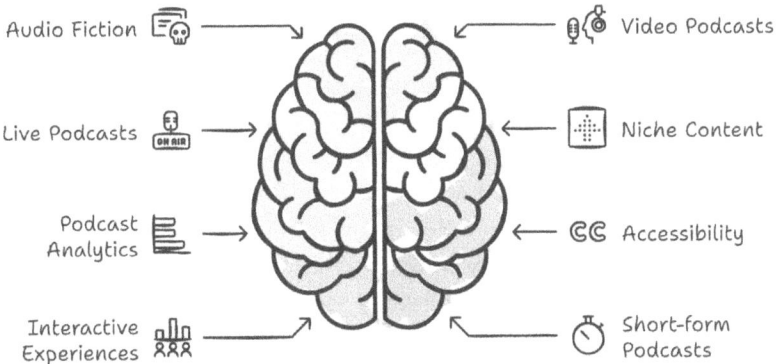

Here are some of the trends the podcasting field has experienced over the years:

- 🎙 **Audio Fiction:** Audio Fiction, comprising scripted audio dramas or narrative podcasts, has gained significant traction recently. This trend presents opportunities for writers, producers, and voice actors to create original, immersive content that captivates listeners and offers a unique storytelling experience. Audio fiction appeals to an audience who wouldn't normally listen to podcasts by offering something unique. They differ from audiobooks in that Audio Fiction is serialized.

- 🎙 **Video podcasts:** The growing popularity of video podcasts present an opportunity for podcasters to reach a wider audience through visual storytelling. Video podcasts enable monetization through video ads, sponsorships, and platforms like YouTube, broadening your podcast's revenue streams. We explain the benefits of and how to get into video podcasting in the The Power of Video Podcasting chapter.

- 🎙 **Live podcasts:** Live podcasts, recorded and streamed in real time, allow for more immediate and interactive audience engagement. Hosting live events, Q&A sessions, or interviews can foster a stronger connection with your listeners and create unique, shareable content.

- 🎙 **Niche content and communities:** As the podcasting space becomes increasingly crowded, carving out a niche and building a dedicated community around specific topics or interests can help set your podcast apart. Focusing on unique content and engaging with your community can lead to a smaller audience of more loyal listeners.

- 🎙 **Podcast analytics and data-driven strategies:** Leveraging podcast analytics to understand your audience's behavior, preferences, and demographics can help you make data-driven decisions to improve your content, marketing strategies, and monetization efforts.

- 🎙 **Podcast accessibility:** Ensuring your podcast is accessible to a diverse range of listeners, including those with disabilities, is increasingly important. Integrating features such as transcripts, captions, and accessible web design can help you reach a broader audience and demonstrate your commitment to inclusivity. You can also make your podcast accessible to people in other languages by using a machine translation service like Google Translate or DeepL.

- 🎙 **Interactive podcast experiences:** Incorporating interactive elements into your podcast, such as listener polls, live chats, or user-generated content, can foster audience engagement and create a more dynamic listening experience.

- 🎙 **Podcasts for kids and families:** There is a growing demand for kid-friendly and family-oriented podcasts, offering opportunities for podcasters to create content that appeals to younger listeners and their parents.

- 🎙 **Short-form podcasts:** As listeners' attention spans become shorter, there is a growing interest in short-form podcasts that deliver valuable content in a concise format. Creating bite-sized episodes that can be consumed quickly during commutes, breaks, or between tasks can help you cater to this audience segment.

- 🎙 **Virtual and augmented reality podcasts:** With the advancement of virtual and augmented reality technologies, there are opportunities for podcasters to create immersive, interactive experiences that blend audio storytelling with visual and sensory elements.

- 🎙 **Profitable Podcasting:** Podcasting has traditionally been crowded with indie podcasters who work on their podcast as something of a hobby or way of meeting new and interesting people; not necessarily as a business. However, as podcasting gets bigger, podcasters have started looking for ways to profit from podcasting. Whether that be by taking on sponsors, attempting to get their audience to fund them, or by interviewing guests who might be interested in your products and services, as we cover in Guest Interviews For Profitable Podcasting, podcasting is more viable as a business venture than ever before.

Ask yourself what trend serves as an interesting opportunity for your podcast. How can you grow your audience, improve your content, and monetize your podcast? Your listeners don't listen to podcasts the same way they did ten years ago, so why should you make podcasts the same way ten years later?

What about artificial intelligence (AI) and other cutting-edge technologies?

AI Applications in Podcasting

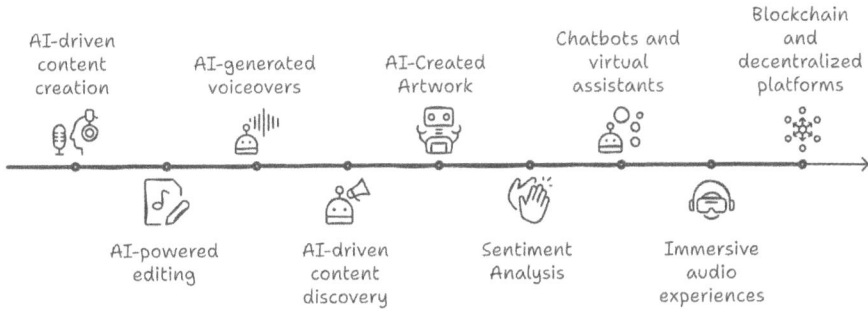

AI-driven content creation	AI-generated voiceovers	AI-Created Artwork	Chatbots and virtual assistants	Blockchain and decentralized platforms

AI-powered editing	AI-driven content discovery	Sentiment Analysis	Immersive audio experiences

Artificial Intelligence has been worked on for decades, and we've used some of these services for years, like machine translation tools such as Google Translate. However, in recent years, machine learning models have gotten good at many more tasks. Once an interesting novelty, many artisans are suddenly concerned about their job security.

Whether it's writing programs, creating artwork, or professional transcription, there are now commercial models out there which can conceivably perform tasks with an acceptable level of quality more quickly than a human can. Some tools can even replace humans altogether, depending on your needs. Of course, these tools are far from perfect and often need a professional in the field to fix the output, but they can certainly save time for professionals.

Professional translators have used machine translation tools as a base to get some output on the page before doing another pass to fix it up for years; this technology is simply becoming available to people in more diverse fields. One of those fields is podcasting. There are other cutting-edge technologies you can leverage, too, but AI tools make the biggest difference.

Here are some examples of this technology and how you can use it in your podcast:

- **AI-driven content creation:** AI can assist in generating ideas, scripts, or even entire episodes of podcasts. As natural language processing (NLP) technology advances, AI can help create more engaging and relevant content tailored to your audience's preferences. Google's Bard and OpenAI's Chat-GPT are examples of Large Language Models (LLMs) the general public can use for this type of content creation using another company's servers. In the near future, there will likely be models users and businesses can host on their own servers and use internally, like Together's Red Pajama project.

- **AI-powered editing:** AI-based tools can streamline the editing process by automatically transcribing your podcast, identifying and removing unwanted sounds or silence, and enhancing the overall audio quality. This can save time and help produce a more polished podcast. Take Adobe Podcast, a service which allows you to enhance the quality of your audio to make it sound as if it was recorded in a professional studio, as opposed to your wardrobe.

- 🎙 **AI-generated voiceovers:** Text-to-speech AI solutions can generate realistic voiceovers, which can be helpful for podcasters who need to create diverse character voices for audio dramas, narrate content in multiple languages, or provide accessibility options for visually impaired listeners. Google is ahead of everyone else in this regard currently, but smaller companies are catching up.

- 🎙 **AI-driven content discovery and recommendations:** AI-powered algorithms can help users discover podcasts that match their interests by analyzing their listening habits, preferences, and demographics. This can lead to more accurate and personalized podcast recommendations, ultimately driving more listeners to your podcast.

- 🎙 **AI-Created Artwork:** You can use AI models like DALL-E or Stable Diffusion to generate artwork for your podcast show. For example, you could generate a cover for your podcast, or for each individual episode. There is some confusion currently regarding copyright for the generated images. In the US, some say any images generated with an AI model are available to the user who generated the image with a prompt under the public domain. However, Getty is attempting to sue Stability AI because it scraped its content and used that content to train its models without permission. This legal case is still ongoing at the time of writing.

- 🎙 **Sentiment Analysis:** AI-powered sentiment analysis tools can help podcasters gain insights into how their audience perceives their content. These tools can identify trends, patterns, and audience sentiment by analysing comments, reviews, and social media interactions, providing valuable feedback for podcasters to refine their content and strategy.

- 🎙 **Chatbots and virtual assistants:** AI-powered chatbots and virtual assistants are a powerful service podcasters can integrate with their websites to provide users a fast way to learn about your podcast and relevant services.

- 🎙 **Immersive audio experiences:** Integrating spatial audio or 3D audio technology can create more immersive and realistic listening experiences, making your podcast stand out and providing a unique value proposition for your audience.

- 🎙 **Blockchain and decentralized platforms:** Emerging blockchain-based podcast platforms can offer podcasters new monetization opportunities, such as funding with cryptocurrency and decentralized ad networks, providing more control and revenue options for podcast creators

Podcasting is no longer just about hitting record and sharing stories; it's about staying adaptable, experimenting with new ideas, and embracing the ever-changing landscape.

Whether it's leveraging AI to streamline your workflow, creating immersive audio experiences, or tapping into niche communities, each trend offers a unique opportunity to stand out and connect with your audience in new ways.

Keep exploring, keep evolving, and remember: the most successful podcasters are those who aren't afraid to try something new.

The future of podcasting is here—time to make it yours!

CHAPTER 54

THE FUTURE OF SOCIAL MEDIA

"Social media is about sociology and psychology more than technology." – **Brian Solis**

Social media has transformed how we connect, share, and grow our businesses—but where is it headed next?

With new platforms, AI-driven algorithms, and changing user behaviors, the landscape is constantly evolving. In this chapter, we'll explore emerging trends, potential game-changers, and how entrepreneurs can stay ahead of the curve.

From virtual reality spaces to hyper-personalized content, the future of social media promises endless opportunities. Get ready to dive into what's next and discover how to make social media work for you in a world that never stops scrolling.

What is the future of social media platforms?

Well, we have no idea!

But let's think about history and make some educated guesses.

Relying on social media for business

Pros	Cons
Large audience reach	Data privacy concerns
Cost-effective marketing	Platform dependency
Direct customer engagement	Risk of account bans
Trend visibility	Negative reviews impact
Easy content sharing	Constant algorithm changes

The rise of Big Tech and the detailed tracking of humans over the past 15 years have started to backfire on these corporations. In the documentary Social Dilemma, they say the only two products that refer to their customers as "users" are software and drugs.

The "users" are starting to wake up. The current generation of kids refers to Facebook as a platform for old people. New platforms are always emerging, and many of those are talking about preserving the privacy of their users.

It's entirely possible people will move to a subscription-based social media experience— sort of like Netflix for Facebook.

LinkedIn already offers upgrades for a deeper use of their platform, for example. After all, your data is valuable, and what you might do in the future is even more valuable to an advertiser. Perhaps there will be an AA for social media in the coming years where people must learn how to get off these platforms.

To respond to growing anger amongst their users, these platforms are likely to go through many changes and may very well hurt the entrepreneurs who rely on it for the survival of their businesses.

In this ever-changing landscape lies massive opportunity. The reality is that these platforms come and go just like governments do. Does the name "MySpace" ring a bell?

But these new corporations have massive wealth behind them. They can pivot into other investment options. Like Google with self-driving cars, Amazon with its space program, and Facebook with virtual reality.

So, let's not try to predict the future; rather, let's design our own.

Many of these social media platforms have attracted young entrepreneurs, especially by allowing them not to worry about building and managing a website. There is a cafe down the road from us which only has a Facebook page, and that's the extent of their online presence.

These entrepreneurs are sold on the basis that "you should go where your customers are". The danger here is that, if they get too many bad reviews, they could easily be banned or locked out with no recourse. What happens if these platforms no longer allow you to go where your customers are?

You want to focus on building a platform where you can attract prospective customers and keep them on your website, not being distracted by the latest shiny object from all manner of other companies on their social media feed.

If you have their email address, you have the one thing these platforms never want to give you and now you probably see why!

With Evolvepreneur.app, we can create multiple front-end websites that all lead to a back-end community site that also helps your customer track their downloads, and orders, and engage in your educational and marketing materials.

At the same time, you can start a podcast or on-demand show that your prospects and customers can subscribe to and get alerted when new content comes out.

Make sure you own your own stuff and tread your own path. Use social media as a tool, not a platform.

🎤 Scripts

To help you implement the strategies outlined in Podcasting Secrets for Entrepreneurs, we've put together a comprehensive Podcast Secrets Resource Kit, which is available for free.

This kit contains tools, templates, and guides to streamline your podcasting process, from the initial planning stages to audience growth and monetization.

https://podcastsecrets.biz/s/kit

CHAPTER 55

PODCAST INTERVIEW SCRIPTS

"Give me six hours to chop down a tree and I will spend the first four sharpening the axe."
– Abraham Lincoln

A n engaging interview doesn't just happen by accident—it's crafted with the right questions, a structured flow, and a warm connection with your guest.

This script is designed to guide you through a seamless interview process, from pre-interview chats to a polished promo video.

By breaking the interview into separate recordings, you make post-production easier and create content that both you and your guest can share. Ready to capture compelling stories, deep insights, and memorable moments? Let's dive into the steps to make each interview a conversation that resonates.

We recommend splitting up your interview into 4 separate recordings to make post-production easier. START and STOP each recording when each section begins and ends:

Enhancing Podcasting Experience

Clever Questions

Asking for Reviews

· LIVE

Interview Ideas

Promo Video

Guest Warm-Up

1. Recording - initial pre-interview discussions
2. Recording - the complete raw interview
3. Recording Promo
4. Recording - the closing stage where there may have been offers discussed.

Ask For Reviews:

In your initial show opening, try to include a line like:

"If you like the show, we would really appreciate a 5 star review, and let your friends know as well."

Promo Video:

We have found a promo video to be very useful in marketing the episode, and recommend you do it at the end of the interview.

Tell the guest in the pre-interview that you will ask them to do a 30-second summary of the interview at the end. Then ask them after the interview (prior to the close step).

Say something like:

To tell the audience what we talked about...As long as this is a separate recording, we can use the video and give it to the guest for them to promote the show.

Start recording and say "[guest name] thanks for being on the show tell me why our audience should tune in"

The guest then says: "My Name is _____, and I was just on the Evolvepreneur After Hours Show with HOST, and you should watch it because we talked about _____"

GUEST WARMUP:

The interview will run about 30 minutes.

We want our audience to understand how to get from your current situation to the future, I would like to ask for details about your business and how you overcame and got through certain challenges. Are you okay if I ask you some tough and specific questions about revenue and metrics?

We ask this so my audience can get a deeper understanding of what level you are at and help them in their own situation. Tell them at the end of the interview. You will give them an opportunity to do some "shameless promotion" so we can focus on the interview first.

Interview ideas:

Ask for 3 accolades or sentences to give them a meaningful introduction to make them look as awesome as possible. The more heartfelt and unique we can make these introductions, the more trust can be immediately built in the process.

The best interviews are when the interviewer listens and asks about what intrigues them. Often if you're curious about something, it's because you have something to add to the conversation. This gives you a chance to lead with vulnerability.

Vulnerable conversations are often heavily connected emotionally. The best way to get someone to be vulnerable, is to lead with vulnerability. As a leader on the podcast, you'll want to practice this frequently... and just watch the magic unfold as you do so. — The more emotions you can get people to feel, the more likely they are to buy. Sadness, happiness, anger, resentment, longing, humour, what frustrates you about your business or the industry?

Implement the Pull podcast close frameworks and bring the conversation around to topics where you can add to the conversation with stories, results or insights into how your company helps your prospects.

Clever Podcast Interview Questions:

- 🎤 What did your parents do for a living?
- 🎤 In your own words, what does the phrase [insert phrase related to your guest's niche] mean to you?
- 🎤 What are you not very good at?
- 🎤 What's your favourite book, and why?
- 🎤 Who would you like to play you in a movie?
- 🎤 What does your morning routine look like?
- 🎤 What makes you feel inspired or motivated?
- 🎤 What's one thing that people are generally surprised to find out about you?
- 🎤 If you were going to live on a desert island but could only take one thing with you, what would it be?
- 🎤 What keeps you up at night?
- 🎤 What's your biggest fear?
- 🎤 Tell me something you think is true that almost nobody agrees with you on?
- 🎤 If you could have dinner with any 3 people dead or alive, who would it be and why?
- 🎤 Who do you look up to the most?
- 🎤 What was the last thing you Googled?
- 🎤 If you could turn back the time and talk to your 18-year old self, what would you tell him/her?
- 🎤 What was your first job?
- 🎤 What one piece of advice would you give to someone just starting out as a [insert your guest's job role]?
- 🎤 How would your parents describe what you do?
- 🎤 What's been the most memorable moment of your career so far?
- 🎤 If you could give one piece of advice to your previous boss, what would it be?
- 🎤 What do you hope the world will look like in 10 years?
- 🎤 Would you rather have more time or more money?
- 🎤 Have you had your "I've made it" moment yet?
- 🎤 What are you looking forward to in the future - personally, or professionally?
- 🎤 How do you want to be remembered?
- 🎤 What should I have asked you but didn't?

With a thoughtful approach, engaging questions, and a touch of curiosity, your interviews can become the highlight of each episode, bringing listeners back for more.

This script doesn't just give you structure—it helps you create an experience for your guest and your audience, sparking genuine conversation and lasting connections.

So prep those questions, hit record, and watch as your interviews transform from simple Q&As to memorable stories that leave an impact.

Here's to interviews that feel natural, flow smoothly, and make every guest look (and feel) like a star!

CHAPTER 56

SAMPLE EPISODE SCRIPT

"In every job that must be done, there is an element of fun." – **Mary Poppins**

This structured show script is designed to create a seamless and engaging experience for both listeners and guests, providing a solid framework that guides each episode from the opening through to the interview.

By following this outline, hosts can maintain a dynamic, professional flow that highlights the guest's expertise, offers actionable insights for entrepreneurs, and keeps the conversation both relevant and inspiring.

Each section of the script helps you introduce the show, set clear expectations, and dive into thought-provoking discussions with guests. The questions included are crafted to uncover your guest's journey, insights, and advice, allowing listeners to walk away with practical takeaways that align with the show's mission and build a stronger connection with the host, guest, and audience.

Show Intro

"Welcome to the [SHOW NAME] Show! I'm your host, [YOUR NAME]. Here, our mission is to help entrepreneurs make a real impact and navigate the often unpredictable world of startups and pivots. Each week, we bring you in-depth conversations with inspiring guests who share insights, strategies, and stories that can fast-track your business journey.

Today's guest is [Guest Name], who is… [Brief Introduction of the Guest's Background and Expertise]. We're thrilled to have them here to share their experiences and expertise with us."

Interview Questions

1. Starting the Conversation
- 🎙 What first inspired you to get into [their field or industry]?
- 🎙 What do you find most fulfilling about the work you do?

2. Exploring Their Journey
- 🎙 Can you tell us about one of the biggest turning points in your career?
- 🎙 What's been a pivotal challenge you've faced, and how did you overcome it?

3. Insights and Advice for Listeners
- 🎙 What's the best piece of advice you've ever received—and how has it shaped your career?

🎙️ What advice would you give to someone just starting out in [their industry]?

4. Connecting with Their Clients

🎙️ How do your ideal clients typically find you, and what makes them want to work with you?

🎙️ Who would you say is your ideal client, and why do you enjoy working with them?

5. Business Growth and Goals

🎙️ What's currently working well for you in attracting new business?

🎙️ Looking forward, what's your main revenue goal for the next 12 months?

6. Challenges and Roadblocks

🎙️ What's the biggest roadblock currently standing between you and your next big goal?

🎙️ If you could overcome that challenge, what impact would it have on your business?

7. Personal Impact and Broader Vision

🎙️ In what ways would achieving this goal change other areas of your life?

🎙️ What legacy do you hope to build through your work?

Show Wrap-Up

"Thank you so much, [Guest Name], for joining us today and sharing your incredible journey and insights. It's been inspiring to learn from your experiences and hear your advice.

To our listeners, if you enjoyed this episode, we'd be grateful for a 5-star review! Share the episode with friends who might benefit from these insights, and make sure to subscribe for more practical takeaways from successful entrepreneurs.

Remember, success in entrepreneurship often starts with that first step toward your vision—so go make it happen. Until next time, stay inspired, and keep pushing forward!"

About The Show—An Example

Evolvepreneur (After Hours) Show features guest stories about entrepreneurs and their journeys from startup, growth to success. If you're looking to succeed with quick start concepts for online entrepreneurs, this brand new show reveals how startup entrepreneurs or someone looking to start, grow or reboot their online business can understand how to create specific strategies to build their list, make offers and connect with their best buyers.

We want to help entrepreneurs make a real difference and navigate the messy world of startup or re-launch.

Also, visit *https://evolvepreneur.app/podcast/show* to grab your free copy of #1 International Best Selling Book *"Evolvepreneur Secrets for Entrepreneurs".* Subscribe and get immediate access!

Want to be a guest on the show?

Apply here: https://evolvepreneur.app/page/guestapplication

Sponsored by Evolvepreneur.app—"Your All In One Business System"

CHAPTER 57

PODCAST EPISODE: CLOSE SCRIPT

"Every exit is an entry somewhere else." – **Tom Stoppard**

A strong closing script doesn't just wrap up the episode—it leaves a lasting impression, motivates your listeners to take action, and reinforces your show's brand.

Here's a sample script for the final section of your episodes, along with tips to make your closing even more effective:

Well, that's a wrap on another awesome guest episode for the Evolvepreneur Secrets for Entrepreneurs Show

Just Before you go...

If you liked this episode we would be very grateful for a 5 star review!

Please also consider recommending the show to a friend or two!

Make sure you subscribe for future episodes at evolvepreneursecrets.show right now.

Until next time and if you an entrepreneur make a start on your next great idea today!

Tips for an Effective Show Wrap-Up

1. Encourage Reviews and Shares Naturally

Instead of a generic call to action, make it feel like a personal request. Mention how reviews help others find the show and build community support, or even call out a few recent reviewers by name in the episode to make the request more personable. Reviews and shares are vital for growth, and a personal touch makes listeners feel valued.

2. Motivate Listeners with a Sense of Purpose

Use the closing to empower listeners, encouraging them to apply what they learned and take the next step in their journey. Simple lines like, "Start with one idea you learned today" or "Keep moving forward—your success story is just getting started!" remind listeners that they're part of a journey alongside your show.

3. Highlight Upcoming Episodes

Tease upcoming guests or topics that your audience will want to hear. Mention something like, "Next week, we'll be talking with [Exciting Guest or Topic], so make sure you're subscribed," to build anticipation and encourage regular listening.

4. Provide a Clear Path to Subscribe

Link directly to your show's main website or subscription page. Encourage listeners to subscribe to avoid missing out on future episodes. This action is especially helpful for those who might be tuning in for the first time and aren't yet regular listeners.

5. Include a Special Offer or Bonus Content

If you have a free resource, exclusive PDF, or mini-ebook related to the episode's topic, mention it here. Direct them to download it from your website, and you'll increase engagement and email subscribers, creating a stronger connection with your audience.

6. Invite Listener Feedback and Engagement

Ask listeners to leave questions, comments, or topic ideas for future episodes. This keeps the audience engaged and allows you to shape future content based on real feedback. Encourage them to reach out via social media or a dedicated email. For example, "Got a question or topic idea? Drop us a line on [Your Social Platform or Email]!"

7. Add a Friendly Sign-Off to Make It Memorable

Find a unique phrase or friendly sign-off that fits your podcast's personality. Whether it's a simple "Catch you next time!" or something more quirky like, "Until then, keep those big dreams alive," a memorable sign-off adds warmth and familiarity to your show's brand.

A strong closing isn't just about wrapping up—it's about building loyalty, engagement, and anticipation for what's next. By combining these strategies, you'll leave listeners with the feeling that they're part of something valuable and impactful.

So get creative, show gratitude, and finish each episode with an open invitation for listeners to join you on this journey.

CHAPTER 58

JOINT VENTURE IDEA SCRIPT

"Great things in business are never done by one person; they're done by a team of people." – **Steve Jobs**

This script is designed for guests open to a collaborative venture, where they offer the podcast interview to their audience and, in exchange, earn a commission on any resulting sales.

Our aim with this partnership is simple: to invite your audience to participate in our top 200 podcast, offering a unique, high-value experience that benefits everyone involved.

The guest gains exposure and credibility; the audience gets an insightful episode on growing an online business; and we, as hosts, get to connect with influential entrepreneurs who might just need our support to elevate their businesses.

Our goal with the partnership is to invite your audience to interview on one of our podcasts. Our podcast interviews are considered a triple-win.

1. *The guest wins, as they get exposure and credibility on a top 200 podcast.*

2. *The audience wins, as they get an amazing episode breaking down the challenges of growing an online business.*

3. *We win as hosts, as we get introduced to an amazing guest who may need our help in growing their business using a podcast.*

Your goal is to invite dream prospects to be interviewed on our podcast simply. We do the rest.

This isn't a conventional partnership or Joint Venture.

This partnership will involve only two things:

You'll need to email your list over 3 days (a total of 5 pre-written emails).

You'll be inviting people on your email list to be interviewed on one of our shows. That's it!

We're looking for 5 Micro-Influencer Joint Venture Partners to Collaborate With Us For Our Podcast.

Requirements:

🎤 *Have an email list or FB Group of over 1,000 people.*

🎤 *Have an audience of entrepreneurs, coaches, consultants and authors*

🎤 *Have an audience who'd be interested in using a podcast to grow their business or looking to take their online business to the next level*

We are looking to interview 6 & 7-figure entrepreneurs, coaches, consultants and authors about the challenges of being an online entrepreneur and starting or growing their business in a low-pressure conversational interview as well as a possible recession and what your worries and concerns are.

Affiliate a fee equal to 3% (Publishing Services) 5% (Ep.app) of the prevailing end-user price (once-off) of the Evolvepreneur.app products for each Converted Sale.

To help you implement the strategies outlined in Podcasting Secrets for Entrepreneurs, we've put together a comprehensive Podcast Secrets Resource Kit, which is available for free.

This kit contains tools, templates, and guides to streamline your podcasting process, from the initial planning stages to audience growth and monetization.

https://podcastsecrets.biz/s/kit

Conclusion

CHAPTER 59

YOUR PODCAST CHECKLIST

"Plans are nothing; planning is everything." – **Dwight D. Eisenhower**

R eady to turn your podcast into a powerful tool for your business? This checklist pulls together the key insights from Podcasting Secrets for Entrepreneurs, breaking down everything from the basics of RSS feeds to maximizing your reach and monetizing your content.

With these essentials in hand, you'll have a roadmap for creating a podcast that engages listeners, builds brand loyalty, and opens doors for growth.

So, whether you're just starting out or looking to take your podcast to the next level, these steps will guide you toward a show that makes a real impact.

Comprehensive Guide to Podcasting for Entrepreneurs

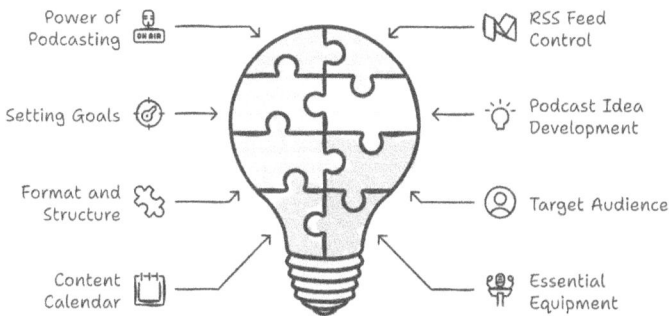

Power of Podcasting

RSS Feed Control

Setting Goals

Podcast Idea Development

Format and Structure

Target Audience

Content Calendar

Essential Equipment

The power of podcasting

Podcasting can be a powerful marketing and communication tool for entrepreneurs, allowing them to reach a targeted and engaged audience.

What is an RSS Feed and Why Do I Care?

Owning your RSS feed gives you complete control over your podcast distribution. If you host your feed on your own domain, you can easily change hosting platforms without losing your feed URL or episode data even if the platform you're using shuts down.

Setting goals and objectives

It is important to have clear goals and objectives for your podcast, and to align your content and marketing efforts with these goals.

Developing your podcast idea

To create a successful podcast, it is important to choose a relevant and interesting topic to your target audience, and to differentiate your podcast from others in the market.

Choosing your format and structure

There are many different formats and structures for podcasts, including solo shows, interviews, and panel discussions. Choosing a format and structure that best fits your goals and target audience is important.

Defining your target audience

To create a successful podcast, it is important to clearly understand your target audience and tailor your content and marketing efforts to meet their needs and interests.

Creating a content calendar

A content calendar can help you to plan and schedule your podcast episodes, and to ensure that you are consistently producing fresh and relevant content.

Essential podcasting equipment

To produce a professional-quality podcast, you will need a microphone, recording software, and other equipment. It is important to choose equipment that is suitable for your needs and budget.

Audio editing software and techniques

Audio editing software and techniques can help you to improve the sound quality of your podcast, and to create a more polished and professional final product.

The art of interviewing and conversation

Interviewing and conversation skills are essential for podcasting, and can help you to create engaging and meaningful content for your listeners.

Tips for improving delivery and sound quality

There are many techniques and best practices that can help you to improve the delivery and sound quality of your podcast, including practicing your delivery, using a microphone stand, and using pop filters.

Maximizing production value

To create a high-quality and professional-sounding podcast, it is important to focus on maximizing production value, including using high-quality equipment, editing carefully, and choosing the right music and sound effects.

Building a website and blog

A website and blog can help you to connect with your listeners and promote your podcast, and can provide a professional platform for your content.

Maximizing visibility and reach

To grow your audience and reach as many listeners as possible, it is important to focus on maximizing your podcast's visibility and reach, including publishing on multiple platforms, optimizing for search, and promoting your podcast on social media.

Monetizing your podcast

There are several options for monetizing your podcast, including advertising, sponsorship, Patreon, and merchandise. Choosing a monetization strategy that is right for your podcast and your audience is important.

Building a loyal audience and engaging with your community

Building a loyal audience and engaging with your community is essential for creating a successful and sustainable podcast. This can be achieved by consistently creating valuable and engaging content, fostering a sense of community, encouraging listener participation, and consistently promoting your podcast.

The legalities of podcasting

There are several legal issues to consider when podcasting, including copyrights, trademarks, privacy, and disclaimers. It is important to be aware of these legalities and to follow them to avoid legal action and financial penalties.

Emerging trends and opportunities

The world of podcasting is constantly evolving, and staying up-to-date with emerging trends and opportunities is important. This includes exploring options such as audio fiction, podcast networks, video podcasts, and live podcasts.

Best practices for staying up-to-date and relevant

To create a successful and sustainable podcast, staying up-to-date and relevant in the industry is important. This can be achieved by staying informed, being flexible, engaging with your audience, and keeping your content fresh.

Congratulations!

With this checklist, you're now armed with everything from podcast fundamentals to pro tips that will have you sounding like a seasoned host.

Remember, every great podcast starts with just one episode, a lot of heart, and probably a few bloopers along the way.

So go ahead—grab that mic, hit record, and get ready to make waves.

The world is out there, earbuds in, waiting for your voice. Now, let's show them what you've got!

PODCAST RESOURCES KIT

Grab it here:

https://podcastsecrets.biz/s/kit

CHAPTER 60

NEXT STEPS FOR SUCCESSFUL PODCASTING AS AN ENTREPRENEUR

"Success is not the key to happiness. Happiness is the key to success." – **Albert Schweitzer**

Congratulations!

You have made it!

You're officially on the path to becoming a podcasting pro...

So, what's next?

Podcasting as an entrepreneur is a bit like training for a marathon—except you're building your brand, connecting with clients, and talking into a microphone instead of pounding the pavement.

Whether it's refining your content, expanding your reach, or finding new ways to monetize, we've got you covered. So, grab your headphones, take a deep breath, and get ready to hit the next level in your podcasting journey!

Steps for Successful Podcasting

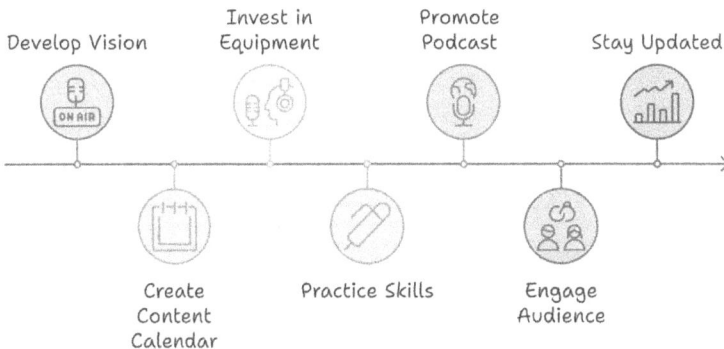

Develop Vision • Invest in Equipment • Promote Podcast • Stay Updated

Create Content Calendar • Practice Skills • Engage Audience

Develop a clear vision for your podcast

Before you start creating your podcast, it is important to develop a clear vision for your show. This includes setting goals and objectives, choosing a topic and format that is relevant and interesting to your target audience, and defining your target audience.

Create a content calendar

To ensure that you are consistently producing fresh and relevant content, it is important to create a content calendar. This can help you to plan and schedule your episodes, and to stay organized and on track.

Invest in equipment and software

To create a professional-quality podcast, you will need to invest in the right equipment and software. This includes a microphone, recording software, and other tools and resources.

Practice your delivery and audio editing skills

To improve your podcast's sound quality and professionalism, it is important to practice your delivery and audio editing skills. This may involve taking online courses or working with a coach or mentor to improve your skills.

Promote your podcast

To grow your audience and reach more listeners, it is important to promote your podcast. This can be done through social media, email newsletters, and other marketing channels.

Engage with your audience

Building a loyal audience and engaging with your community is essential for creating a successful and sustainable podcast. Make an effort to connect with your listeners, respond to their feedback, and foster a sense of community around your show.

To stay relevant and successful in the world of podcasting, it is important to stay up-to-date with industry trends, news, and events, and to be flexible and adapt to new technologies and platforms.

You did it!

You've got the tools, the vision, and—most importantly—the drive to take your podcast to the next level. Now it's time to go from planning to action, from ideas to impact. Whether you're creating your content calendar, refining your promotion strategy, or engaging with your audience, every step brings you closer to building a show that not only grows but thrives.

Remember, podcasting as an entrepreneur isn't just about getting heard; it's about connecting, inspiring, and creating a platform that serves your business and your listeners alike.

So, go on—hit record, keep pushing forward, and watch your podcast become the unforgettable voice that brings your brand to life.

The world is listening!

Our final "There is a better way!"

POWERFUL YET SIMPLE "ALL IN ONE" PODCAST SOLUTION

Launch Your Podcast Show in Minutes!

- Create or transfer your own podcast to our platform and handle every aspect in one place.
- No messy hosting issues or complex setup.
- Build your Professional Show Page in minutes
- Easily Manage and Promote Your Guests
- Grow Subscribers with auto episode alerts

https://podcastsecrets.app

To help you implement the strategies outlined in Podcasting Secrets for Entrepreneurs, we've put together a comprehensive Podcast Secrets Resource Kit, which is available for free.

This kit contains tools, templates, and guides to streamline your podcasting process, from the initial planning stages to audience growth and monetization.

https://podcastsecrets.biz/s/kit

OTHER BOOKS FROM THE AUTHOR

EVOLVEPRENEUR SECRETS FOR ENTREPRENEURS: HOW TO CREATE SPECIFIC STRATEGIES TO BUILD YOUR LIST, MAKE OFFERS AND CONNECT WITH YOUR BEST BUYERS

176 Pages / $14.95 / 978-1979285773 / Paperback / eBook / Hardcover /AudioBook

Available from: https://getmybook.store/s/ep-secrets

The ultimate guide for entrepreneurs who want to discover simple and effective ways to get started that don't cost a fortune.

Find out the best steps for each strategy and the most important areas you should focus on to connect with your best buyers.

If you're looking to succeed with quick start concepts for online entrepreneurs, this brand new book by John North reveals how startup entrepreneurs or someone looking to reboot their online business can understand how to create specific strategies to build their list, make offers and connect with their best buyers.

Discover how to fast-track your idea to startup without risking large amounts of capital investment. Learn how to create your own marketing strategies to quickly test your market and grow your idea with our 5-step system.

In this Amazing Book, you will discover...

- The perfect mindset for startup entrepreneurs or someone looking for reboot their online business at this point that would virtually guarantee their success.
- The big opportunities in quick start concepts for online entrepreneurs that many beginner, or even experienced entrepreneurs might be missing.
- The #1 mistake entrepreneurs make in the area of quick start concepts.
- The things that entrepreneurs are most likely to overpay for, and how they can avoid having their money sucked out of their pockets.
- How podcasting can be a quick and easy way to market your book or ideas!
- Simple and effective ways to get started that don't cost a fortune in time or money, the best steps for each strategy we teach, the most important areas to focus on, and even how to connect with your best customers and foster your own online community.
- How to create specific strategies to build your list, make offers and connect with your best buyers.
- Everything you need to know about how an entrepreneur can quickly start their own online business and starting creating their own community of buyers!

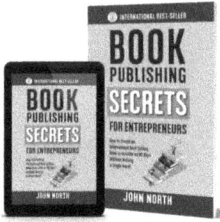

BOOK PUBLISHING SECRETS FOR ENTREPRENEURS: HOW TO CREATE AN INTERNATIONAL BEST-SELLING BOOK IN AS LITTLE AS 90 DAYS WITHOUT WRITING A SINGLE WORD!

194 Pages / $14.95 / 978-1979285773 / Paperback / eBook / Hardcover

Available from: https://getmybook.store/s/publish

Having a published book is one of the most powerful ways to gain authority in your industry. It's the ultimate marketing strategy that sells itself!

And with these 5 Book Publishing Secrets, getting your book written, published, and into the hands of as many people as possible has never been easier!

We speak to many entrepreneurs every day, and this question eventually comes up..."What's the fastest and easiest way to boost my marketing and get more customers?"

Almost without exception, we say, "a book!" You can base your book around your business or use it to start a whole new business. The great thing about writing a book is that it not only ensures that you get crystal clear on what you do, but also how you do it.

Check out www.evolveglobalpublishing.com for more information.

Look inside to get free instant access to our special book bonus. Your "Secret Publishing Kit" includes:

- 🎙 Checklists for the 90-Day Book Publishing Plan
- 🎙 Publishing Cheat Sheets
- 🎙 Sample Book Marketing Plan
- 🎙 Sample Marketing Images
- 🎙 Promotional Marketing Ideas
- 🎙 Sample Media Kit
- 🎙 Special "Would You Like to Create a Quality Book That Attracts Clients Like Crazy?" Report

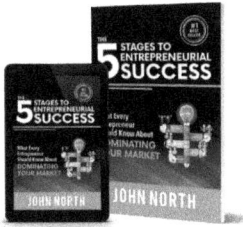

THE 5 STAGES TO ENTREPRENEURIAL SUCCESS—WHAT EVERY ENTREPRENEUR SHOULD KNOW ABOUT DOMINATING YOUR MARKET

226 Pages / $14.95 / 978-1979285773 / Paperback / eBook / Hardcover

Available from: https://getmybook.store/s/5stages

It's a common question, but what makes a successful entrepreneur?

It's my belief that success isn't just about making money. Most people start a business for the freedom they expect it to give them. The cold hard reality is that most entrepreneurs end up working longer hours and for a lot less than a typical wage for an average job.

Entrepreneurs commit to "the hustle" because they have a much bigger vision for their future than the average person. But, if they work harder than an average worker, then why doesn't every entrepreneur become massively successful?

The fact is, many entrepreneurs are making the same mistakes year after year. Learn what those are and how to avoid them in The 5 Stages to Entrepreneurial Success.

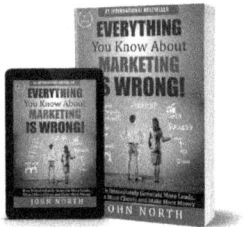

EVERYTHING YOU KNOW ABOUT MARKETING IS WRONG!—HOW TO IMMEDIATELY GENERATE MORE LEADS, ATTRACT MORE CLIENTS, AND MAKE MORE MONEY

218 Pages / $19.95 / 978-1943843138 / Paperback / eBook / Hardcover

Available from: https://getmybook.store/s/everything

We believe that everything you've ever learnt or ever tried—it's all wrong!

In this #1 best-selling book, we'll reveal the strategies you can immediately deploy that will enable you to out-think, out-market, and out-sell your competition.

What we want to do in this book is to teach you a system for marketing your business ... to a point where it becomes instantly obvious to your prospects that they would be an idiot to do business with anyone other than you ... anytime, anywhere, or at any price.

What most business owners will focus on is generating more leads at any cost, but this isn't the best way to attract prospects to your business.

We can help you build a million-dollar or even multi-million-dollar business. Also, make sure you take advantage of the free bonuses found in the book!

EVOLVEPRENEUR (AFTER HOURS) SHOW VOLUME 1

156 Pages / $19.95 / 978-0648623267 / Paperback / eBook / Hardcover

Available from https://getmybook.club/s/afterhours

"Evolvepreneur (After Hours) Show - Volume 1," curated by John North, is a unique anthology that brings together the insights of seven seasoned entrepreneurs, each an expert in their respective field.

Each chapter in this book provides a unique perspective on entrepreneurship, covering topics from innovative business strategies to digital marketing, financial management, and leadership. This anthology is not just a collection of strategies; it's an exploration of the experiences and insights of successful entrepreneurs.

"Evolvepreneur (After Hours) Show - Volume 1" is a must-read for anyone aspiring to succeed in the entrepreneurial world. It's packed with actionable advice and real-life examples, inviting readers to explore the essence of entrepreneurship and unlock their full potential. This book is an essential guide for budding entrepreneurs and seasoned business owners alike, providing a comprehensive look at the path to success in business.

ABOUT EVOLVEPRENEUR.APP

My journey to entrepreneurship, and generating more than $25 million in revenue to date is certainly an interesting and varied one. About Evolvepreneur.app

My journey to entrepreneurship, and generating more than $25 million in revenue to date is certainly an interesting and varied one.

Entrepreneurial Journey and Lessons

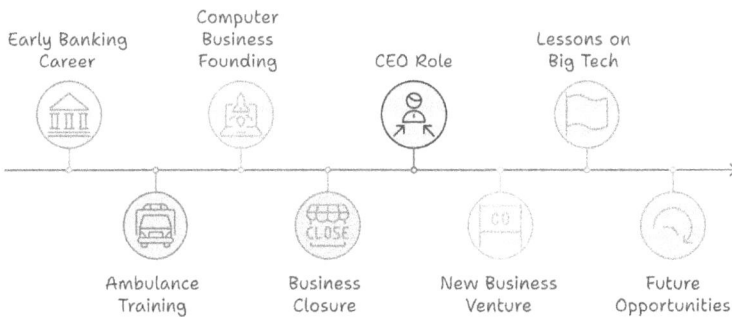

After leaving school at age 15, I started my first job as a bank employee in a small country town. Throughout the next 12 years, my roles in the bank included: front office, supervision, legal, and lending. I learned many skills while at the bank, including management, systems, and procedures, as well as how to handle unhappy customers!

Along the way, I trained as an ambulance and state emergency services officer. I even received an Australia Day award for services to the local community.

In 1989, I started getting very interested in the emerging computer revolution and founded a part-time computer and accounting software business. I soon realized the huge opportunity emerging, so I resigned from the bank and started working full-time. In a few years, it quickly grew to more than $1.5 million per year in recurring revenues.

In 2000, Australia introduced a new sales tax "GST" system and my business went from boom to bust — the new tax drove businesses to computerize en masse for the reporting they needed to do, and it sucked all new revenue from future years.

I faced my first major business failure and was forced to close the business, but was fortunate enough to get a new job working as the CEO for my accounting software supplier in Sydney.

After six months of being an employee, I made a successful bid to take over their Australian operations as their sole distributor and become a self-employed entrepreneur again. Within a few years, with annual revenues in excess of $2.5 million (nearly 80% recurring) we became #2 in the world for a major accounting software brand.

I learned a lot about developing recurring revenue, software development, negotiation, marketing, sales, and people management throughout those years.

In 2013, I sold the distribution company to focus on my new venture, Evolve Systems, providing digital marketing services for clients. Along the way, I became a hybrid book publisher and was involved in publishing more than 2,000 books.

My next venture will draw on all of my previous experience and then some!

The internet certainly has changed the world and made it easier to start a new business, but not everything has changed. In reality, the true art of business hasn't changed significantly. The way people decide what to buy is much the same as it always has been.

What has changed is the volume of information a prospect can uncover and how quickly they can research their options.

With the rise of social media platforms, it has become so easy to generate interest for your product or service by creating a social media page, running some ads, and writing posts to accumulate likes. You even can create a special interest group to attract conversations with your best buyers. Many businesses today are only present on social platforms but do not have a website.

These platforms deliberately make it easy for you to outsource your customers to them, while simultaneously restricting the information you need to contact them later.

With the recent push for individual privacy protections and better government regulation for Big Tech, these social media platforms are now pulling the ladder up behind them and keeping the majority of the meaningful data for themselves.

These social media platforms might be free and easy to use, but they come with a cost — and it's something that many online businesses don't see until it's too late. Accumulating likes and followers on social media is a bit like renting a nice apartment. It's clean and fancy, but it's not really yours.

If you break any of their rules — both the reasonable and the draconian — you risk losing access to your followers by being banned or blocked. In fact, they often penalize posts that contain off-site web links, because they don't want their users leaving their site. Past a certain point, this stops being a symbiotic relationship and starts costing you more than you're earning. You hit a ceiling, and you need to break past it if you want to grow your business.

On top of this, the cost of advertising on these platforms is only going up, because the majority of their customers are now big corporations.

What does this all mean to you?

As a time-poor, typically underfunded online entrepreneur who receives so much conflicting advice about the best ways to grow your business, how can you compete with the big end of town without any of the resources they have at their disposal?

Let's imagine that you send some traffic to your social profiles.

You should then focus on building a closer relationship with your prospects by moving them from that site to your own community platform.

Notice I didn't say website.

Let me explain what a community platform means for an online entrepreneur.

The major challenge that most online business owners face is providing a world-class website experience since it can be complicated and expensive. It often means cobbling several solutions together using plugins and third-party tools to get a functioning website capable of engaging and convincing visitors to buy from you.

As the number of businesses relying on the internet for day-to-day operations has grown, a new type of software system has arisen. It's called SaaS - Software as a Service.

I remember when I first started selling accounting software - you often had to buy multiple unconnected products to manage your cashbook, invoicing, payroll, and asset management. Over time, these functions merged into powerful, interconnected single-system solutions at a fraction of the cost of all the individual components.

Individually, these systems often are costly and labor-intensive to maintain. When I started working for clients in digital marketing, if I ran into a problem, I knew there was "an app for that". Whilst this is great, it also opens your business up to problems if one app fails or someone misses an update or forgets to sync all of these unconnected applications.

I believe the next-level SaaS "social platform" or "all-in-one business system" will be a significant opportunity in the marketplace for entrepreneurs.

If you want to create a real growth-based sustainable business, my advice is to focus on building your own complete system; become independent from "Big Tech" so you can't be banned or throttled. Use them to send traffic to your own assets like a website, recurring membership, online e-commerce shop, or e-learning platform, and build your own audience.

As a marketing consultant, after thousands of hours of consulting and deploying marketing systems, the following is a blueprint for what I believe a typical online entrepreneur needs to be successful in today's highly-competitive marketplace:

- Your major focus should be the overall customer experience. You will also want to try to be as frictionless as possible throughout. At the same time, employ as much automation as possible.

- You should start with a mobile-ready website that tightly integrates your content-based assets, such as your podcast channel, on-demand videos, courses, memberships and blogs.

- Seamlessly build up your subscriber database and automatically email subscribers when new content is available. Your marketing module should trigger emails or actions based on your prospect's behavior, as well as help them progress through your courses and products.

- You will need to design some pages to promote free checklists, blueprints, and/or ebooks to build your subscriber database. You will want your visitors to be able to buy your products & services and handle the delivery of your digital download or physical product on the same site. At the same time, you may wish to upsell products at checkout. By segmenting your prospects, you can build powerful followup emails.

🎤 You should have multiple payment gateways. This reduces the risk of one portal withholding funds if you grow too fast. You could also sell products in different currencies to lower buyer resistance.

🎤 You may want the ability to create a recurring membership system where you can charge users at regular intervals and allow them to easily update their records with you.

🎤 You may want different front-end websites, but they should all lead back to your eCommerce and backend member area so you can manage them easily. This allows you to promote different angles of your business without splitting up your audience or resources.

🎤 To grow your business, you should create an affiliate program and encourage referrers or affiliates to share your products and services for rewards.

🎤 At the end of the process, the prospect or customer should finish their initial journey in your back-end membership area, which includes all of their invoices, downloads, and bonus content. You don't want your customers fumbling around with separate websites looking for all of this information!It's vital to have a ticketing system or similar service system to support your customers.

🎤 The next step is to create a highly-engaged community for your clients and prospects that provides extra value behind a secure login and keeps them coming back for your content. To further engage users, you need to gamify your community through status badges and rewards systems.

🎤 Think about creating courses where your members can learn online at their own pace. Your course system should allow them to progress step-by-step as they do each lesson, not necessarily on a weekly release schedule where they could quickly get behind and give up. You should also encourage students to engage with other students.

🎤 What if they didn't need to download a worksheet PDF they never actually complete? You need a system to allow them to leave their responses as they work through the lessons. This will give you the ability to see all their answers, which means you also know where they are in the course. This means no one is left behind! A useful feature is to be able to assign a task to your students as they progress through the course. You could also create a coaching program based on their task list.

🎤 You also need a powerful analytics reporting system that tells you exactly where your traffic is coming from and what they're clicking on to help make decisions for your marketing campaigns.

🎤 You will also want a single dashboard to view statistics, create content, and manage your business.

🎤 Ideally, you should build a procedure system (Knowledge Base) so your staff and outsourcers can run your processes the same way every time. Make it easy to create step-by-step instructions rather than having to continually re-train staff.

🎤 What if you wanted to create a mastermind group? It would be best if you could group people together and allow users to be able to access Q&A calls, group tasks, and results in a logical and centralized way.

- 🎤 It would also help to have a project management system to help you and your team manage your projects as well as client ones.
- 🎤 Most importantly, your platform needs to have fast loading times, or you risk driving customers away!

How long do you think it would take to implement all of this?

Maybe a year or longer!

I've spent thousands of dollars and many fruitless hours in search of the best all-in-one platform that had most of the features I wanted. But as far as I could tell, that system doesn't exist. In frustration, I set out on a journey to develop my own unique platform, completely based around the needs of entrepreneurs, coaches, consultants, authors, podcasters, publishers, and mastermind groups.

I called it evolvepreneur.app. My mission is to start a revolution to help entrepreneurs establish their own complete business system that can compete with mainstream social media platforms.

Don't become a cog in the machine; create your own machine.

I challenge you to focus on building your own complete business community platform.

Take control of your destiny and sleep better a night!

GLOSSARY

A

» **Advanced Analytics:** In-depth metrics beyond basic download counts, including listener demographics and engagement.

» **Affiliate Fee:** A percentage commission paid for referrals or sales generated through affiliate partnerships.

» **Amplify:** Strategies to enhance the reach of your podcast, often involving promotion across social media, email marketing, and collaboration with other podcasters.

» **Audience Engagement:** Interactions with listeners, measured through comments, shares, likes, and other forms of listener participation.

B

» **Back Catalogue:** The collection of all past episodes of a podcast, accessible to listeners.

» **Branding:** Consistent visual and audio elements, such as logos and theme music, that create a recognisable identity for the podcast.

C

» **Closed Captioning:** Text for audio content, commonly used in video podcasts to improve accessibility.

» **Content Calendar:** A pre-planned schedule for publishing podcast episodes, helping maintain consistency.

» **Conversion Rate:** The percentage of listeners who take a desired action after hearing a call-to-action (CTA).

D

» **Data Breach Notification:** Requirement to notify authorities and affected individuals in case of a data breach, ensuring compliance with GDPR.

» **Demographic Characteristics:** Attributes of your target audience, such as age, occupation, and lifestyle, essential for targeted content creation.

» **Downloads:** The count of times an episode is requested, which serves as a primary metric for audience size.

E

» **Email Funnel:** A series of follow-up emails designed to nurture podcast listeners toward becoming customers or subscribers.

» **Episode Trailer:** A brief preview of an episode, meant to generate interest and attract listeners.

» **Episode Completion Rate:** The percentage of listeners who complete an episode from start to finish.

G
- » **GDPR Compliance:** Legal requirements under the General Data Protection Regulation, including data collection and processing safeguards.
- » **Guest Landing Page:** A dedicated webpage for potential podcast guests, providing details and application instructions.

H
- » **Hashtag Strategy:** Using specific hashtags on social media to improve episode discoverability and foster engagement.
- » **Hosting Platform:** A service that stores and distributes podcast audio files via an RSS feed to platforms like Apple Podcasts and Spotify or PodcastSecrets.app

I
- » **Interview Format:** A podcast style where the host interviews guests, popular for engaging listeners through expert insights and storytelling.

J
- » **Joint Venture (JV) Proposal:** A partnership plan outlining the roles, responsibilities, and benefits of collaboration between podcasters and other businesses.

K
- » **Key Performance Indicators (KPIs):** Essential metrics tracked to gauge a podcast's success, such as downloads, listener retention, and episode completion rates.

L
- » **Listener Engagement:** Interaction and response from listeners, often measured through comments, shares, and retention rates.
- » **Listener Retention:** The percentage of an episode that listeners complete, reflecting engagement levels.

M
- » **Media Kit:** A promotional document summarizing a podcast's key details, used for attracting sponsors, guests, and media.
- » **Metadata:** Information embedded in the podcast RSS feed, including title, description, and tags, essential for search and discovery.
- » **Monetization:** Revenue-generating strategies for a podcast, including ads, sponsorships, and premium content offerings.
- » **Music Licensing:** Legal permission required to use copyrighted music in a podcast, typically involving mechanical and public performance licenses.

O
- » **OP3.dev:** The Open Podcast Prefix Project, a community-driven, privacy-focused analytics tool for tracking downloads and engagement.
- » **Organic Growth:** Audience growth achieved through unpaid methods, like SEO and social media sharing.

P
- » **Podcast Checklist:** A comprehensive guide or list of steps for launching and promoting a podcast effectively.
- » **Prefix URL:** A tracking code added to episode file links for gathering analytics data on downloads and listener behavior.
- » **Production Value:** The quality of sound, editing, and overall presentation of a podcast.

R
- » **RSS Feed:** A structured XML file used to syndicate podcast episodes across platforms like Apple Podcasts and Spotify.

S

» **SEO for Podcasts:** Search engine optimisation strategies to increase podcast discoverability in search results.

» **Social Media Shares:** The number of times an episode or podcast content is shared on social media platforms.

» **Sponsor:** A company or individual who provides financial support in exchange for promotional opportunities on a podcast.

T

» **Target Audience:** The specific demographic or group of listeners a podcast aims to attract and serve with its content.

» **Transcripts:** Written versions of podcast episodes, used for accessibility and SEO benefits.

U

» **Unique Listeners:** Distinct individuals who download or stream an episode, providing an accurate view of the podcast's audience size.

» **Upsell Opportunity:** Additional products or services offered to listeners to generate further revenue.

V

» **Visitor Tracking:** Monitoring the traffic generated from podcast links to websites or social media, often used to evaluate engagement and marketing efforts.

W

» **Website Clicks from Podcast Links:** The count of clicks from episode links to a website, helping assess the effectiveness of CTAs.

INDEX

www.ingramcontent.com/pod-product-compliance
Lightning Source LLC
Chambersburg PA
CBHW050808270326
41926CB00026B/4619